The iPhone
PocketGuide
Fourth Edition

ChristopherBreen

Ginormous knowledge, pocket-sized.

**Peachpit
Press**

The iPhone Pocket Guide, Fourth Edition
Christopher Breen

Peachpit Press
1249 Eighth Street
Berkeley, CA 94710
510/524-2178
510/524-2221 (fax)

Find us on the Web at: www.peachpit.com
To report errors, please send a note to errata@peachpit.com.

Peachpit Press is a division of Pearson Education.

Executive editor: Clifford Colby
Editor: Kathy Simpson
Production editor: Myrna Vladic
Compositor: David Van Ness
Indexer: Rebecca Plunkett
Cover design: Peachpit Press
Cover photography: Scott Cowlin
Interior design: Peachpit Press

ISBN-13: 978-0-321-64724-5
ISBN-10:   0-321-64724-6

9 8 7 6 5 4 3 2 1

Printed and bound in the United States of America

Dedication

To my ceaselessly loving and encouraging mother, Patricia Whitney.

About the Author

Christopher Breen has been writing about technology since the latter days of the Reagan administration for such publications as *MacUser*, *MacWEEK*, and *Macworld*. Currently a senior editor for *Macworld*, Breen pens its popular "Mac 911" tips-and-troubleshooting column and blog, routinely opines about digital media in its Playlist blog, and hosts the *Macworld Podcast*. He's the author of Peachpit's *The iPod & iTunes Pocket Guide*, *The iPod touch Pocket Guide*, and *The Flip Mino Pocket Guide*. When not engaged in technological pursuits, he's a professional musician in the San Francisco Bay Area.

Acknowledgments

This book would be just another take on just another unrealized intriguing idea if not for the dedication of the following people.

At Peachpit Press: Publisher Nancy Ruenzel, who continues to support these efforts; Cliff Colby, who, mere minutes after the iPhone's announcement, sidled up and said, "So I suppose you'd like to write a book about this"; Jim Akin, who edited the first edition; Kathy Simpson, who did everything that needed doing after the manuscript left my computer and took up residence on hers; production pro Myrna Vladic, who, with barely an anxious ripple, turned our work into the lovely book you hold now; David Van Ness, who made words and pictures fit so attractively within the confines of these pages; and Rebecca Plunkett, who performed a book's most thankless yet necessary job: indexing.

At home: My wife, Claire, who not only put up with the late hours and missed weekends, but also reminded me time and again just how cool her iPhone is; and my daughter, Addie, who gave her father a huge smile and welcome hug at the end of every working day (and then asked to borrow my old iPhone so she could watch *Harry Potter and Fill in the Blank* for the 194th time).

Abroad: Ben Long for hacking the iPhone so we could include screen shots of the interface in the first edition and for being my partner in crime for Macworld Expo's iPhone Supersessions; Macworld Expo's Paul Kent for letting us be the iPhone guys year after year; Erica Sadun for creating the utility that made the screen shots possible; *Macworld* Editorial Director Jason Snell, who never said, "I'd like exclusive rights to that brain full of iPhone goodness"; and the boys from System 9 for their continued cool-cattedness.

And, of course, the sleep-deprived designers, engineers, and other Apple folk who gave birth to the original iPhone, did it all over again for the iPhone 3G, and came back for a third helping with the iPhone 3GS. Congratulations!

Contents

Getting Started

I really, *really* appreciate your purchasing this book. And because I do, it would be rude of me to delay, even for an instant, the pleasure you'll gain from using your cool new iPhone. Allow me to offer a few quick steps for firing up what will soon be your new best friend.

When the original iPhone was released, you had the option to take it with you and activate it later. With the iPhone 3G, you were compelled to purchase and activate it in a store such as a retail Apple Store or

AT&T outlet. Now, with the iPhone 3GS (and the older iPhone 3G, which is still for sale), you have three options:

■ Travel to Apple's online store at www.apple.com/iphone/buy, fill out a preauthorization form, and then trek down to your local Apple Store to pick up the phone.

■ Travel to that same Apple online store and fill out a very similar pre-authorization form. (Which form you complete depends on whether you're a new iPhone customer or someone upgrading from an old iPhone.) Apple will ship the phone to your door.

> **note** You'll need an Apple ID to purchase an iPhone in this way. During all this form-filling, you'll be given the opportunity to acquire an Apple ID. Yes, a credit card is required.

■ Waltz into a retail Apple Store, AT&T outlet, or other emporium that sells these things, and scream *"Gimme iPhone now!"* After you're politely but firmly escorted from the building, don a false beard so that you can return (Yes, even if you're a woman. That'll fool 'em!), request a new iPhone in a more genteel manner, sign up for a voice and data plan, and receive your phone.

With the iPhone finally in your possession, follow these steps:

1. Download iTunes 8.2 or later.

   If you don't already have the latest version of iTunes, travel to www.apple.com/itunes/download and grab a copy. Versions are available for Windows PCs as well as Macs. You must be running version 8.2 or later to use the iPhone 3.0 (or later) software, which lets your phone work its magic.

2. String the included USB cable from your computer to the iPhone.

   Attach the USB end of the cable to a free USB 2.0 port on your Mac or PC. Then plug the dock connector into the bottom of the iPhone.

tip   Use one of the ports on your computer or a powered USB 2.0 hub.
A USB port on your keyboard won't provide enough power to charge
the iPhone.

3. Do iTunes' bidding.

    - If you purchased your iPhone at a retail store, it's likely already
      set up to the point where you can make a call, use the Internet
      features, and take pictures and shoot movies (if you purchased an
      iPhone 3GS).

    - If, however, the phone was delivered to your door, when you plug it
      into your computer, iTunes will launch and ask for a little informa-
      tion so that AT&T (or the carrier in your country) can activate the
      phone at its end. With AT&T, you'll be asked to provide your billing
      zip code and the last four digits of your Social Security number;
      your phone number should already be filled in. (Yes, this process is
      meant to ensure that the intended person received the phone.) The
      activation process should take no more than a couple of minutes.
      During that process, iTunes or your phone may prompt you to
      do one thing or another, such as disconnect and then reconnect
      the phone. Just follow its lead. When everything's complete, your
      iPhone is ready to make a call.

4. So make a call, already.

    I know that you're eager to load some music and video on your iPhone
    and maybe download a few applications from the App Store, but first,
    you should call someone and brag about having the coolest phone on
    the planet. If the device has been plugged in for an hour, you should
    have enough juice to brag with the best of 'em.

tip   If the battery is low, and you plan to brag for a long time, jack the
dock connector into the bottom of the iPhone. The phone will charge
while you talk.

Just tap the Phone icon in the bottom-left corner of the iPhone's screen, tap the Keypad icon at the bottom of the resulting screen, tap in a number on the keypad that appears, and tap Call. Then brag.

5. Configure iTunes.

   If you've unplugged the iPhone from your computer, plug it in again. It should appear in iTunes' Source list.

6. Choose which media to sync.

   iTunes is likely to present you with a screen that reads Set up Your iPhone. On this screen, you'll have the option to sync your music and photos automatically. If you don't have a massive amount of music and photos, feel free to let iTunes fill your iPhone. If, however, you have more music in iTunes than will fit on your iPhone, you have a couple of options:

   ■ **Let iTunes choose some music.** If you leave the option for syncing music checked, iTunes will eventually report that it can't fit all your music on the iPhone. Instead, it will offer to select a collection of music on its own and then sync that collection. If that arrangement sounds good to you, leave the option checked.

   ■ **Do your own music choosing.** If, on the other hand, you want complete control of the music that's placed on your phone, uncheck the option and choose your music later (which I show you how to do in this book).

7. Check out your options.

   Select your iPhone in iTunes' Source list, and the iPhone preferences pane fills most of iTunes' main window. Note the Info, Ringtones, Music, Photos, Podcasts, Video, and Applications tabs. These tabs are where you choose what to sync to your iPhone.

8. Obtain some content.

   Put an audio CD in your computer's media drive. iTunes will offer to import its tracks. Let it do so. Then click the iTunes Store entry in iTunes' Source list, and after signing up for an iTunes account, download a few podcasts and buy a TV episode. (I show you how to do all these things later in the book, if these terse instructions won't do.)

9. Enable the Manually Manage Music and Videos option, and put that content on your iPhone.

   You find this option when you select your iPhone in iTunes' Source list and select the Summary tab—down there in the Options area. With this option checked, you can drag music and videos to your iPhone. Delve into the Music, Movies, TV Shows, and Podcasts areas of your iTunes Library (available by clicking the appropriate headings in iTunes' Source list), and drag some music, videos, and podcasts onto the iPhone icon. This content will be copied to the iPhone.

10. Plug the included headset into the top of the iPhone, and jam the business ends of the earbuds into your ears.

11. Tap the iPod entry at the bottom of the iPhone's screen.

    You'll be able to find and play your media by tapping Playlists, Artists, Songs, and Videos. If you'd like to search for media in other ways, tap the More icon at the bottom of the iPhone's screen. The resulting More screen displays Albums, Audiobooks, Compilations, Composers, Genres, and Podcasts.

12. Find out where you are.

    Unplug your iPhone, step outside, click the Home button (the single button at the bottom of the screen), tap the Maps icon, and then tap the small icon in the bottom-left corner of the screen. Using GPS (Global Positioning System), the iPhone will pinpoint its location on the map that appears. This information will be used by other applications on your iPhone, so now is as good a time as any to orient the phone.

13. Find out *which way* you are.

    If you have an iPhone 3GS in your hand, tap that small icon in the bottom-left corner one more time. The blue dot that indicates your position now has a fan spreading out toward the top of the phone. Turn to face in another direction, and marvel as the map rotates to indicate the new direction in which you're pointing the phone.

    This is a cool reflection of the compass capabilities that are built into your phone. I discuss these capabilities along with the Compass application later in the book.

> **note** It's possible that your iPhone will be a little confused about the direction in which it's facing. If it is, the Compass application will prompt you to wave the phone in a figure-8 pattern. Yes, you're going to feel silly, but you won't be the only person who was ever prompted to do this (I was too).

14. Read the rest of this book.

    Everything you need to know to make the most of your iPhone is within its pages. Enjoy your stay!

Meet the iPhone

On January 9, 2007, Apple, Inc.'s Steve Jobs took the stage at San Francisco's Moscone West convention center to open the annual Macworld Expo. Close to the 30-minute mark of his presentation, he moved, with these words, to the main subject of the day:

"Today, we're introducing three revolutionary products of this class. The first one is a widescreen iPod with touch controls. The second is a revolutionary mobile phone. The third is a breakthrough Internet communications device.

"A widescreen iPod, a mobile phone, and a breakthrough Internet communications device," he repeated and repeated again until the crowd finally caught on with a roar.

Rather than describing three separate devices, Jobs was introducing one: the iPhone.

That device, with its sleek design and multiple personalities, went on to change the face of the mobile-phone industry. No longer did people use their phones simply to make calls. Rather than ignore a slew of features deemed too convoluted to explore, iPhone owners actually put the device's communications and media features to good use—some, in fact (including your humble author), rarely even using the iPhone to make a call.

Fast-forward to March 6, 2008, when Apple previewed its iPhone 2.0 software, which let you purchase third-party applications via an App Store application listed on the iPhone's Home screen. Additionally, the software made the iPhone compatible with many corporate servers— a feature missing from the original iPhone that made it less than attractive to corporate IT departments. The announcement hinted that a new iPhone model was in the works, and sure enough, Jobs unveiled just such a model—the iPhone 3G—in early June 2008.

Leaping ahead another year, in March 2009 Apple offered a sneak peek at the iPhone 3.0 software—a version that features cut, copy, and paste; support for MMS (Multimedia Messaging Service; a system for sending media files along with text messages); support for *tethering* (using the iPhone's Internet connection with a computer); landscape view in a greater number of applications; and a way to search the phone's many files. Apple released that software in June 2009 along with the iPhone 3GS, a faster iPhone that provides a built-in video camera, voice dialing, control of some iPod functions via Voice Control, and direction data thanks to built-in magnetometer circuitry.

note   As I write this chapter, the iPhone's U.S. carrier, AT&T, hasn't implemented tethering and MMS messaging, though it intends to. My fervent hope is that by the time you read this book, AT&T's pokiness will be a thing of the past.

Like the iPhone 3G that preceded it, the iPhone 3GS has a black or white plastic back and is compatible with high-speed third-generation (3G) wireless technology and Global Positioning System (GPS) circuitry, a technology for pinpointing the location of the GPS-compatible device. It has a better-quality camera than its predecessor, however, capturing 3 megapixels rather than 2, and it's a faster iPhone overall, thanks to its greater memory (256 MB versus 128 MB in the older phones) and faster processor.

iPod, Phone, Internet Device, and More

Now, nearly three years after its debut, does the iPhone live up to Jobs' three-faced claims?

- **Widescreen iPod? Yes.** Indeed, the iPhone was the first widescreen-video-capable iPod, with a unique interface for browsing your music collection by album cover and a beautifully bright 3.5-inch display on which you can view pictures, TV shows, music videos, and movies in a widescreen way. Thanks to the inclusion of the iTunes Store on the phone, you can even purchase music and video and download it directly to the iPhone over a Wi-Fi or 3G network.

note If you attempt to download a file larger than 10 MB over a 3G network—whether that file is a video or an iPhone app—your phone will tell you "Nuh-uh." Files larger than 10 MB can be downloaded only over Wi-Fi or directly from the iTunes Store on your computer.

- **Mobile phone? Yes.** As a mobile phone, the iPhone offers many of the finest features of today's sophisticated phones (and a few features that these "smart" phones haven't even thought of), offering such options as speakerphone, conference calling, SMS (Short Message Service) and MMS messaging, voice dialing, contact syncing with a computer or Internet service, and a Visual Voicemail scheme that allows you to choose quickly just those messages you want to listen to.

- **Internet communications device? Yes.** As an Internet communications device, the iPhone offers a full-blown browser capable of displaying real Web pages, email, maps, helpful applications for quickly getting information on weather and stocks, and even streamed YouTube videos. And more? Yes, lots more. To begin with, the beauty of the iPhone is that these three major elements work hand in hand. It's the work of a moment to search for a nearby pizza joint in the Maps application, click its contact information link, and call to order your dinner.

- **And more? Yes.** Add to all those features the iPhone's unique multi-touch screen, which lets you use natural finger motions and virtual onscreen controls to manage your phone; a sensor that detects the phone's vertical or horizontal orientation and rotates its images accordingly; and built-in Wi-Fi, GPS, 3G, magnetometer (iPhone 3GS only), and Bluetooth capability, and you've got a fairly formidable hunk of technology in your pocket.

- **Even more than that.** Should the built-in applications not be enough, there's always the App Store. With it, you can add such a host of capabilities to an iPhone that it becomes a computer in your pocket. Need a wireless remote control for your iTunes Library or Apple TV? Apple's free Remote application for the iPhone and iPod touch provides it. Want to learn about all the restaurants within a 10-mile radius? You can get apps for that too. Care to send an instant message to a friend rather than burn up your SMS messages? Just turn to one of the instant-messaging (IM) clients available from the App Store. Need to send a quick tweet or update your Facebook page? Yes, there are apps for that. The possibilities are nearly endless—and growing by the day as new applications are created and added.

Oh, and did I mention that the iPhone works with both Windows PCs and Macs? Or that the computer application that handles the handshake between your computer and the iPhone is one you're already familiar with? Yes, that would be the same iTunes you now use to load your iPod with music, podcasts, games, movies, and TV shows.

In this inaugural chapter, I look at the items that come in the iPhone box, as well as the physical features and controls that make up this three-in-one wonder.

Boxed In

The squat black box holds more than the iPhone. Within, you'll find these goodies.

iPhone

Well, of course. You didn't lay out $100, $200, or $300 (or more, depending on the kind of service plan you qualified for and the variety of phone you purchased) with the dream of getting an electric shaver, did you? Lift the top of the box, and the iPhone is the first thing you see, suspended in its plastic tray.

Stereo headset

Yes, you can press the iPhone against your face just as you can any other telephone, but if you do, you miss the opportunity to use your iPhone to check your stocks or surf the Web as your mother complains, for the 37th time, that the old coot across the way has been nipping at her nasturtiums. The stereo headset, with its onboard microphone, not only frees your hands for playing with the iPhone's other features, but also lets you listen to your favorite tunes; serves as an audio aid when you're watching a video; and (if you have an iPhone 3GS) allows you, through voice control, to demand that your phone dial a friend or play the catalog of a favorite artist.

The headset's mic—the small gray plastic cylinder located about 5 inches down the line from the right earbud—is also a switch. Here's how you use it:

- To adjust the volume of the headset, press the top of the switch to increase volume or the bottom of the switch to turn things down. These volume buttons aren't of the press-and-hold variety. Volume goes up or down only when you press and release the button. To increase volume by two increments, press the top button twice in succession.

- While listening to music or watching a video, press the switch once in the middle to pause playback.

- Press it twice to move to the next track when listening to music.

- Press it three times in succession to move to the previous track when listening to music.

- Press the switch twice in rapid succession while you're watching a video, and if the video has chapter markers, you'll skip to the next chapter. (If the video has no chapters, nothing happens.) If you press three times in rapid succession while watching a video with chapters, you move back to the beginning of the currently playing chapter. Stop playback with a single click and press the switch three times quickly, and you go back to the previous chapter.

- When the phone rings, press it once to answer the call and again to end the call.

- To decline a call, press and hold for a couple of seconds; then let go. The iPhone beeps twice to acknowledge your action.

- While you're in the middle of a call, press once to answer an incoming call and put the first call on hold.

- To end the current call and answer an incoming call or switch to a call on hold, press and hold for 2 seconds; then let go.

- Again, if you have an iPhone 3GS and you're not in the middle of a call, press and hold the center of the switch for a couple of seconds to call up the Voice Control screen. (I discuss all that is Voice Control in Chapters 3 and 6.)

Documentation

Inside the black paper envelope beneath the plastic tray are three hunks of paper: Finger Tips, a short guide to using your iPhone (unnecessary, as you're holding this much larger guide); a safety information guide, which you may be able to read if you wear 6x reading glasses; and a sheet that bears two white Apple stickers, appropriate for placing anywhere you want to let your Apple flag fly.

USB power adapter

With the iPhone 3G and 3GS, Apple bundles a redesigned power adapter that looks very much like those three-prong-to-two-prong plug adapters that you find at the local hardware store. On one side are the two blades you plug into a power outlet; on the other is a USB port into which you plug the iPhone's dock connector-to-USB cable.

Dock connector-to-USB cable

Speaking of that cable, this is the one you string between the dock connector port on the bottom of the iPhone or a Dock (if you have one) and either the USB power adapter or a USB port on your computer. When it's connected to a computer, this cable acts as both data and power link between the iPhone and computer. Without it, you can't sync media and information from the computer to the iPhone, as the iPhone—wireless wonder though it may be—syncs only via the cable.

SIM eject tool

Should you someday want to remove your iPhone's SIM card (currently, you have very few good reasons for doing so), you can insert the end of this tool (a glorified unbent paper clip) into the small hole at the top of the iPhone, give it a push, and pop out the SIM card holder. You'll find this little baby inside the documentation envelope.

On the Face of It

Thanks to its touchscreen display, the iPhone sports very few buttons and switches. Those that it does possess, however, are important (**Figure 1.1**).

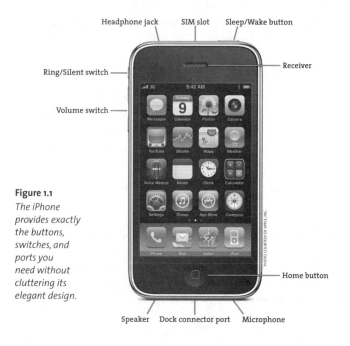

Figure 1.1
The iPhone provides exactly the buttons, switches, and ports you need without cluttering its elegant design.

Up front

After peeling the plastic off your iPhone and flipping it in your hand a time or two, you will come to a remarkable realization: The thing apparently has but one button! No number keys, no tiny joystick, no Answer and Hang Up buttons—just an indented round button at the bottom of the display. This button is the Home button, and as its name implies, it takes you to the iPhone's Home screen nearly every time you click it once.

(OK, I'll end the suspense: You also use the Home button to wake up your sleeping phone. When you do, you don't go Home; rather, after unlocking the phone, you see the last screen that was visible when the phone dozed off. Also, when you're already looking at the first screen of the Home screen and you click this button, you're taken to the Spotlight screen, where you can search for items on your iPhone.)

Click it quickly twice in succession, however, and its behavior changes, depending on how you've set up the Home button—a topic that I examine more closely in Chapter 2.

The front of the iPhone also bears a small slit near the top. This slit is the receiver—the hole through which you listen to the person you're speaking with when you operate the phone in traditional phone-to-face mode.

On top

Look a little more carefully, and you discover a few more mechanical controls and ports. On the top edge of the iPhone 3G and 3GS is a tiny silver switch. Apple describes this switch as the Sleep/Wake button, which you also use to turn the iPhone on and off.

To lock the phone, press this button. (To unlock the phone, click the Home button and slide your finger where you see the words *Slide to Unlock*.) To switch the phone off, press and hold the Sleep/Wake button for a few seconds until a red slider, labeled *Slide to Power Off*, appears onscreen. Drag the slider to the right to switch off the phone (or tap Cancel to belay that order). "Drag?" you ask. Yes, the gesture is exactly what it sounds like. Place your finger on the arrow button and slide it to the right. (I describe all these maneuvers in the "Full Gestures" section later in this chapter.)

To turn the phone on after shutting it off, press and hold the Sleep/Wake button until you see the Apple logo on the display.

Next to the Sleep/Wake button is a very thin strip of plastic. This strip is the edge of the SIM (Subscriber Information Module) card, which holds a programmable circuit board that stores your personal subscriber information. This card allows the iPhone to work. Without it, you've got a pretty hunk of metal, glass, and acrylic that can use all its media and email and Internet functions, but can't make or receive calls, or send or receive text messages. Unlike some other mobile phones, the iPhone comes with this removable card preinstalled.

Hunkered down in the top-left corner is the Headphone jack, which accommodates the iPhone's white headset plug. On the original iPhone, this jack was recessed, meaning that although it accommodated Apple's ultrathin headphone plug, it was too narrow for most other headphone jacks. Apple saw sense with the iPhone 3G (and continues to see sense with the iPhone 3GS), so this jack is now flush, letting you use any set of headphones you like without an adapter.

Down below

Smack-dab in the middle of the iPhone 3G's bottom edge is the familiar-to-iPod-owners dock connector port. This port is a proprietary 30-pin connector used for syncing the iPhone and attaching such accessories as power adapters, FM transmitters, and speaker systems.

The hole in the bottom-left corner of the iPhone is for the device's built-in speaker, used for both speakerphone and audio playback when nothing is plugged into the Headphone jack.

The hole in the bottom-right corner is for the phone's microphone.

To the left

Unlike some other mobile phones, the iPhone has a physical Ring/Silent switch. You'll find this silver toggle switch on the top-left side of the phone. When the switch is toggled toward the face of the phone, the iPhone is in the Ring position. Push the switch toward the back of the phone to silence the ringer. That orange dot you see above the switch tells you that it's in the Silent position.

note When the Ring/Silent switch is set in the Ring position, the iPhone makes noise when you receive a call, voice-mail message, text message, or email message; when an appointment or alarm-clock alarm goes off; when you lock the phone; and when you type with the iPhone's keyboard (provided that you haven't switched off that sound in the Sounds setting). When the switch is set to Silent, the phone makes noise when an alarm-clock alarm goes off. It also makes noise if you've used MobileMe's Find My iPhone feature (which I discuss in Chapter 10) to track down the whereabouts of your iPhone and, in the process, asked the iPhone to make a noise to help you find out where it is (under a couch cushion, for example).

Below the Ring/Silent switch is the Volume rocker switch. Press it up to increase the volume on a call or when listening to music or watching a video; press it down to decrease the volume.

Icon See That

When operating your iPhone, you'll see a variety of small icons in its status bar. Here's what they mean:

 Cell signal: This icon indicates how strong a signal your phone is receiving. The more bars, the better the signal. If you're out of range of your carrier's network, you'll see *No Service*.

 Airplane mode: All functions that broadcast a signal—making a call, using Wi-Fi or EDGE networks, connecting to Bluetooth devices—are shut off when you switch the phone to airplane mode.

 Wi-Fi: This icon indicates that you're connected to a Wi-Fi network. The stronger the signal, the more bars.

 3G: If 3G is available to your phone, this icon appears.

 EDGE: This icon indicates that you're within range of your carrier's EDGE network.

 GPRS: The iPhone supports General Packet Radio Service, a data-moving technology on GSM (for Global System for Mobile communication) networks that's more common outside the United States. If your carrier offers GPRS (and yes, AT&T does), and its GPRS network is available, you see this symbol.

 VPN: The iPhone displays this symbol if you're connected to a VPN network.

 Network activity: If your iPhone is busy syncing or talking to a network, you see the Mac OS X–like "I'm doing something" symbol.

Icon See That (continued)

 Call forwarding: If you've turned on call forwarding for your phone (a feature that I discuss in Chapter 3), this symbol appears.

 Lock: Your phone is locked.

 Play: Your iPhone is playing music.

 Alarm: You've set an alarm.

Bluetooth: If you see a blue or white Bluetooth icon, the iPhone is linked to a Bluetooth device. If you see a gray Bluetooth icon, Bluetooth is on, but the phone's not linked to a Bluetooth device.

Battery: This icon indicates the battery level and charging status. A battery icon with a lightning bolt tells you that the phone is charging. When you see a battery icon with a plug icon, the battery is connected to a power supply and fully charged. A battery icon without a lightning-bolt or plug icon tells you that the iPhone isn't plugged into power. The solid portion of the battery icon tells you approximately how much power is left in the battery. If, on an iPhone 3GS, you've switched on the Battery Percentage feature (tap Settings > General > Usage), you'll see the percentage of remaining battery charge—94%, for example—listed to the left of the battery icon.

TTY: If the iPhone is configured to work with a TTY (teletypewriter—a telecommunications device used by the audibly impaired to translate spoken text into type), this symbol appears.

The back

Other than the shiny Apple logo, the iPhone name, the iPhone's capacity, and some really tiny print, the only thing you'll find on the back of the phone is the camera lens.

note And by "the only thing," I do mean that you won't find a lever, switch, or button to open the iPhone for the purpose of replacing its battery. Like the iPod, the iPhone doesn't offer a user-replaceable battery. When your iPhone's battery gives up the ghost, you must have it serviced. See Chapter 10 for more on the iPhone's battery.

Applications

Steve Jobs wasn't kidding when he claimed that the iPhone is a wide-screen iPod, a mobile phone, and an Internet communications device. As I write these words, Apple bundles 19 applications with the iPhone 3GS and 18 with the iPhone 3G. (The difference is the Compass application, which isn't included in the iPhone 3G.) You access these applications from the iPhone's Home screen, which you can summon easily by clicking the Home button on the face of the phone.

The Big Four

The iPhone's four most powerful applications—the ones that act as the gateway to the device's phone, music, video, email, and Web browsing functions—appear at the bottom of the Home screen, much like the Dock in Mac OS X.

Phone
Tap the Phone icon on the Home screen, and you're taken to the main Phone screen, where you can make calls, pull up a list of your

contacts, view recent calls, and listen to your voice mail. I describe this area in rich detail in Chapter 3.

Mail

This application is the iPhone's email client. As with the email client on your computer, you use the iPhone's Mail app to compose and send messages, as well as to read and manage received email. I look at Mail in Chapter 4.

Safari

Safari is Apple's Web browser. Unlike other mobile phones, the iPhone carries a real live Web browser rather than a "baby browser" that grudgingly allows you to view only a small portion of the material a Web page offers. When you pull up a Web page in the iPhone's Safari, it looks and behaves like a real Web page. Chapter 5 is devoted to Safari.

iPod

Perhaps the coolest iPod ever made is incorporated into your iPhone. Capable of playing both audio and video, the iPhone is a wonderful on-the-go media player. Look to Chapter 6 for the ins and outs of the iPod functions.

The stores

An iPhone running version 2.0 or later of the iPhone software lets you purchase music and videos and download podcasts from the iTunes Store and buy iPhone and iPod touch applications from Apple's App Store. These tasks are handled by the iTunes and App Store applications, respectively. I devote all of Chapter 7 to these stores.

The Littler 14 (plus 1)

The built-in applications don't stop with the Big Four and the store applications. The iPhone also includes smaller applications that handle things like text messaging, calendars, stocks, and weather.

Messages

No, this app isn't a full-blown IM client, though it looks like one (specifically, like Mac OS X's iChat). This application is for sending and receiving SMS text messages. I look at the Messages application in Chapter 3.

Calendar

When you sync your iPhone, you can transfer calendar events and alarms from Apple's iCal and from Microsoft's Entourage and Outlook. If you have a MobileMe or Microsoft Exchange account, you can sync the calendar information from these services automatically over the air. These transferred and synced items appear in the iPhone's Calendar application. You can also add events directly to the phone by using the iPhone's keyboard and then sync those events with your computer or a MobileMe or Exchange server. I discuss Calendar in more detail in Chapter 4.

Photos

Tap the Photos icon, and you see a list of photo albums—the first holding the pictures you've taken with the iPhone's camera; the next, the complete collection of all synced photos on the iPhone; and then any albums or folders you've synced with the phone. Chapter 8 offers more details on the iPhone's photo capabilities.

Camera

Use this application to snap a picture with the built-in 2-megapixel (iPhone 3G) or 3-megapixel (iPhone 3GS) camera. If you have an iPhone 3GS, you can also shoot and edit videos with the Camera app. The camera, photos, and movies shot with the iPhone 3GS are the subjects of Chapter 8.

YouTube

With this application, you can view streamed YouTube videos on your iPhone. YouTube, being a visual-based application, is examined in Chapter 8.

Stocks

Similar to the Stocks widget in Apple's Mac OS X, the iPhone's Stocks application lets you track your favorite stocks in near real time. All widgety things are detailed in Chapter 9.

Maps

Lost? A street map is just a tap away. Based on Google Maps, this application quickly provides not only maps, but also current driving conditions, satellite views, the locations of businesses within each map, GPS, and (if you have an iPhone 3GS) directional information. Chapter 9 covers the Maps app.

Weather

Much like another Mac OS X widget, the Weather application displays current conditions, as well as the six-day forecasts for locations of your choosing. Like I said, Chapter 9 is great.

Voice Memos

A feature that appeared with the iPhone 3.0 software update, Voice Memos allows you to record and play back audio through the iPhone's microphone. You just know that I'm going to discuss it in Chapter 9.

Notes

Notes is the iPhone's tiny text editor. Use the phone's virtual keyboard to create lists, jot down reminders, compose haiku, or remind yourself to look in Chapter 9 for more details.

Clock

Find the time anywhere in the world, as well as create clocks of favorite locations. You also use the Clock application to create alarms and to invoke the stopwatch and countdown timer. Yeah, see Chapter 9 for this one too.

Calculator

Still can't figure out an appropriate tip without using your fingers? Pull up the iPhone's Calculator to perform common math operations (and, with the Scientific Calculator view that appears when you turn the iPhone to a horizontal position, not-so-common math operations too). You're not going to make me write it again, are you? *Sigh.* OK, Chapter 9.

Settings

Settings is the "plus one" application in this list. Though Settings technically isn't an application, a tap of the Settings icon produces a preferences window for configuring such features as airplane mode, Wi-Fi, 3G, data fetching, phone use, sounds, brightness, wallpaper, general settings (including date and time, autolock, password lock, network,

Bluetooth, and keyboard), mail, phone, Safari, iPod, and photos. Some third-party applications plant their settings in this screen as well. Though I discuss Settings in regard to specific applications throughout this little tome, I provide the big picture in Chapter 2.

Compass (iPhone 3GS only)

As I mention earlier in this chapter, the iPhone 3GS has a built-in magnetometer. This impressive-sounding bit of circuitry tells the iPhone the direction in which it's pointing—northeast or southwest, for example. To glean this kind of information, tap the Compass app to view . . . well, a compass. The Compass gets its moment in the sun in Chapter 9 as well.

Contacts

Some people objected to the iPhone's contacts being buried in the Phone area of the device, so with version 2.0 of the iPhone software, Apple took the Contacts application that it created for the iPod touch and added it to the iPhone's suite of applications (and it remains part of that suite with software version 3.0). I mention this app in Chapter 9, but all you really need to know is that it provides almost exactly the same functions as the Contacts entry in the iPhone area.

Full Gestures

The iPhone's screen is deliberately touchy: Touching it is how you control the device. This section covers the gestures you use to navigate and control your phone.

Tap

You're going to see the word *tap* a lot in this book. When you want to initiate an action—launch an application, control the phone's iPod play-back features, flip a object around, or move to the next screen—this

gesture is the one you'll likely use. If you've turned on the iPhone 3GS'
VoiceOver accessibility features—a feature that help the visually and
aurally impaired use the phone—a single tap selects an item. I cover
accessibility in Chapter 2.

Tap and hold

You use the tap-and-hold gesture when editing text—either to bring up
the magnifying-glass icon to help insert a cursor or to initiate the process
for cutting, copying, and pasting text. The iPhone 3.0 software introduces
cut, copy, and paste to the iPhone, allowing you to work more readily
with text or Web-site content. See "Entering and Editing Text" later in this
chapter for more on cut, copy, and paste.

Double tap

Sometimes, just one tap won't do. Double-tapping often enlarges or
contracts an image—zooms in on a photo or Web-page column, for
example, or returns it to its normal size after you've enlarged it. Other
times, it can make items return to the previous view.

When the VoiceOver feature is on, a double tap acts like a single tap ordi-
narily does. With VoiceOver engaged, one tap tells you what you're touching, and a double tap launches the application or item you want to use.

If you engage the Zoom feature—another accessibility option—a double
tap with three fingers zooms the display.

Flick

If you want to scroll up or down a long list rapidly on your iPhone, zip
through a selection of album covers in the iPhone's Cover Flow view (a
view that allows you to browse your music and podcast collection by
album cover/artwork), or flip from one photo to another, you use the flick

gesture. As you flick faster, the iPhone attempts to match your action by scrolling or zipping more rapidly. Slower flicks produce less motion on the display.

To stop the motion initiated by a flick, just place your finger on the display. Motion stops instantly.

Two-finger flick

With the iPhone 3.0 software, Apple expands the iPhone's gestures to accept multifinger touches. If you download Apple's Remote app from the App Store (a wonderful application for controlling iTunes remotely on your computer or on Apple TV), you'll find that when controlling an Apple TV device, a two-finger flick to the left causes a video playing on Apple TV to back up 10 seconds. I expect that we'll see more of this gesture as the iPhone matures.

Three-finger flick

As far as I know, the three-finger flick is used only when VoiceOver is on. In that situation, this gesture is used for scrolling.

Drag

For finer control, drag your finger across the display. Use this motion to scroll in a controlled way down a list or email message, or to reposition an enlarged image or Web page. You also drag the iPhone's volume slider and playhead when you're in the iPod area.

Three-finger drag

This multifinger gesture works only with the Zoom accessibility feature. When Zoom is on, a three-finger drag moves the screen so that you can see the parts hidden by the zoom.

Rotor

This is another special gesture reserved for when VoiceOver is turned on. You place two fingers on the iPhone's screen and turn them as though you were turning a dial. I'll talk more about this gesture when I discuss accessibility in Chapter 2.

Stretch/pinch

To expand an image, such as a photo or Web page, place your thumb and index finger together on the iPhone's display and then stretch them apart. To make an image smaller, start with your thumb and finger apart and then pinch them together.

Touch and drag

You use this gesture when you want to change the positions of icons. Tap and hold icons on the Home screen, for example, and they start wiggling, indicating that they can be moved. Touch and drag one of them to move it to a different place, or touch and drag it to the edge of the screen to move it to another Home-screen page. In the iPod's More area, you'll find the option to swap out icons along the bottom of the display by touching and dragging new icons into place. You also touch and drag entries in the On-The-Go playlist to change their positions in the list.

Entering and Editing Text

Taps, pinches, and drags help you navigate the iPhone, but they won't compose email messages for you, correct spelling mistakes, or delete ill-considered complaints. The iPhone's keyboard and a well-placed finger will do these jobs.

Touch typing

The iPhone's virtual keyboard largely matches the configuration of your computer's keyboard. You'll find an alphabetic layout when you open most applications (**Figure 1.2**). To capitalize characters, tap the up-arrow key (the iPhone's Shift key). To view numbers and most punctuation, tap the .?123 key. To see less-used characters (including £, ¥, and €), choose the numbers layout by tapping the .?123 key and then tapping the #+= key. The Space, Return, and Delete keys do exactly what you'd expect. You can produce alternative characters, such as those with accents or umlauts, by tapping and holding the most appropriate character and then waiting for a pop-up menu of characters to appear. Tap and hold the letter *E*, for example, and you get a menu that includes such characters as *è, é, ê,* and *ë*.

Figure 1.2
The iPhone's keyboard.

To make typing easier, the keyboard's layout changes depending on the application you're using. In Mail, for example, the bottom row holds the @ symbol along with a period (.). Tap and hold that period key, and a pop-up menu displays .net, .edu, .org, and .com; append these extensions simply by sliding your finger over the one you want and then pulling your finger away. While you're working in Safari, the default layout shows period (.), slash (/), and .com keys along the bottom. Tap and hold the .com key to see a pop-up menu that also includes .net, .edu, and .org. In the bad old days before the iPhone 3.0 software, only Safari allowed you to type in landscape orientation—providing you a keyboard that offered more space between keys. Now all of Apple's applications that support text input offer landscape orientation. Just turn the iPhone on its side, and the screen swivels and displays the broader keyboard.

> **tip** When you type a character, its magnified image appears as you touch it. If you tap the wrong character, leave your finger where it is and slide it to the character you want; the character won't be "typed" until you let go of it.

Editing text

The iPhone offers a unique way to edit text. You needn't tap the Delete key time and again to work your way back to your mistake. Instead, tap and hold the line of text you want to edit. When you do, a magnifying glass appears (**Figure 1.3**), showing a close-up view of the area under your finger. Inside this magnified view is a blinking cursor. Drag the cursor to where you want to make your correction—after the word or letter you want to correct—and then press the Delete key to remove the text. In most cases, you can also tap between words to insert the cursor there.

Figure 1.3
Tap and hold to magnify your mistakes.

Cut, Copy, and Paste

Let the heavenly trumpets blare: Cut, copy, and paste are now possible with the iPhone! What's more, they're easy to do.

Editing text

To select text for cutting or pasting in editable text—such as an email message or note—tap where you want to insert a cursor and then tap the cursor that you just inserted. A balloon appears that includes the words *Select, Select All,* and (if you've already copied something) *Paste.* To select the word closest to the cursor, tap Select. To select everything on the page, tap Select All.

When you do either of these things, the balloon changes to display the words *Cut, Copy,* and *Paste;* the text is highlighted in blue; and blue handles appear at the beginning and end of the text (**Figure 1.4**).

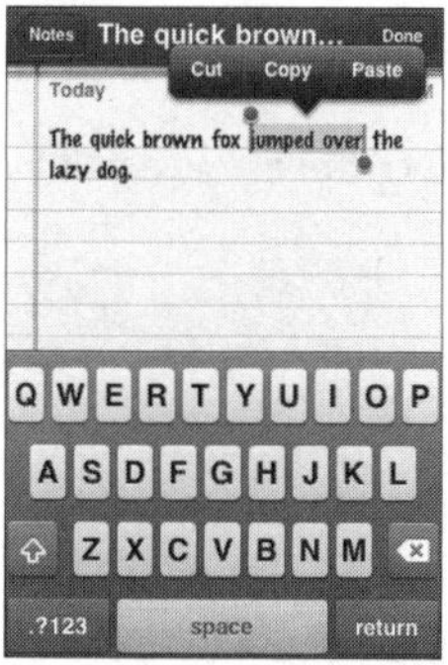

Figure 1.4
With a couple of taps, you can cut, copy, and paste on your iPhone.

To alter the size of the selection, just drag the handles. When you've selected what you want, tap Cut to make the selected text disappear and add it to the iPhone's clipboard (a virtual holding area for storing cut and copied items), Copy to leave the text where it is but also place a copy of it on the clipboard, or Paste to replace the selected text with whatever is currently on the clipboard.

To paste material on the clipboard, just tap somewhere to place the insertion cursor, tap that cursor, and select Paste in the balloon.

If you want to copy *jumped over* from the phrase *The quick brown fox jumped over the lazy dog* in the Notes application, for example, you do this:

1. Tap next to the *j* in *jumped* to insert the cursor.

2. Tap the cursor to select *jumped* and produce the Select, Select All, Paste balloon.

3. Tap Select, and drag the blue handle at the end of *jumped* to the end of the word *over.*

4. With *jumped over* now selected, tap Copy.

Now, to insert the phrase *jumped over* into an email message, do this:

1. Return to the Home screen by clicking the Home button.

2. Tap the Mail application, and create a new email message.

3. Tap to place the cursor in the message.

4. Tap that cursor to produce the Select, Select All, Paste balloon.

5. Tap Paste to insert *jumped over* at the cursor location.

Copying Safari text

You can copy (though not cut) content from Safari as well, even though that text is not editable. Launch Safari, and tap the text you'd like to copy. The magnifying-glass icon appears, and you can choose a selection point. Then, just as you do with text in an email or SMS message, you can expand the selection and copy it.

> **tip**   If you'd like to copy an entire block of text—a column of text on a Web
> site, for example—just tap the edge of that block, away from any
> specific text. Everything in the block is automatically selected, and a Copy
> balloon appears.

Once more, here's a real-world example.

You're in a wedding band and preparing for the next client's trip down
the aisle. The bride and groom have requested Nirvana's "Smells Like
Teen Spirit." The band leader launches Safari, uses Google to search for
Smells Like Teen Spirit lyrics, and taps one of the many links that produce
those lyrics.

On the resulting Web page, she discovers that the lyrics are contained
within a block. She taps one of the edges of the block to highlight all the
text in the block and then taps Copy to copy it.

Next, she clicks the Home button, taps Mail, creates a new email
message, taps in the body of the message to insert the cursor, taps the
cursor, and taps Paste in the balloon that appears. The lyrics are pasted
into the message. Finally, she addresses the message to the band's singer
and sends it.

Copying Safari images

You can also copy images in Safari. To do that, just tap and hold an image.
A screen pops up from the bottom of the display, listing either three or
five options.

If the image acts as a hyperlink (meaning that when you tap the image,
you're taken to a Web page linked to that image), you'll see five buttons:
Open, Open in New Page, Save Image, Copy, and Cancel (**Figure 1.5** on the
next page).

Figure 1.5
*Tap and hold a
linked image in
Safari, and you
see these options.*

Above these buttons is the destination address (or *URL*). They work
this way:

- **Open** takes you to the Web page that's linked to the image.

- **Open in New Page** saves the current page and opens a new browser
  page in Safari. (I cover this multiple-page Safari stuff in Chapter 5.)

- **Save Image** places a copy of the image in the Photos application.

- **Copy** places on the clipboard a copy of the URL that's linked to the image.

- **Cancel** does exactly what it suggests.

If the image isn't linked to anything but is simply a picture, when you tap
it, you see the Save Image, Copy, and Cancel buttons:

- **Save Image** places a copy of the image in the Photos application.

- **Copy** copies the image to the clipboard, thus providing you the opportunity to paste it into an email message.

- **Cancel** does . . . you know.

tip   Cut, copy, and paste aren't limited to Notes, Safari, and Mail. You can
copy and paste the contents of SMS messages in the Messages application and numbers that appear in the Calculator application's results field.
Also, because the cut, copy, and paste features are available to anyone who
creates iPhone applications, you'll find them used in a variety of apps that you
can purchase from the App Store.

2

Setup, Sync, and Settings

In this book's important first pages, I outline how to lay hands on and activate an iPhone. Having followed those instructions, you now hold an iPhone that's capable of making a call and performing a few Internet-related tricks. What say you add the last bits of magic that let your phone play music and movies, display contacts and events, and glom onto your email?

Setting Up the iPhone

Now that your phone is activated, it's time to establish a relationship between the phone and iTunes to make the phone comfortable with your media, email accounts, and personal information.

Get iTunes

iTunes is, in nearly all instances, the conduit for passing information between your computer and the iPhone. Without it, your iPhone will be a pretty limited hunk of technology. Therefore, if you don't have a copy of iTunes 8.2 or later, now's the time to make a beeline for www.apple.com/itunes/download. The iPhone 3GS (or any iPhone running the 3.0 software) can't be synced without this version (or later) of iTunes, and Apple doesn't include it or any other software in the iPhone box.

iTunes is available in both Macintosh and Windows versions. For the iPhone to work with your Mac, you must be running Mac OS X 10.4.11 or later, and your Mac should have a 500 MHz G3 processor or better. PC users must be running Windows XP (with Service Pack 2) or Vista on a 500 MHz Pentium processor or better.

Plug in the iPhone

Plug the included USB cable into a free USB 2.0 port on your Mac or PC. Then plug the data-connector end of the cable into the bottom of the iPhone. When you do, iTunes should launch automatically and display the Set Up Your iPhone screen. (You may also see a friendly offer to search your iTunes Library for songs that can be turned into ringtones. Feel free to ignore it for now.)

What initially appears on the setup screen with regard to the iPhone depends on whether you've previously jacked an iPhone into your computer. If not, you see a Name field containing something like *Joe Blow's iPhone* and, below that, the Automatically Sync Contacts, Calendars, Email Accounts, and Bookmarks option. (I discuss this option shortly.)

If you've plugged an iPhone into this computer before—if you had an original iPhone or iPhone 3G and have upgraded to the iPhone 3GS, for example—you'll be offered the opportunity to set up your iPhone as a new device or restore it from a backup from your previous phone (**Figure 2.1**).

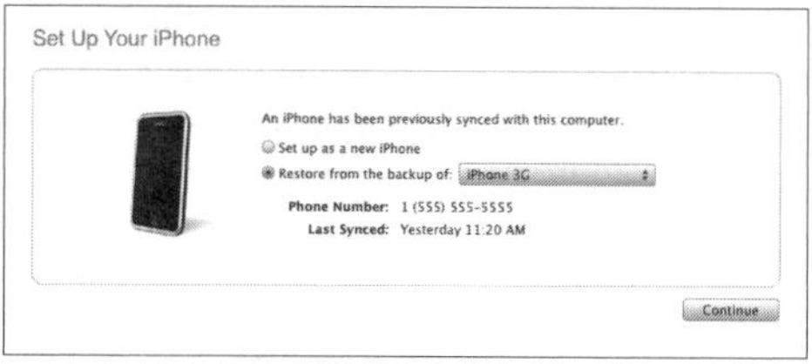

Figure 2.1

Setting up your iPhone when you've already synced an iPhone with this computer.

Set Up Your iPhone

An iPhone has been previously synced with this computer.
○ Set up as a new iPhone
◉ Restore from the backup of: iPhone 3G ⌄
Phone Number: 1 (555) 555-5555
Last Synced: Yesterday 11:20 AM

Continue

To restore your iPhone with this old information, simply select the Restore from the Backup of . . . radio button, click the pop-up menu to the right, choose the backup you'd like to restore from (the Last Synced entry below the menu tells you the age of this backup), and then click Continue. The iPhone displays *Restore in Progress* while iTunes restores it with the data from the backup you selected.

If this iPhone is your first, you won't see these choices but simply a screen in which you can name and automatically sync your phone.

If you're using a Mac, iTunes syncs the iPhone with your Address Book contacts, iCal calendars, Apple Mail accounts, and Safari bookmarks.

If you're using a Windows PC, iTunes syncs contacts from Yahoo Address Book, Windows Address Book (called Windows Contacts in Windows Vista), Google Contacts, or Microsoft Outlook; calendars from Outlook; and email accounts from Windows Mail (included with Vista), Outlook Express (Windows XP), or Outlook.

Notes are synced on a Mac to Apple's Mail and on a PC to Outlook.

note   An iPhone running the 2.0 or later software can also sync contacts, calendars, and email from a Microsoft Exchange account, but it won't do so when you first set up the iPhone because it doesn't know your Exchange information. After you create an Exchange account on your iPhone (one created for you at your place of work, for example), the Exchange server will automatically send (or *push*) contacts, calendars, and mail to your iPhone.

If you'd rather tell iTunes exactly what information to sync, you can do this later and in a more specific fashion. To choose the manual method, simply uncheck the Automatically Sync Contacts box in this window and then click Done.

Tabtastic

If you've synced a display-bearing iPod with your Mac or PC lately, you won't be startled by the iPhone Preferences window in iTunes. Like the iPod Preferences window, this one contains a series of tabs for syncing data to the iPhone. Those tabs shake out as follows.

Summary

As its name suggests, the Summary tab provides an overview of your iPhone. Here, you find the iPhone's name (which you can change by click-ing it in iTunes' Source list and entering a new name), its capacity, the software version it's running, its serial number, and its phone number (**Figure 2.2**).

Figure 2.2
The iPhone's Summary tab.

In the Version portion of the window, you learn whether your iPhone's software is up to date. (You can make sure that you have the latest version by clicking the Check for Update button.) Here, you also find a Restore button for placing a new version of the iPhone software on the device. I revisit this button in Chapter 10.

The Summary tab provides four or five options, depending on the model of iPhone you've plugged into your computer. The first, Automatically Sync When This iPhone Is Connected, does exactly that: It tells iTunes to sync your phone whenever you dock it. If iTunes isn't running when you dock the iPhone, the phone launches automatically and starts syncing. Disable this option if you don't want iTunes to replace any of the iPhone's content automatically. This setting is carried with the phone, which means that regardless of which computer you jack the phone into, it does what this setting instructs.

tip   **The Devices panel of the iTunes Preferences window contains an option similar to this one: the Disable Automatic Syncing for iPhones and iPods check box. The option in the Summary tab applies only to an individual iPhone; the iTunes setting applies to *all* iPhones and iPod touches. When you check Disable Automatic Syncing for iPhones and iPods, no iPhone or iPod touch connected to the computer will sync.**

The second option—Sync Only Checked Songs and Videos—tells the iPhone to sync only those checked items in your iTunes Library. If you want greater control over what is planted on your iPhone, you can check some songs or videos on a playlist in your iTunes Library but not others. The check boxes appear next to the names of the items—"Love Me Do" and *Casablanca*, for example. When this option is turned on, when you sync the iPhone, it syncs only the items you've checked.

The third option—Manually Manage Music and Videos—makes it possible to drag content from your iTunes Library to the iPhone in iTunes'

Source list. You can't do this to add music from another computer's library; the iPhone can be synced with only one iTunes Library.

 tip **This option is a good one to use when you want to add something to the iPhone quickly, without going through the whole syncing rigmarole.**

When you check Encrypt iPhone Backup, which is the fourth and last option if you have anything but an iPhone 3GS, you ask iTunes to back up your iPhone and password-protect your data. You might do this with a company-issued iPhone containing sensitive information that you back up to your computer.

When you select this option, you'll be prompted to enter and verify a password. Thereafter, your iPhone will be backed up completely (even if you just backed it up recently), and the backup will be protected. Should you want to change the password—say, because foreign agents weaseled it out of you by tickling your tootsies—click the Change Password button, enter your old password, and then enter and verify a new password.

 tip **Encrypting a backup can take iTunes a very long time. You might consider starting this process just before you go to bed. It should be complete when you awaken in the morning.**

If you have that iPhone 3GS, you'll also see a Configure Universal Access button at the bottom of the options list. Click it to open a Universal Access window, where you can choose which (if any) of the iPhone's accessibility features to switch on (**Figure 2.3**).

Figure 2.3
Click the Universal Access button in iTunes to configure accessibility options for the iPhone 3GS.

Info

The Info tab is where you choose which data—contacts, calendars, notes, mail accounts, and browser bookmarks—you'd like to sync to your iPhone (**Figure 2.4**). This tab is also where you configure iTunes to push email, calendars, contacts, and bookmarks from Apple's MobileMe service to the iPhone.

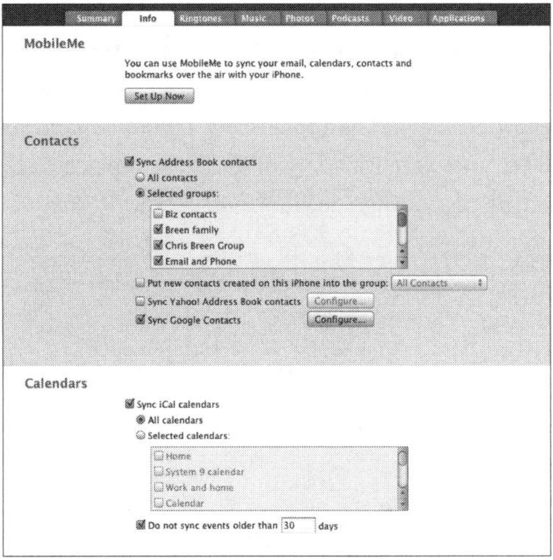

Figure 2.4
The iPhone's Info tab.

MobileMe

To set up MobileMe, you first have to have a MobileMe account, which costs $100 annually. You can sign up for just such an account at www.apple.com/mobileme. (Apple offers a 60-day free trial if you'd like to test the service before committing.)

Having signed up, click the Set Up Now button in the MobileMe area of the iPhone's Info tab. A MobileMe Setup page appears in your default browser. Here, you find links for setting up Macs as well as Windows PCs. Essentially, the steps break down this way:

1. After downloading iTunes 8.2 or later, sync your contacts, calendars, and bookmarks with your iPhone.

   You enable these options in the Info tab.

2. Sync your data with MobileMe.

   You do this on a Mac from within the MobileMe system preference. Just choose MobileMe in System Preferences; click the Sync tab; enable the Synchronize with MobileMe option; check the Bookmarks, Calendars, and Contacts boxes in the list box; and click Sync Now (**Figure 2.5**). A MobileMe Sync Alert dialog box appears; via a pop-up menu, it lets you Merge All Data, Replace Data on Computer, or Replace All Data on Mobile Me. Choose the setting you want, and click Sync. Your data will be synced.

Figure 2.5
The MobileMe preference's Sync tab on a Macintosh.

On a Windows PC, choose the MobileMe Preferences item in Windows' Control Panels area. (This control panel is installed when you install iTunes 8.2 or later.) Click the Sync tab, and as you would on a Mac, enable Contacts, Calendars, and Bookmarks. As I mention earlier in this chapter, for contacts, you have the option to sync Google, Outlook, Yahoo Address Book, and Windows contacts. Only Outlook calendars are supported. Also, you can sync either Internet Explorer or Safari bookmarks. Just like on the Mac, when you click Sync Now, you see an alert box that offers you the option to merge or replace data.

3. Configure MobileMe on the iPhone.

Tap the Settings button on the Home screen; tap the Mail, Contacts, Calendars entry; and ensure that Push is set as the Fetch New Data option. If it isn't, tap Fetch New Data, and switch the Push option on in the resulting Fetch New Data screen.

If you haven't yet added your MobileMe account to the iPhone, now's the time. Tap Mail, Contacts, Calendars, and in the screen that appears, tap Add Account. In the resulting Add Account screen, tap MobileMe. In the sheet that appears, add your name, MobileMe address (such as *example@me.com*), MobileMe password, and a description of the account (such as *Chris' MobileMe*). Tap Save to add the account.

Return to the Mail, Contacts, Calendars screen; tap the MobileMe entry; and choose those kinds of data—Mail, Contacts, Calendars, and Bookmarks—that you'd like to sync with your iPhone. Just flick the On/Off slider to On for those bits of information. When everything is set up the way you want it, tap the Mail arrow in the top-left corner of the screen, and your settings will be saved.

And . . . say what? Oh, yes—the Find My iPhone entry at the bottom of your MobileMe screen. I address that entry fully in Chapter 10, but to help you hold out until then, I'll explain that if you have a MobileMe account, you have the ability to trace your phone's whereabouts, whether it's hiding under the fridge, resting in the back yard where your dog buried it, or chugging away in the back of a sardine trawler. When you switch on the Find My iPhone option, this wonder becomes possible. When the option is off, nuh-uh.

Contacts

Here, you find settings for syncing all your contacts or just selected groups that you've created in Address Book (if you use a Mac) or in Windows Address Book, Outlook, Yahoo Address Book, and Google Calendars. (On a Mac, the Yahoo and Google options are listed at the

bottom of the Contacts area. Click the Configure button next to either
one, agree to the license agreement, and enter your Yahoo or Google user
name and password. When this option is enabled, your Yahoo Address
Book and Google contacts will make their way to the iPhone too.)

Below this area, you see the option to put new contacts that you create
on the iPhone in a specific group within Address Book or Outlook. You
also see an option for syncing your online Yahoo Address Book and
Google contacts.

Calendars

This area works similarly. You can choose to sync all your calendars or, if
you're using a Mac, just selected calendars you've created in Apple's iCal
(your work calendar, for example, but not your personal calendar). With
the iPhone 2.0 software and later, the iPhone displays multiple calendars in its Calendar application. I discuss calendars in greater depth in
Chapter 4.

Web Browser

In this area of the Info window in the Macintosh version of iTunes, you'll
find a Sync Safari Bookmarks check box. On a Windows PC, a pop-up
menu provides the option to sync Safari or Internet Explorer bookmarks.

Notes

Notes is an on/off option. Enable Sync Notes in the Mac version of iTunes,
and any notes created on the iPhone will be synced to the Notes area
of Mail—Apple's email client. Likewise, if you create a note in Mail and
have this option enabled, that note will be synced to your iPhone.) On a
Windows PC, notes are be synced to Outlook (and vice versa here, too).
I take a closer look at Notes in Chapter 9.

Mail Accounts

iTunes looks for email account settings in Mail on a Mac and in Outlook, Microsoft Mail, and Outlook Express on a Windows PC. (It looks for the settings only; syncing mail accounts doesn't sync messages.) The settings that it finds appear in a list in the Mail Accounts area of the Info tab. You have the option to select the email account(s) you'd like to access with the iPhone.

tip If, after allowing iTunes to add email accounts to the Info tab automatically, you add a different account (maybe you've changed Internet service providers or taken on a MobileMe account, for example), iTunes will add the account to the Mail Accounts area automatically when you next sync your iPhone.

The Mail/Entourage Relationship

Although the iPhone doesn't support pulling account information from Microsoft's popular Macintosh email client, Entourage 2004 and 2008, it can sync Entourage contacts and calendars, but in an indirect way. Recent versions of Entourage include a new Sync Service feature, which you find in Entourage's Preferences window. Choose Sync Services, and you find the option to synchronize contacts with Apple's Address Book and .Mac (now called MobileMe). Likewise, you can synchronize Entourage events and tasks with iCal and MobileMe. (Entourage's Notes, however, are not supported by the iPhone.) When this option is switched on, Address Book, iCal, and Entourage swap data as you add it.

Enable Sync Services, and any events and contacts you've stored in Entourage are synced to your iPhone. Leave it off, and your Entourage data remains missing in action.

Advanced

Finally, the Advanced area offers a nifty little workaround when you plug your iPhone into another computer. For this feature to work, you must first choose at least one option above—say, Sync Address Book Contacts—and then choose the options you want in that area (choose to sync a specific group of contacts, for example). Now enable the related option in the Advanced area (you'd choose Contacts if you enabled Sync Address Book Contacts). When you click the Apply button in the bottom-right corner of the window, iTunes overwrites the selected information that's currently on the iPhone with the information stored on the computer to which the iPhone is connected.

Note the word *overwrite*. If you do this, the information you had on the iPhone is deleted.

Ringtones

The iPhone can play ringtones that you purchase from the iTunes Store. In this tab, you choose which ringtones to sync with your iPhone—all or just selected ringtones (**Figure 2.6**). I discuss creating and purchasing ringtones in Chapter 7.

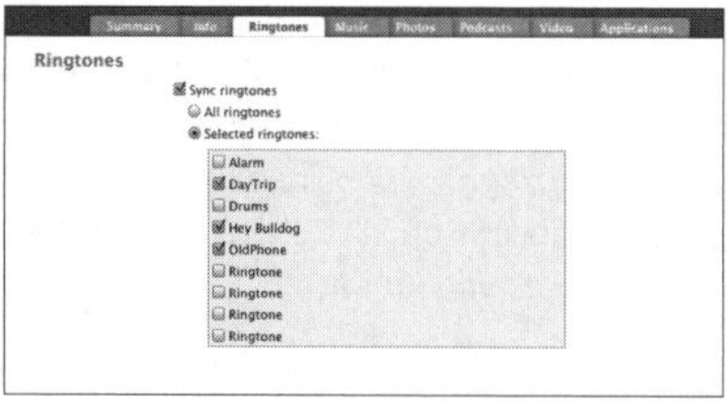

Figure 2.6
*The iPhone's
Ringtones tab.*

Music

The Music tab is exactly like the one in the iPod Preferences window (**Figure 2.7**). Enable the Sync Music option and then choose to sync All Songs and Playlists or just Selected Playlists. (All the playlists in your iTunes Library appear in the list box; you can select just some of them to sync to your iPhone.) At the bottom of the window, you find the option to include music videos and voice memos when you sync your iTunes music. In Chapter 6, I discuss how to sync music most efficiently.

Figure 2.7
The iPhone's Music tab.

Photos

If you use a Mac, the iPhone can sync photos with Apple's iPhoto and Aperture, as well as with your Photos folder or a different folder of your choosing (**Figure 2.8** on the next page). On a Windows PC, it can sync with your My Pictures folder (called simply Pictures in Windows Vista), a different folder of your choosing, or photo albums created with Adobe Photoshop Elements 3.0 or later or Adobe Photoshop Album 2.0 or later.

When syncing with an application that supports albums—iPhoto, for example—you can select specific albums to sync with. If you're syncing with a folder, you'll see the option to sync with specific folders within that folder.

Figure 2.8
*The iPhone's
Photos tab.*

I cover photos in rich detail in Chapter 8.

Podcasts

Just as you can on an iPod, you can listen to podcasts on your iPhone.
Because people tend to listen to lots of podcasts, some of which tend
to be long (their files therefore taking up significant amounts of room),
iTunes lets you manage which ones are synced to your iPhone (**Figure 2.9**).

Figure 2.9
*The iPhone's
Podcasts tab.*

As in each one of these tabs, you have the option to not sync this content,
but if you choose to do so, you have plenty of options. You can choose
all podcasts, all unplayed podcasts, or all new podcasts. Or you can play
1, 3, 5, or 10 of the following: the most recent podcasts, the most recent
unplayed podcasts, the least recent unplayed podcasts, the most recent

new podcasts, or the least recent new podcasts. These settings apply to all your podcasts or just to those you've selected.

tip Video as well as audio podcasts are listed in this tab. Because video can consume a lot of storage space, be careful how you choose your video podcasts.

For more on podcasts, check Chapter 6.

Video

This tab is where you configure the transfer of movies you've rented from the iTunes Store and the syncing of TV shows and movies. I cover movie rentals in Chapter 7. For now, all you need to know is that the movies you rent from the iTunes Store first appear in the top portion of this pane. From there, you can transfer them to your iPhone or video-capable iPod.

The TV Shows and Movies sections below work very much like the Podcasts tab. To help you sync exactly the video you want, the TV Shows and Movies areas of this tab allow you to sync very specifically (**Figure 2.10**).

Figure 2.10
The iPhone's Video tab.

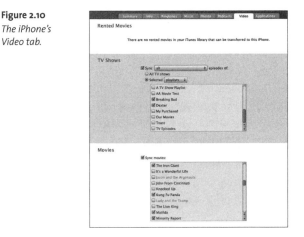

In the TV Shows area, you see all the TV programs listed in the TV Shows category in iTunes' Source list. You can sync all or the 1, 3, 5, or 10 most recent TV shows among all TV shows or just the selected shows or play-lists in the list of shows below. Or you can sync all unwatched or the 1, 3, 5, or 10 most recent unwatched or least recent unwatched episodes of all TV shows or selected TV shows or playlists.

tip What's with all this "least recent unwatched episodes" jazz? If you've downloaded a season of a TV show, you'd choose this option so that the shows sync in order from the beginning of the season to the end. If, instead, you chose the most recent unwatched episodes, playback would start with the last show and then work its way backward. (If that won't spoil the suspense, I don't know what would!)

The Movies area of the Video tab is very straightforward. You'll find a simple Sync Movies check box that you enable if you want to sync movies to the iPhone. Just select from the list the movies you want to sync. This list is derived from the movies that fall within the Movies category in iTunes' Source list.

Applications

Your iPhone can use applications sold at Apple's App Store. This tab is where you manage which apps are synced to your iPhone. I look at the App Store in greater detail in Chapter 7, but if you'd like to take a look now, here's what you're looking at: All applications that you download from the App Store (either from within iTunes or from your iPhone or an iPod touch) are listed in this tab. Those applications that you downloaded from the phone or iPod touch are moved to iTunes only when you sync.

Within this tab, you can choose to sync all applications or just those that you've checked in the list box (**Figure 2.11**).

Figure 2.11
The iPhone's
Applications tab.

Down Below

I would be remiss if I left the iPhone Preferences window without
mentioning the Capacity bar at the bottom (**Figure 2.12**). Familiar
to iPod owners, this bar details how your iPhone's storage space is
being used. Here, you view the total capacity of your iPhone, along
with statistics for Audio, Video, Photos, Apps, Other (a category that
includes contacts, calendars, and applications, for example), and Free
(as in free space).

Figure 2.12
The iTunes
Capacity bar.

By default, the amount of storage consumed by a particular item
appears below its heading (Video 1.25 GB, for example). But if you
click the Capacity bar, the statistics labels change—first to the number of items in each category and then, with another click, to the
amount of time it would take to play all the videos and audio stored
on the iPhone (2.5 days, for example).

To the right of the Capacity bar is the Sync button. Click this button
to sync the iPhone right now rather than wait for the next time you
dock the thing.

(continues on next page)

> **Down Below** (continued)
>
> If you make a change in your sync settings—change photo albums,
> for example, or choose a new movie or podcast to sync—the Sync
> button disappears, and Cancel and Apply buttons take its place. To
> sync the iPhone immediately with the new settings, click Apply. If
> you think better of your choices, click Cancel to undo your changes.

Settings

Although you'll control much of your iPhone's behavior within its applications, some global settings have some bearing on how it performs. You
access these settings by tapping the Settings icon in the iPhone's Home
screen. Here's what Settings contains (**Figure 2.13**).

Figure 2.13
*The Settings
screen.*

Airplane Mode

Modern mobile phones are far more than just devices for annoying patrons
in restaurants and movie theaters. Like the iPhone, they can play music and
videos, as well as display pictures. Although some airlines offer on-board

Wi-Fi, the bulk of today's flights lack this modern miracle. In fact, attempting to use the iPhone's wireless communication features can interfere with an aircraft's navigation system. Thus was born airplane mode, which switches off these features—calling, email, Web browsing, and location services, for example—but allows you to use the phone's other features.

This mode is a simple On/Off setting. When it's on, you can't make or receive calls, use email, browse the Web, locate yourself in the Maps application, or use a Bluetooth accessory. (Neither can you get the best from a third-party application that requires wireless communication, such as a chat or Twitter client.) You can continue to listen to music, watch videos, check your calendar, listen to your Visual Voicemail, view pictures, play with the Compass on an iPhone 3GS, and read email and text messages stored on the phone.

tip If you're interested in getting the longest media play time out of your iPhone, turn on airplane mode regardless of where you are. Enabling the wireless features—even without using them—pulls power from your battery.

Wi-Fi

The iPhone supports 802.11 wireless networking. In this screen, you can turn Wi-Fi on or off. Turning it off saves some battery power. I describe the workings of the iPhone's Wi-Fi settings in the "Network" section later in this chapter.

Sounds

In the Sounds screen (**Figure 2.14** on the next page), you choose among the iPhone's 25 built-in ringtones, as well as any custom ringtones you've added. You can adjust the volume of these rings by dragging the Volume slider just above the Ringtone entry.

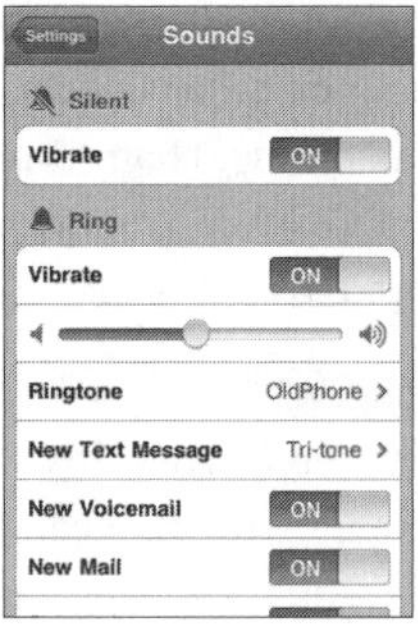

Figure 2.14
*The Sounds
screen.*

You also use the Sounds setting to determine which phone behaviors and events are assigned alert sounds and which aren't. You can set sounds to accompany the arrival of new voice mails, text messages (for which you can choose among six sounds), and emails; the successful sending of email; and calendar alerts, lock sounds, and keyboard clicks. By default, all these actions make sounds; you can turn these sounds off and on, but you can't customize them. To turn one off, just drag its slider from On to Off.

The Sounds setting screen also lets you specify vibrate alerts by using two separate Vibrate switches. When the Vibrate switch below the Silent heading is switched to On, the iPhone vibrates instead of making an audible alert whenever you turn off the ringer with the Ring/Silent switch on the side of the phone; otherwise, the phone issues no alert at all when it's silenced. When the Vibrate switch below the Ring heading is set to On, the iPhone vibrates at the same time that it issues an audible alert.

Brightness

By default, the iPhone's display brightness is adjusted automatically, based on the light it senses around it. When you're outdoors on a sunny day, for example, the screen brightens; when you're inside a dark room, the display dims. If you'd like to override the automatic brightness settings—when you want to save battery power by making the display dimmer than the iPhone thinks necessary, for example—you do so in this screen. Turn auto-brightness off and drag the slider to adjust brightness up or down.

Wallpaper

On the iPhone, *wallpaper* refers to an image you choose, which appears when you unlock the phone or when you're talking to someone whose contact information doesn't have a custom photo attached. To set and adjust your wallpaper picture, tap the Wallpaper control and then navigate to an image file in the collection provided by Apple (listed below the Wallpaper heading), pictures you've taken with the phone's camera, or the images you've synced to the iPhone. Just tap the image, and the iPhone shows you a preview of it as wallpaper (**Figure 2.15**).

Figure 2.15
Changing wallpaper.

You can move any of your images by dragging them around or enlarge them by using the stretch gesture (see Chapter 1). When you're happy with the picture's orientation, tap Set Wallpaper. Interestingly enough, you can't resize any of the images that Apple includes in its Wallpaper collection (because, one assumes, they're perfect just as they are).

General

The General settings are . . . well, pretty general. The grouping consists of a hodgepodge of miscellaneous controls (**Figure 2.16**).

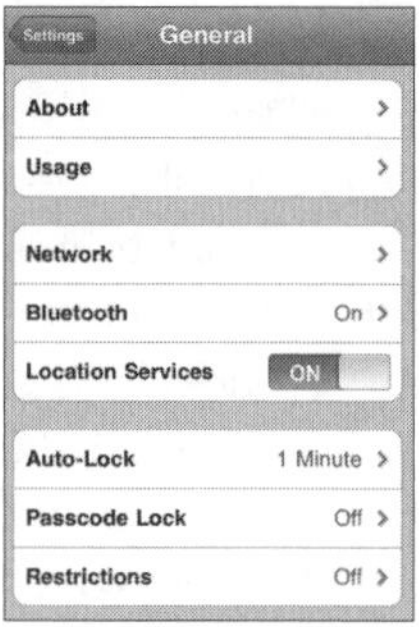

Figure 2.16
*The General
settings screen.*

About

This screen provides your phone's vital statistics—the name of your network; the number of audio tracks, videos, photos, and applications on the iPhone; total capacity; how much storage space remains; software version; carrier (AT&T in the United States); serial and model numbers; Wi-Fi and Bluetooth addresses; the International Mobile Frequency Identity (IMEI) and Integrated Circuit Card Identifier (ICCID); the modem firmware number; and a Legal command that, when tapped, leads to a seemingly endless screen of legal mumbo jumbo.

Usage

If you're wondering how long it's been since your iPhone was fully charged or how many minutes you've yakked, here's where to look. The Usage screen includes information on when you last charged the iPhone fully, how long the iPhone has been in standby mode since the last full charge, the number of minutes you've talked in the current billing period and over the life of the phone, and how much data you've sent and received over the network.

To reset the current call time period and network statistics, tap Reset Statistics. The time since last full charge and lifetime call-time statistics remain after a reset.

On the iPhone 3GS, you see one additional (and useful) entry: Battery Percentage. If you'd like a better idea of exactly how charged your iPhone's battery is, switch this option on. In addition to the iPhone's battery icon—which gives you a very broad notion of how much juice is left in the phone—the Battery Percentage display provides this information in specific percentages, such as 87% (**Figure 2.17**).

Figure 2.17
Get a better idea of the life left in your battery with the iPhone 3GS' Battery Percentage readout.

Network

The Network setting includes settings for turning 3G and data roaming on, initiating Internet tethering, and configuring VPN (virtual private networks) and Wi-Fi.

The Enable 3G and Data Roaming options are straightforward. If you're not within a service area that offers 3G, or if you want to save some wear and tear on your battery charge, you turn 3G off here. The Data Roaming option (a feature for getting data from a network other than the one supplied by your carrier) is there to help you avoid being charged enormous fees when you travel abroad. Turn Data Roaming off, and your phone won't be able to access email, the Web, or other 3G or EDGE services from another network. (You can still use these services over Wi-Fi for no additional charge.) In addition, you may not be able to access Visual Voicemail. You're welcome to switch Data Roaming back on and incur those usurious roaming charges if you like.

Internet tethering is an iPhone 3G and 3GS feature new with the iPhone 3.0 software. This feature allows you to use your iPhone as a wireless modem to connect your computer to the Internet. You set it up this way:

1. Tap General > Network > Internet Tethering.

2. Tap Internet Tethering in the resulting screen.

3. In the Internet Tethering screen, slide the On/Off switch to On.

4. Make the connection.

   If you want to use a USB connection, use the iPhone's data cable to attach the iPhone to a spare USB 2.0 port on your computer. Choose the iPhone from the list of available network options on your Mac or PC.

   To use a Bluetooth connection, initiate Bluetooth pairing on your computer, and choose the iPhone as the device you want to pair with. On the iPhone, wait for a message from your computer—a prompt to accept or the request to enter a code.

5. Celebrate.

   If you've tethered successfully, you should see a blue bar at the top of the iPhone's display that reads *Internet Tethering*.

A VPN is an encrypted network protocol used by many companies that allows authorized outsiders to join the company network, regardless of their locations. When you choose VPN, you're shown the VPN window, which includes a switch for turning VPN on or off; the Choose a Configuration area, which includes any VPN networks you've created; and an Add VPN Configuration button that you tap to view an Add Configuration screen with a list of fields to fill in, including Server, Account, and Password. You can also choose among L2TP, PPTP, and IPSec networks.

> **note** Configuring a VPN is beyond the mission of this small book. The IT department at your company will be able to tell you how to configure VPN on your iPhone.

When you tap the Wi-Fi entry in the Network screen, you're taken to the Wi-Fi Networks screen, atop which appears an On/Off switch for enabling or disabling Wi-Fi on your iPhone. (Disabling Wi-Fi conserves power.) Below that is the Choose a Network area. Any visible Wi-Fi networks within range appear in a list below; those that have a lock icon next to them are password-protected. To access a password-protected network, simply tap its name, enter the password with the keyboard that appears, and tap Join.

To see detailed network information, tap the blue symbol to the right of the network's name. A new screen appears, listing such information as IP Address, Subnet Mask, Router, DNS, Search Domains, and Client ID. At the bottom of one of these screens, you see an HTTP Proxy area with the choice of Off, Manual, and Auto. Again, an IT or ISP representative will tell you if you need to muck with these settings.

> **tip** If a network that you never use routinely appears in this list, you can instruct your iPhone to avoid using it by tapping Forget This Network in the resulting screen.

Finally, the bottom of the Wi-Fi Networks screen includes the Ask to Join Networks option. Leave this option set on (as it is by default), and your iPhone will join known networks automatically and ask to join a network if no known network is available. If you switch the option off, you'll have to join networks manually without being asked. To do so, tap Other; then, using the keyboard that appears, enter the name of the network and password (if required).

Bluetooth

This setting is a simple on/off option. When you turn it on, the iPhone becomes discoverable and searches for other Bluetooth devices. Turning Bluetooth off can save power. Any Bluetooth devices you've paired your phone with are listed in the Devices area.

note The iPhone 3.0 software provides improved Bluetooth support. You can now use Bluetooth stereo headphones with the iPhone, for example. You still can't do several other desirable things, however, such as use a Bluetooth keyboard with your iPhone, copy files between the phone and your computer over a Bluetooth connection, initiate a call by pressing a Bluetooth headset's Call button, or wirelessly sync your iPhone over Bluetooth.

Location Services

The iPhone is one smart smartphone. Unlike some other mobile phones, it knows its location at most times. It performs this trick via three methods: cell-tower triangulation (guessing where it is based on the signal strength of nearby cell towers), Wi-Fi location (its proximity to wireless routers whose location is known), and GPS (Global Positioning System). This feature is slick, but it can eat up the iPhone's battery charge. When you want to conserve power, switch this option off.

Auto-Lock

The iPhone equivalent of a keypad lock, Auto-Lock tells the touchscreen to ignore taps after a customizable period of inactivity. Use these controls to specify that interval: 1, 2, 3, 4, or 5 Minutes, or Never. To make the iPhone pay attention again after it autolocks, click the Home button.

When the iPhone is locked, it can still receive calls and SMS (Short Message Service) text messages, and you can still use the iPhone's Volume switch to change the volume when listening to music or placing calls. The button on the headset's mic works when the iPhone is locked, too.

Passcode Lock

You'd hate to lose your iPhone. Worse, you'd hate to lose your iPhone and have some ne'er-do-well dig through it for your email, contacts, and schedule. If you fear that your iPhone could fall into the wrong hands (and yes, that may just mean your surly teenage daughter), create a passcode. To do so, tap Passcode Lock; then enter and re-enter a four-digit password with the numeric keypad (**Figure 2.18**).

Figure 2.18
The Passcode screen.

The next screen offers the option to turn the passcode off (useful if you decide that you no longer require a passcode), change it (for . . . well, you know), and a Require Passcode area that offers the options Immediately and After 1, 5, 15 Minutes or After 1 or 4 Hours.

After you set a passcode on an iPhone 3GS, you'll see a Voice Dial option. Switch it off, and the Voice Control feature can't be used for dialing (though Voice Control will continue to work for music playback).

Regardless of which iPhone you have, you can configure Passcode Lock to destroy its data (wipe email, contacts, calendars, and media from it), via an Erase Data option, if the wrong passcode is entered ten times.

Restrictions

With the iPhone 2.0 software came a form of parental controls called *restrictions*. The 3.0 software gives you finer control of the kind of content you get from the iTunes and App stores. Tap Restrictions, and in the top part of the screen labeled Allow, you see options for shutting off Safari, YouTube, and the iTunes Store. You can also disable application instal-lation, the camera, and the iPhone's location features. In the Allowed Content area. you can switch off in-application purchases (add-on levels for games, for example), choose ratings for specific countries (Australia, Canada, France, Germany, Ireland, Japan, New Zealand, United Kingdom, and the United States), disallow playing explicit music and podcasts, select allowed movies by rating (G, PG, PG-13, R, and NC-17), select allowed TV shows (TV-Y, TV-Y7, TV-G, TV-PG, TV-14, and TV-MA), and allow apps by age ratings (4+, 9+, 12+, and 17+). By default, restrictions are turned off, meaning that everything is allowed.

To impose restrictions, first tap Enable Restrictions at the top of the screen. You'll be asked to enter and confirm a four-digit password. When you do, you're allowed to use On/Off switches for functions in the Allow section and for the In-App Purchases option. In the Allowed Content area, you tap one of the entries and then tap the ratings restriction you want to impose (**Figure 2.19**). When you're ready to free all the phone's func-tions, tap Disable Restrictions. You'll be asked to enter the restrictions password. When you do, all functionality is restored.

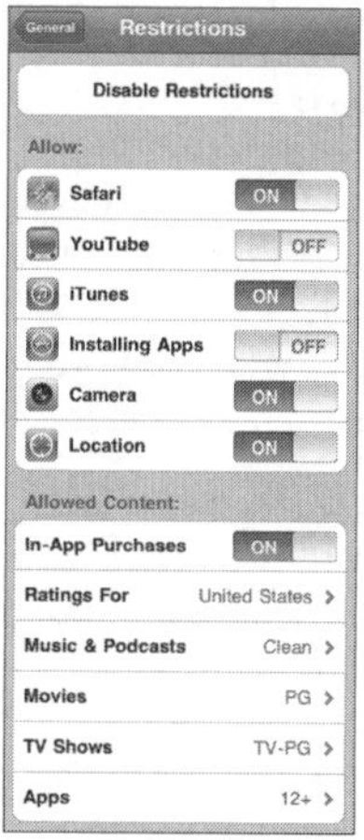

Figure 2.19

All the options available in the Allowed Content area of the Restrictions setting.

Home button

The Home button on the iPhone's face can do more than just transport you to the Home screen. In this setting, you determine what happens when you give the Home button two rapid clicks. Options are Home, Search, Phone Favorites (the default), Camera, and iPod.

Below is an iPod Controls switch. When this switch is on, and you're playing music, double-clicking the Home button shows the iPod play-controls overlay, regardless of how you've set the double-click function.

Date & Time

The Date & Time settings include a switch for enabling 24-hour time and a Set Automatically switch. When this switch is set to On, the phone syncs to your carrier's clock; when it's set to Off, you can enter a time zone, date, and time manually by tapping the Time Zone and Set Date & Time entries on this screen.

Search

With the iPhone 3.0 software come ways to search your iPhone. The obvious way to search is to visit the first page of the Home screen and swipe your finger to the right to produce the Search screen. (You can also click the Home button once while you're on the first page of the Home screen to produce the Search screen.)

The power of search goes beyond this screen, however; it's spread throughout the iPhone applications. When you launch the Contacts application or tap Contacts in the Phone application, for example, you'll find a Search field at the top of the screen. This same kind of Search field appears in other applications, including Mail, Notes, and iPod. In these applications, however, the Search field doesn't appear by default. To produce it, just flick your finger down the screen. The Search field bounces down into view.

You can configure what kind of results you get from the main Search screen by tapping the Search Results entry at the bottom of the Home setting screen (in the General setting). Here, you see a list of items you can search for on your iPhone (Figure 2.20). Search results appear in this order, but you can change that order by dragging items up or down in the list by using the drag handles on the right side of the screen.

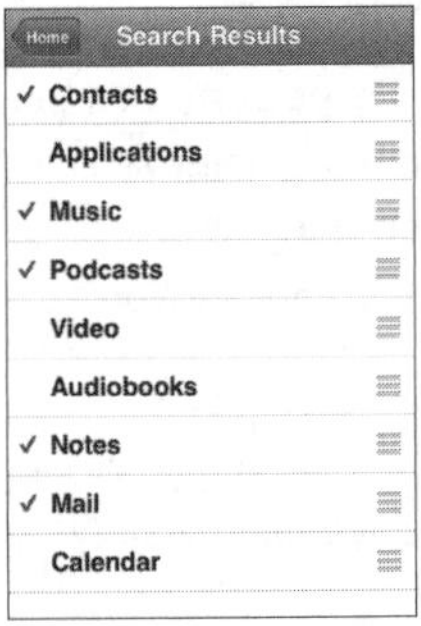

By default, all these options are enabled. If you don't want certain kinds of items to appear when you search—podcasts and calendar items, for example—just tap them to uncheck them.

Figure 2.20
You can limit what your iPhone searches for.

Keyboard

Are you sensitive enough about your iPhone autocorrecting your typing errors that you want to disable that feature? Care to turn autocapitaliza- tion on or off (*on* means that the iPhone automatically capitalizes words after a period, question mark, or exclamation point)? Or to enable or disable Caps Lock (a feature that types in ALL CAPITALS when you double- tap the keyboard's spacebar)? Or configure the iPhone so that when you tap the spacebar at the end of a sentence, the iPhone types a period and adds a space? Here's where you do these things.

Below these four On/Off options, you see International Keyboards. Tap it, and you're taken to a Keyboards screen, where you can switch on additional keyboards. Do so, and when you're using an application that requires the iPhone's keyboard, a small Globe icon appears to the left of the spacebar. Tap it, and you can switch keyboards. The name of the selected keyboard appears briefly on the spacebar. The number of acti- vated keyboards is reflected next to the International Keyboard entry in the Keyboard screen—*International Keyboards 5*, for example.

International

The International setting is where you choose the language for your iPhone, which supports 30 languages, including English, French, Japanese, Chinese, Korean, German, Italian, Portuguese, Romanian, Behasa Indonesian, and Polish.

On an iPhone 3GS, you'll see a Voice Control command below the Language entry. Tap it, and you discover that you can speak to your iPhone in one of 21 languages. The iPhone not only listens for commands in the language you select, but also tells you what it's doing in a robotic form of that language. VoiceOver, the iPhone 3GS' screen reader, speaks in the language that you've chosen here.

tip U.S. iPhone owners who want a tonier-sounding iPhone—yet one that still understands their commands—should choose English (United Kingdom) from this list to hear responses delivered with a feminine British accent.

The Keyboards command appears in the International screen as well. Tap it, and you're taken to your old friend the Keyboards screen, where you can enable additional keyboards.

At the bottom of the International screen, you discover the Region Format command. Tap it, and you can choose among a seemingly endless list of countries supported by the iPhone. Choose a country, and the format for date, time, and telephone number changes.

Accessibility (iPhone 3GS only)

Apple has taken its world-class VoiceOver technology feature from Mac OS X and adapted it for the iPhone. Now the blind and visually impaired can navigate an iPhone's touchscreen—something that many people thought would be impossible—thanks to the voice cues and modified commands offered on the phone.

The accessibility feature offers not only the VoiceOver screen reader— which speaks the name of onscreen elements as well as items under your finger—but also a Zoom feature for enlarging the screen; a White on Black toggle that inverts the iPhone's screen colors, making it easier to read for some visually impaired users; Mono Audio, which mixes the left and right channels of a stereo track into both the left and right earbuds; and Speak Auto-Text, which alerts the user to autocorrections and capitalizations with VoiceOver's voice (**Figure 2.21**).

note You can enable either VoiceOver (the screen reader) or Zoom, which does exactly as its name implies, but not both.

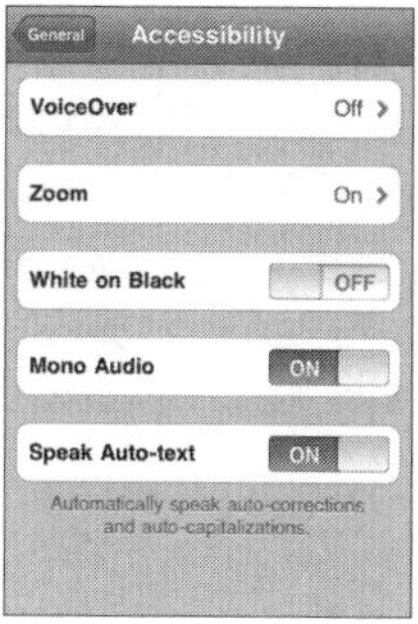

Figure 2.21

The Accessibility screen offers options for the vision- and hearing-impaired.

When you tap VoiceOver, you have a few options:

- You can activate or deactivate the Speak Hints option, which reads items on a screen to you.

- You can adjust the speaking rate with a slider. (I find the voice too fast in the default setting.)

- You can determine what kind of typing feedback VoiceOver gives you: characters, words, characters and words, or nothing.

VoiceOver isn't difficult to learn, but it takes practice. If you're a Mac user who's familiar with VoiceOver on the Mac, the workings of this feature will be familiar to you. Selecting letters and typing on a virtual keyboard take some getting used to, however.

The applications that ship with the iPhone are all compatible with VoiceOver, and because VoiceOver is built into the operating system, third-party applications take advantage of it as well. The one iPhone 3.0 software feature that isn't supported by VoiceOver is cut, copy, and paste.

Reset

To remove information from your iPhone without syncing it with your computer, you use this screen, which includes a variety of options:

- **Reset All Settings.** This option resets your iPhone's preferences (your Network and Keyboard settings, for example) but doesn't delete media or data (your mail settings, bookmarks, or contacts, for example).

- **Erase All Content and Settings.** If your iPhone is packed with pirated music, and the Recording Industry Association of America is banging on the door, this option is the one to choose. It erases your preferences and also removes data and media. After you've performed this action, you'll need to sync your iPhone with iTunes to put this material back on the iPhone.

- **Reset Network Settings.** Choose this option, and any networks you've used and your VPN settings are erased. Additionally, the phone switches Wi-Fi on and off, thus disconnecting you from the network you're connected to.

- **Reset Keyboard Dictionary.** As you type on your iPhone's keyboard, word suggestions occasionally crop up. This feature is really handy when the iPhone guesses the word you're trying to type. If the word is correct, just tap the spacebar, and the word appears complete onscreen. But if the iPhone always guesses particular words incorrectly—your last name, for example—you can correct it by tapping the suggestion and continuing to type. The dictionary will learn that word.

  When you tap Reset Keyboard Dictionary, the dictionary returns to its original state, and your additions are erased.

- **Reset Home Screen Layout.** You can move icons on the Home screen around by tapping and holding them until they wiggle, at which point you can move them to another position on that screen or move them to a new screen by dragging them to the right or left edge of the iPhone's display. When you invoke this command, the icons on the Home screen return to their default locations, and third-party applications are arranged in alphabetical order.

▪ **Reset Location Warnings.** The iPhone will warn you when an application wants to use the iPhone's location services. After you OK the warning a second time for a particular application, the iPhone no longer issues the warning for that application. To reset the iPhone so that it starts asking again, invoke this reset.

> **note** Fear not that a slip of the finger is going to delete your valuable data. The iPhone always pops up a panel that asks you to confirm any Reset choice.

And more

The iPhone includes seven more Settings screens by default: Mail, Contacts, Calendars; Phone; Safari; Messages; iPod; Photos; and Store. (In truth, you may see several more, because some third-party applications that you download from the App Store place their settings commands in the Settings screen too.) Because these settings are tied to iPhone functions, I discuss them in the chapters devoted to those subjects.

3

Phone and Messaging

Given the number of hats the iPhone wears—Internet communicator, music and video player, camera, camcorder, compass, picture viewer, personal information organizer, and ... oh, yeah, telephone—you can imagine Apple's marketing department scratching its collective head about the iPhone ad campaign.

"Best iPod ever?"

"The Internet in your pocket?"

"The mobile phone for the rest of us?"

"Room deodorizer?"

OK, maybe crossing the last one off the list was pretty easy. The point is, though, that the iPhone is far more than just a phone. But to be a success, it can't be anything less. It must be capable of making and answering calls as well as sending and receiving text and media messages. The iPhone is designed to do all that—and more, as I show you in this chapter.

Calling All Callers

You've synced your contacts to your iPhone, and you're ready to make a call. The iPhone offers multiple ways to do it.

Call the old-fashioned way

Tap the Phone icon and then tap the Keypad icon at the bottom of the screen. On the keypad that appears, use the keys to tap out the number you want to call. When you enter a number that belongs to someone in your list of contacts, that person's name appears below the number. Tap Call, and start talking (**Figure 3.1**).

Figure 3.1
The old-school keypad.

Favorites | Contacts | Voicemail
Recents | Keypad

To bring up the last number you called, tap Keypad and, with the number field empty, press the Call button.

Connect with Contacts

Tap the Contacts icon; locate a contact; tap the contact's name; and in the resulting Info screen, tap the number you want to call. (You can also reach the Contacts screen via the Contacts application on your iPhone's Home screen.)

Revisit Recents

If you recently had a phone conversation with someone, that person's number is likely in the Recents list. To find out, tap Recents and seek out the number. When you find that number and/or the contact associated with the number, tap it to place a call.

Favor Favorites

If, while browsing through your phone, you added a person to the iPhone's Favorites list (the procedure for which I describe later in the chapter), tap Favorites and then tap that person's name. The iPhone will call him.

In Chapter 2, I point out that you can change the behavior of the Home button when it's double-clicked. Tap Settings > General > Home, and you'll find that you can configure the phone to move to your Favorites list by double-clicking the Home button.

Command it (iPhone 3GS only)

The iPhone 3GS can place calls by voice command. Click and hold the Home button until the Voice Control screen appears, and speak these words: "Call Joseph Blow" (*Joseph Blow* being the name of a person in your iPhone's list of contacts). If you have more than one number listed in the intended contact's Info window, you'll be asked which number you'd like to call—Mobile, Home, or Work, for example. Say "Mobile" if you want to call that number, and the call is placed. To avoid this questioning, you can cut to the chase by saying "Call Joseph Blow at home" or "Call Joseph Blow mobile" (**Figure 3.2**).

Figure 3.2
Calling with
Voice Control.

Christian Fletcher
calling mobile…

Cancel

You'll also avoid further questioning by using the person's full name. Although you can say "Call Jane," if the iPhone has more than one Jane in its list of contacts, you'll be asked which of those many Janes you want to speak with. On the other hand, if you have a friend named Agamemnon or Beelzebub, there's a pretty good chance that you can speak the first name only.

You can also say a number ("Call 810-555-1212"). Be sure to say the name of each digit—"eight, one, zero" rather than "eight-ten." The iPhone doesn't recognize such shortcuts except in the case of 800, for which you can say "eight hundred" rather than "eight, zero, zero."

Also, if you like, you can use the word *dial* instead of *call.* And should you need to correct your phone when it makes a mistake, just say "Wrong," "Not that one," "Not that," "No," or (and I'm not making this up) "Nope."

If you try any of these techniques when you're out of reach of your phone's cellular network, you'll hear this message: "Voice dialing is unavailable when there is no cellular connection."

tip If you have to place calls while driving, please, please, *please* take advantage of this feature. It works remarkably well, and as it allows you to keep your eyes on the road, it may save your life (and mine).

Exploring In-Call Options

When you place the iPhone against your face while making a call, its screen fades elegantly to black, but its advanced phone features remain at the ready. Pull the phone away from your face, and you'll see a series of option icons in the middle of the iPhone's screen (**Figure 3.3**). The following sections explain these options.

Figure 3.3
In-call options.

Mute

If your spouse interrupts a call to ask whom you're talking with, I advise you to tap this icon before issuing any reply along the lines of "That blowhard Charlie." Doing so turns the Mute icon blue and allows you to hear what the other party is saying but mutes the iPhone's microphone. To unmute the phone, just tap Mute again.

Keypad

When a call is in progress, tap this icon to display a keypad if you want to enter additional digits. This feature comes in handy for automated phone attendants that require you to enter account numbers, menu choices, and/or your second cousin's height and weight before you can Speak To A Representative. To make the keypad disappear, tap Hide Keypad.

Speaker

The iPhone has speakerphone capabilities. To hear the call from the speaker, tap this icon; tap it again to listen to the iPhone's headset or receiver port.

note If your iPhone is paired with a Bluetooth device (a headset or hands-free automobile system, for example), this button is called Audio Source. In this case, tapping the button lets you choose among the Bluetooth device, the iPhone (in wired-headset or against-the-face mode), and speakerphone.

Add Call

If you've ever tried to create a conference call on another phone, you know how complicated it can be. Not on the iPhone. The process works like this:

1. Tap the Add Call icon.

   The person you're speaking with is put on hold. (You might warn her first that you're going to do this.)

2. Place another call.

You can use the keypad (tap the Keypad icon to access it) or choose a contact (tap the Contacts icon to view your contacts). When that other caller connects, the Add Call icon turns into Merge Calls.

3. Tap Merge Calls (**Figure 3.4**).

All three of you will be on the same call.

Figure 3.4
Tap the Merge Calls icon to create an instant conference call.

You can add more callers (a conference can have as many as five total callers, including you) by repeating this procedure.

To boot someone from the call, tap the Conference icon that appears; tap the red Hang Up button next to the call; and then tap the End Call icon that appears.

If you'd like to commiserate privately with one of the other callers in the conference, tap Conference and then tap the Private button next to the caller (**Figure 3.5**). When you're ready to join the parties together again, tap Merge Calls.

Figure 3.5
While you're on a conference call, you can speak privately to one person.

If you'd like to add someone who's calling in to your conference, tap Hold Call + Answer and then tap the Merge Calls icon.

Hold

You know. Tap again to unhold.

Contacts

As I've pointed out before, this icon is helpful when you're using the Add Call feature. You can also browse your contacts while you're on a call.

tip In addition to browsing your contacts while you're on a call, if you're connected to a Wi-Fi or 3G network (but not EDGE), you can do pretty much anything other than use the iPhone's audio functions (including iPod and YouTube, as well as any third-party audiocentric applications you may have downloaded from the App Store). Check your stocks, look at the weather in Tasmania, tap out your grocery list, browse your photo collection, or use the Calculator to decide how much you're going to charge this client for taking your time. When you're ready to hang up or perform some other call-specific action, you can return to the call screen by tapping the green bar at the top of the iPhone's screen.

Other buttons

Other buttons can appear during a call:

- **Ignore.** If a call comes in while you're on another call, and you'd rather send it to voice mail than speak with the person, tap the Ignore button that appears.

- **Hold Call + Answer.** To answer that incoming call and put the current caller on hold, tap Hold Call + Answer.

- **End Call + Answer.** For those "Whoops, that's the cheesemonger on the other line. Gotta go!" moments, tap End Call + Answer to drop the current call and answer the incoming call.

- **Swap.** You've put the Party of the First Part on hold to speak with the Party of the Second Part. To return to the PotFP and hold the PotSP, tap Swap, or tap the first caller's entry at the top of the screen.

- **Emergency Call.** I hope you never have to tap this button. The iPhone, like all mobile phones in the United States, can make emergency calls to special numbers (911, for example) when you're out of range of the network and even if your phone doesn't have a SIM card installed. But if you've locked your phone with a passcode and don't have time to unlock it, bring up the keypad, tap the Emergency Call button, and then tap out the emergency number.

Phone Settings

The iPhone lets you take advantage of special calling features built into your plan. The means for managing those features is the Phone screen, which you access via the Settings screen. Tap Phone on this screen, and you'll see these options:

My Number: By default, your iPhone's phone number appears next to the My Number entry. Interestingly enough, you can change it to a different number. Just tap the number, and up pops the My Number screen. You're welcome to tap the X icon to erase what's in the field and enter a different number—your landline number, for example.

International Assist: Enable this option, and when you take your iPhone overseas, you can call numbers in your home country without having to preface them with prefix or country codes.

Call Forwarding: Tap it to access the On/Off slider.

Call Waiting: Ditto.

Show My Caller ID: If you don't want people to know who's calling (or the number you're calling from), flip this option on.

TTY: This accessibility feature allows you to connect your iPhone to a compatible TTY (Teletype) machine via the optional iPhone TTY Adapter cable. People use this technology to create messages that can be read by the deaf and hearing-impaired.

Managing Your Calling Plan

When the iPhone first hit the street, Apple placed the Phone application icon in prime position: in the first spot among the four major apps at the bottom of the Home screen. Tap that Phone icon, and you see one of the five Phone application screens: Favorites, Recents, Contacts, Keypad, or Voicemail. (Which screen appears depends on the last one you accessed before moving back to the Home screen or to another application.) A row of menu icons along the bottom of all five screens (refer to Figure 3.1) lets you navigate quickly among these screens. Because you may be in a hurry to place a call, I'll discuss them out of order.

Keypad

The function of this icon couldn't be much more obvious. Tap Keypad, and you see . . . a telephone keypad. To place a call, just tap the digits you want. As you tap, each digit appears in order at the top of the screen, nicely formatted with the area code in parentheses followed by the number—(555) 555-1212, for example.

In addition to the number keys, star (*), and pound (#), the keypad includes these icons:

- **Delete.** Tap the Delete icon to erase the last digit you entered. Tap and hold to delete a string of numbers quickly.

- **Call.** Tap Call to call the number you've entered.

- **Add Contact.** The Add Contact icon to the left of Call lets you create a contact quickly based on the number you've tapped in.

  Suppose that your dentist calls; he leaves a message that he needs a new boat and that your previously unmentioned impacted wisdom tooth will help him with the down payment. He asks you to call him back at 555-1234. You tap in the number, tap the Add Contact icon, and then choose Create New Contact if you have no contact for him or Add to Existing Contact if you don't have his new office number. (Or you can tap Cancel if you've thought better of the whole thing.)

Voicemail

The iPhone offers a unique voice-mail system dubbed Visual Voicemail. What makes it different from other phones' systems is that you needn't wade through half a dozen messages to get to the one you really want to hear. Instead, all received messages appear in a list. You tap just the ones you want to listen to.

No one can be available 24 hours a day. Here's how to set up and use voice mail when you're not available to take a call:

1. Tap the Voicemail icon.

   When you first tap Voicemail, you'll be prompted to enter a password and record a voice greeting. When recording that greeting, it's not a bad idea to be somewhere quiet with good phone reception so that your greeting is as clear as possible.

   If you don't care to record a greeting, tap Voicemail and then tap Greeting. Tap the Default button, and callers will hear a canned greeting put together by your carrier.

   note   To create a greeting at another time, just tap the Greeting button at the top of the Voicemail screen and then tap Custom. Tap Record; say your piece; then tap Done. Tap Play to listen to what you've recorded, and if you like it, tap Save.

2. Locate a message you want to hear.

   Messages are named for the person who called (if known). The time (or date, if the call was made on a different day) appears next to the caller's name. If the caller is in the iPhone's list of contacts, a blue icon appears next to her name. Tap that icon to be taken to her contact Info screen. A blue dot marks each unheard message.

3. Select the message you want to listen to, and tap the Play icon on the left side of the message entry.

The icon changes to a pause symbol while the iPhone downloads the message and then plays it (**Figure 3.6**).

To pause a playing message, tap the Pause icon (the two vertical lines) to the left of the caller's name. Tap the Play symbol (the right-pointing triangle) to resume playing the message.

Figure 3.6
Playing a voice-mail message.

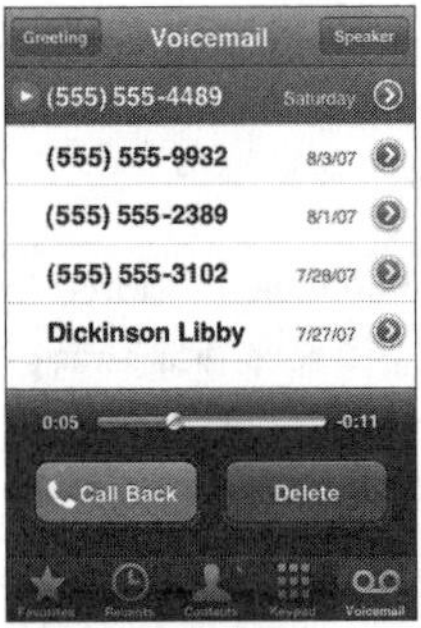

When you begin playing a message, a sheet appears that contains a scrubber bar and Call Back and Delete icons. To move through a message quickly—if your father tends to go on and on about this season's gopher issues before getting to the meat of the message, for example—drag the playhead to later in the message. If the phone was able to obtain a number through Caller ID, you have the option to call that person back immediately by tapping Call Back.

To listen to a message again, simply select it again and tap the Play icon. If listening once was enough, tap Delete.

note   Deleted messages aren't completely gone. At the end of your voicemail list, you'll see a Deleted Messages entry. Tap this entry and then
tap the message you'd like to listen to again. You can undelete a message by
tapping it in the Deleted Messages screen and then tapping Undelete.

4. Create a contact.

   If someone who isn't in your list of contacts calls, and you'd like to add
   him, tap the blue icon next to the message heading. In the sheet that
   appears, tap either Create New Contact (if this contact is new to you)
   or Add to Existing Contact (if the caller is already a contact, but you
   don't have this particular number). Then choose a contact to add the
   number to.

Remote Control

Even though you own the coolest phone in the galaxy, you can do
things with other phones that will enhance your iPhone experience,
such as listen to your iPhone's messages from another phone. To do
so, dial your iPhone's number, wait for the phone to answer and send
you to voice mail, press star (*), enter your voice-mail password, and
press pound (#).

This feature is more than a mere convenience. Checking Visual
Voicemail from your iPhone counts against your monthly minutes.
Call from a landline, however, and the call is free.

Similarly, you can record a greeting for your iPhone from another
phone—not a bad idea, as a landline phone may produce a better-
sounding message. Again, just dial your iPhone's number; press star;
enter your password; press pound; and follow the canned voice's
instructions to get to the greetings area, where you can record a
greeting or an extended-absence message for your iPhone.

If you've created a contact for a caller, you can also add him to your Favorites list, which is described in greater detail later in this chapter. Just tap the blue icon and then tap Add to Favorites.

5. Listen later.

The iPhone lets you know if you have voice-mail messages waiting. If you have missed one or more calls, received one or more voice-mail messages, or both, a red dot appears in the top-right corner of the Phone application icon in the Home screen. A number inside the dot denotes the combined number of missed calls and unheard messages. When you tap the Phone icon, a similar red dot appears over the Voicemail icon, indicating how many unheard messages you have.

Recents

Like other modern mobile phones, the iPhone keeps track of calls you've made and received—both those you've participated in and those you've missed. You'll find a list of those most recent calls by tapping the Recents entry at the bottom of the iPhone's screen.

In this screen, you may see any (or all) of the following:

- **Names,** if the callers or recipients are in your phone's list of contacts

  If a name appears, you'll also see the kind of number the call came from (mobile, home, or work, for example).

- **Phone numbers,** if the callers or recipients aren't in the phone's list of contacts and the numbers aren't blocked

  For a number, you also see the location of the number (such as Anytown, AK).

- **The word** *blocked,* if a phone number is blocked

Contacts that you've attempted to reach multiple times have a number next to them—Jane Blow (3) or 555-1243 (2), for example—indicating the number of calls made.

To see all calls, tap the All button at the top of the screen (**Figure 3.7**). Missed calls are shown in red. To see just your missed calls, tap the Missed button at the top of the screen. As in Voicemail, you see the time or day when the call was made. Tap the blue icon to be taken to one of a few screens, depending on what your iPhone "knows" about the phone number for each call you've placed or received.

If a number belongs to someone listed in your contacts, tapping the blue icon takes you to a screen that displays that person's contact info. Additionally, you see the kind of call (outgoing or incoming), the time and date of the call, and the length of the call. (This entry will read *Cancelled*

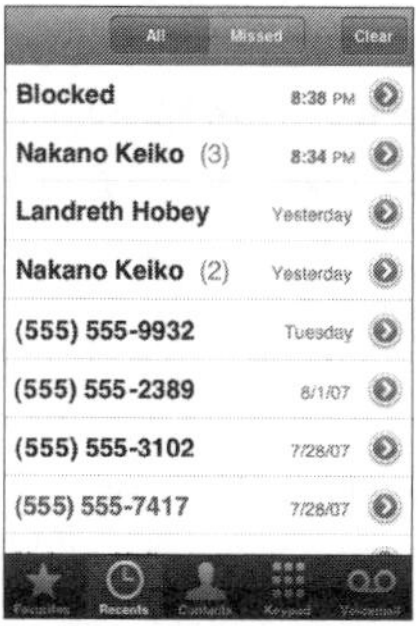

Figure 3.7
The Recents screen.

All	Missed	Clear
Blocked	8:38 PM	
Nakano Keiko (3)	8:34 PM	
Landreth Hobey	Yesterday	
Nakano Keiko (2)	Yesterday	
(555) 555-9932	Tuesday	
(555) 555-2389	8/1/07	
(555) 555-3102	7/28/07	
(555) 555-7417	7/28/07	

Favorites Recents Contacts Keypad Voicemail

if the call didn't go through.) At the bottom of that screen are icons marked Text Message, Share Contact, and Add to Favorites.

Tap Text Message to open a blank text message directed to that person. (If the person has more than one phone number in her contact info, a sheet appears and asks you to choose the number to use.)

When you tap Share Contact, if you've enabled MMS on your phone (see "Sending Them Messages" later in this chapter), a sheet rolls up to offer you three options: Email, MMS, and Cancel. When you tap Email, a new, unaddressed email message opens that contains that person's contact information saved as a vCard attachment. (vCards are a universal format for exchanging contact information between devices.) To send that message, just enter a recipient in the To field and type something in the Subject field. (You can learn far more about email and the iPhone in Chapter 4.) Tap MMS, and a new MMS message opens in the Messages application that contains the vCard as part of that message.

Tap Add to Favorites, and that's just what happens: The person is added to your list of favorites, and you can access his info by tapping Favorites at the bottom of the screen.

If you place a call to a number that isn't in the iPhone's list of contacts, or if you capture an unrecognized Caller ID number from a received call, the phone number is displayed, and you can tap the blue icon to view these options: Call, Text Message, Create New Contact, Add to Existing Contact, and Share Contact.

If the number came from a blocked number, the entry reads *Blocked Caller*, and tapping the icon tells you only the date and time when the person called. Tap Clear to clear the Recents lists.

Favorites

Use the Favorites list to store those very special contacts you call routinely (**Figure 3.8**). Here, you'll find the numbers you've added by tapping the Add to Favorites button in a contact's Info screen or by tapping Favorites, tapping the plus (+) icon, and then navigating through your list of contacts to find a name. Only those contacts that contain phone numbers are eligible to be added to Favorites. Should you tap a contact that doesn't have a phone number, you'll find that an Add to Favorites button is missing as well.

Figure 3.8
The Favorites screen.

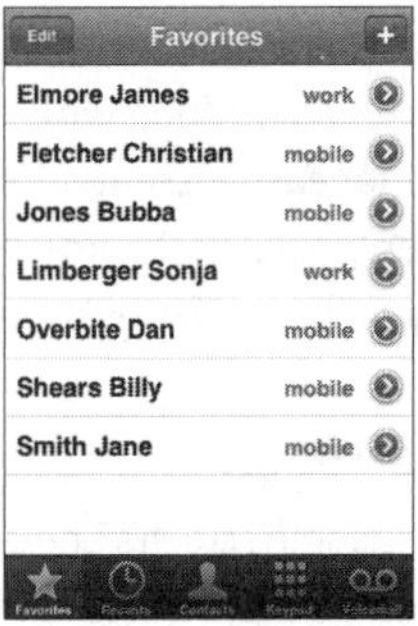

Just like those in Recents and Voicemail, each entry in the Favorites list bears a small blue icon. Tap it to view that person's Info screen.

This may sound silly, but some people care very much where they rate in your Favorites list. If your husband or mother isn't at the top of the list and should be, here's how to put things right: While you're in the Favorites screen, tap Edit; then drag contacts around, using the bars to the right of each name. If someone no longer rates enough to be a favorite, tap the red minus (–) icon next to his name to reveal the Remove button. Tap Remove, and that person will be removed from Favorites (but not from your contacts).

Contacts

Last but hardly least is Contacts. Because your friends, family, and associates are the worthiest people on Earth, they deserve their own section.

Working with Contacts

Contacts is the Big Kahuna of the Phone applications—a Kahuna that makes its presence known in just about every iPhone application save the iPod area. Although you'll find it more convenient to ask your address-book application to do the heavy lifting with regard to creating and editing contacts (because it's far easier to enter information from a real keyboard than on the iPhone's virtual keyboard), you can do a lot of cool things with contacts directly on your iPhone.

Entering the people you know

Tap the Contacts icon or launch the Home screen's Contacts application, and you see a list of your contacts in alphabetical order (**Figure 3.9**) and, above that, a Search field for seeking out contacts. As a bonus, when you access Contacts from within the Phone application (not the Contacts application) and flick your finger down the screen, you see the phone number entered in the My Number area of Phone settings. (You'd be amazed how many people don't know their mobile number, and this feature is a great reminder.)

Figure 3.9
The Contacts screen.

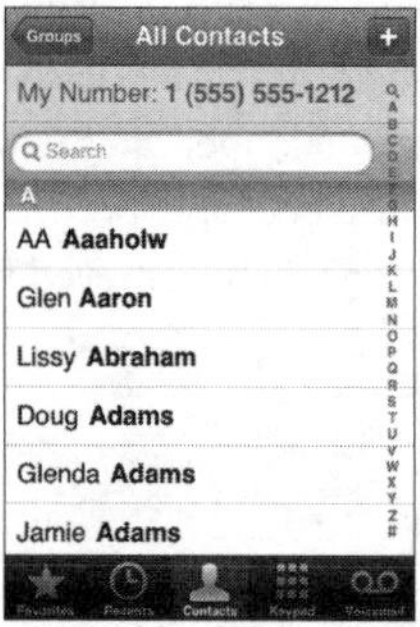

This list works very much like any long list of items you see in the iPhone's iPod area. A tiny alphabet runs down the right side of the screen. Tap a letter to move immediately to contacts whose names (first or last, depending on how you've configured name sorting in Phone preferences) begin with this letter. Alternatively, tap in the Search field, and when the iPhone's keyboard swoops up from the bottom of the screen, start typing some letters in your contact's name. As you type, fewer names appear as the choices narrow.

When you tap a name, you're taken to that contact's Info screen (**Figure 3.10**). Here, you can find information including the following:

Figure 3.10
A contact's Info screen.

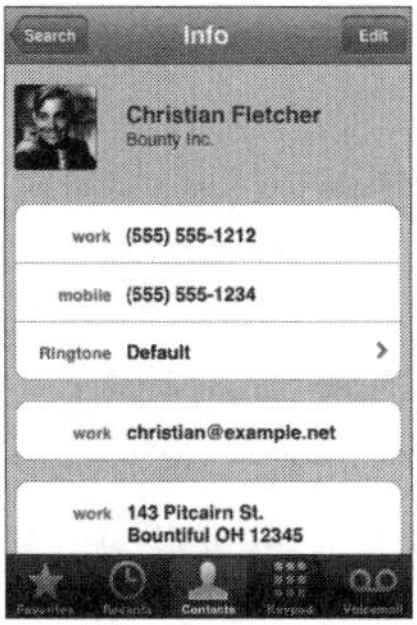

- Photo

  This item can be a photo you've added in Address Book on a Mac, by tapping Add Photo and choosing a picture from your Photos collection, or by assigning a picture to a contact in the Photos or Camera application.

- Name

- Company

- Phone number

  Possible phone headings include Mobile, iPhone, Home, Work, Main, Home Fax, Work Fax, Pager, and Other.

- Ringtone

- Email address

  This item includes Home, Work, and Other options as well as any custom labels you've created.

- URL (for the contact's Web site)

- Home address

- Work address

- Other address

- Other fields

You won't necessarily find all these entries in a contact's Info screen; this list just shows you what's possible to include.

Organizing contacts in groups

Although you see a list of all your contacts when you first tap Contacts, the Contacts application has an organizational layer above the main list. If, in the Info iPhone preference within iTunes, you've chosen to sync your address book with select groups of contacts, or if your full address book contains groups of contacts, those groups will appear in the Groups screen, which you access by tapping the Groups button in the top-left corner of the Contacts screen (**Figure 3.11**).

Figure 3.11
The Groups screen.

Organizing in groups makes a lot of sense if you have loads of contacts. Although Apple made traversing a long list of contacts as easy as possible, easier still is tapping something like a Family group and picking Uncle Bud's name out of a list of 17 beloved relatives.

tip I've found it really helpful to create a group that includes just contacts that have phone numbers and email addresses. The iPhone will sync all your contacts, whether or not they include phone numbers, but more than anything else, I need phone numbers and email addresses on my phone.

In Apple's Address Book, you can create just such a group easily. Choose File > New Smart Group, and configure the resulting pane to read *Contains Cards Which Match All of the Following Conditions: Phone Is Set. Email Is Set.* This step places all contacts that contain a phone number and email address in their own group. Then you can sync this group to your iPhone so that you don't have to bother trying to call or email contacts you don't have this information for.

Regrettably, iPhone-compatible Windows applications (Outlook, Outlook Express, and Windows' Address Book) with address-book functionality don't have this kind of easy-does-it feature.

Making contacts

The best way to become familiar with the iPhone's contacts is to make some of your own. To do that now, tap Contacts and then the plus icon in the top-right corner of the iPhone's screen.

Viewing the New Contact screen

The New Contact screen contains fields for the elements I list in "Organizing contacts in groups" earlier in this chapter—Photo, First and Last Name, Phone Numbers, Ringtone, Email Addresses, URL, Physical Addresses (Home, Work, and Other, for example)—as well as an Add Field entry (**Figure 3.12** on the next page). To add information to one of these fields, tap the field or the green plus icon to its left. In the resulting screen, you'll find a place to enter the information.

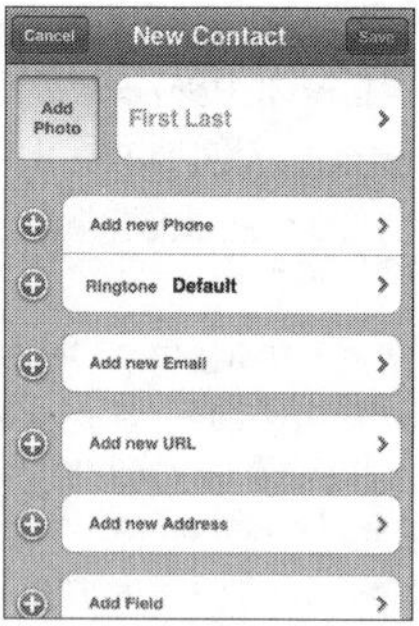

Figure 3.12
*The New Contact
screen.*

Here are the special features of each screen:

Add Photo. Tap this entry to display a sheet containing buttons marked
Take Photo, Choose Existing Photo, and Cancel. Tap Take Photo, point it at
the object you'd like to capture (ideally, something more pleasing than
the back end of your cat), and tap the green camera icon. If you don't
like what you've taken, tap Retake, and do just that. You can resize and
reposition the picture by pinching the image and dragging it around the
screen. When you settle on a view you like, tap Set Photo.

You can edit this picture later, if you like. Tap Edit, and you get the
options Take Photo, Choose Existing Photo, Edit Photo (which takes you
to the Move and Scale screen, where you can pinch and reposition), and
Delete Photo.

When you tap Choose Existing Photo, you're taken to your Photos library,
where you can select a picture. Just as you can with the pictures you take,
you can move and scale these images and then tap Set Photo to attach
them to the contact.

And why all the fuss about a contact's picture when it appears in this tiny
box? The photo appears across much of the iPhone's screen when that
person calls you and stays there as you talk to that person on your iPhone.

Name. In this screen, you enter first, last, and company names. Tap Save to return to the New Contact screen.

Add New Phone. As the name says, this field is where you add a phone number. In the Edit Phone screen, you tap in the number from the keypad and then choose the kind of phone number: Mobile, iPhone, Home, Work, Main, Home Fax, Work Fax, Pager, or Other. If you've added any custom labels within the iPhone, Apple's Address Book (Mac), or Outlook (Windows), those custom labels will appear below these entries. At the very bottom you'll find an Add Custom Label button that, when tapped, lets you type a label of your own making—*Dirigible* or *Private Train Car*, for example.

note The numeric keypad contains a key that reads +*#. Tap it, and these three characters appear on the keypad's bottom three keys, along with the word *pause*, which enters a comma (,) character. What good are they? They're used by automated answering systems for performing certain functions. Some phone systems, for example, require you to press the pound key and then a key combination to unblock a hidden phone number or append an extension. The comma character is commonly used to insert a 1-second delay. It's useful when an automated answering service demands that you wait a second before punching in another string of numbers.

Ringtone. You can choose a unique ringtone for each contact, and here's where you do it. Tap Ringtone, and the default ringtone for your phone will appear at the top of the ringtone list with a check mark next to it. You can choose a different ringtone from the list below—a list that first includes any custom ringtones you've added via iTunes' Ringtones tab and then a list of the standard 25 ringtones included with the iPhone. This feature is a great way to know who's calling without having to pull the iPhone out of your pocket.

Add New Email. Enter your contact's email addresses here. The iPhone's keyboard in this screen contains @ and period (.) keys to make the process easier. Tap and hold the period key, and a menu appears that contains .net, .edu, .org, and .com. Just slide your finger over to the extension you want, and let go to enter it.

Add New URL. Similar idea here. The more-convenient keyboard is in evidence, but instead of an @ symbol, you'll find period (.), slash (/), and .com. You can apply a Home Page, Home, Work, or Other label to the URL as well as any custom labels on your phone.

Add New Address. In the United States, the default Edit Address screen contains two Street fields and areas for City, State, and Zip. Ah, but tap the country field and choose a different nation from the list that appears (these lists are divided into geographic regions such as Europe and Oceana), and these fields change. If you choose Belarus, for example, the bottom fields change to Postal Code, City, and Province. Tap the Location icon next to the Country icon to choose the nature of this address: Home, Work, or Other and, as you might expect, one of those custom labels.

Add Field. Tap Add Field, and you can add more fields to a contact's Info screen. These fields include Prefix, Phonetic First Name, Phonetic Last Name, Middle Name, Suffix, Nickname, Job Title, Department, Birthday, Instant Message, Date (Anniversary and Other are the options), and Note. Both the Birthday and Date screens contain the iPhone's spinning date wheel for selecting month, day, and year quickly.

Working with existing contacts

When you have contacts on your iPhone, you can delete them, edit the information they contain, or use that information to perform other tasks on your iPhone.

To delete a contact, just tap the Edit icon that appears in the contact's Info screen, scroll to the bottom of the screen, and tap the big red Delete Contact button. You'll be asked to confirm your choice.

To edit a contact, tap that same Edit icon in the contact's Info screen, and make the edits you want (**Figure 3.13**). You can add information by tapping a field that begins with the word *Add* (or just tap its green plus icon). To delete information, tap the red minus icon next to the information and then tap the now-revealed Delete button. When you're finished editing the contact, tap Done.

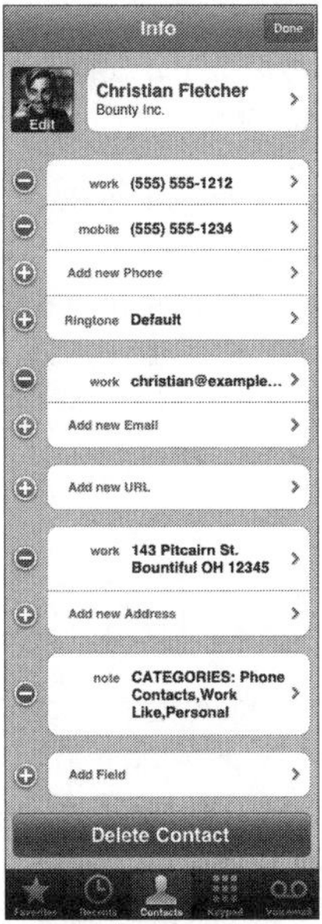

Figure 3.13
An elongated view of the contact edit screen.

As for initiating actions on your iPhone via a contact's Info screen, most of the elements in the screen are *live*, meaning that if you tap them, something happens. If you tap a phone number in the Info screen, for example, the iPhone dials that number; tap an email address, and a New Message window appears in the Mail application, addressed to that person. If you tap a URL, Safari opens and takes you to that Web page. Tap an address, and Maps opens to show you its location.

At the bottom of an Info screen that contains at least one phone number, you'll find Text Message, Share Contact, and Add to Favorites buttons. Because Text Message and Add to Favorites require a phone number, you can see why they're present here but not in Info screens that don't bear phone numbers. Share Contact appears for all contacts and, again, offers you the option to send an email or MMS message that contains that person's contact information in the form of a vCard.

You already know about Favorites. When you tap Text Message, if the contact has more than one phone number in the Info screen, a sheet rolls up that contains each phone number. Tap the phone number you'd like to use, and the Messages application opens with the contact's name at the top of the screen.

And gosh, speaking of Messages . . .

Sending Them Messages

When Steve Jobs first demoed the iPhone, it appeared to contain an instant-messaging client similar to Apple's iChat. That turned out not to be the case. The iPhone's SMS (Short Message Service) application, Messages (formerly called Text), looks very much like iChat, but it's not. It's a standard messaging service much like the ones you find on other mobile phones.

When Apple announced the iPhone 3.0 software in March 2009, one of the features it revealed was support for MMS (Multimedia Messaging Service)—a way to send not just text messages, but messages that can also include audio, video, pictures, and rich text. (MMS is not supported on the original iPhone.)

Sending text messages

Using Messages is pretty straightforward. Tap Messages in the iPhone's
Home screen, and you'll see a Messages screen. Tap the New Message
icon in the top-right corner of the screen to compose a new message.

In the middle of the resulting New Message screen, you'll see the text
field, with a To field for your recipient's name or phone number above
and the iPhone's alphabetic keyboard below.

To enter a name in the To field, tap it and then begin typing the name of
the person you want to message. As you type, a list of matching names
from your contacts appears (**Figure 3.14**). Continue to type, and the list
narrows. To select a recipient, just tap that person's name.

Figure 3.14
*Start typing a
name in Text,
and your iPhone
will suggest
recipients.*

Alternatively, you can tap the plus icon in the To field, which brings up
the iPhone's Contacts list. Navigate to the contact you want to contact,
and tap that person's name to add it to the To field.

tip Why type a name when you can choose a contact? The Contacts
screens include *all* your contacts—even those that don't contain
phone numbers. When you begin typing on the alphabetical keyboard, only
those contacts with phone numbers appear in the list.

Finally, you can simply enter a phone number. Tap the 123 icon at the bottom of the alphabetical keyboard to produce the numeric keypad. Use the keypad to enter the number of the person you want to call.

Tap in the text field, and start typing. The field will show seven lines of text before the first line scrolls out of sight. When you're ready to send your message, tap Send (**Figure 3.15**).

Figure 3.15
An SMS message session in progress.

tip
With the first iteration of the iPhone software, you could send a message to a single recipient. That's changed. Now you can send a text message to multiple recipients. Just tap the New Message button and then start adding contacts. Regrettably, there's no way to send a message to an existing group in Contacts; you must add addresses one by one. (If one of the contacts is a phone number that you're entering by hand, tap Return before entering the next contact.) When someone replies to one of these group text messages, you'll be the only person to see it unless the sender creates a group text message of her own that contains the reply.

Sending MMS messages

Sending an MMS message isn't much different. Before doing so, you'll need to configure your iPhone 3G or iPhone 3GS to use MMS. To ensure that it's ready to go, tap Settings > Messages. In the resulting Messages screen, make sure that the MMS Messaging slider is set to On. While you're there, go ahead and slide the Show Subject Field to On.

Launch Messages, and tap the New Message button in the top-right corner. The resulting New Message screen is a little different from the one offered in previous versions of this application. What's different is the small camera icon next to the Send field and the word *Subject* that appears at the top of this field. (It appears there because you just switched on the Show Subject Field option.) This button is for sending still images or movies (iPhone 3GS only) via MMS.

 If your carrier doesn't support MMS messages, you won't see the Camera icon and will be unable to send or receive MMS messages.

Sending images or video

Sending images or video in an MMS message works this way:

1. Tap the camera icon.

    The sheet that appears offers three buttons: Take Photo or Video (on the iPhone 3G, the first button will read *Take Photo*), Choose Existing, and Cancel.

2. Tap Take Photo or Video to launch the Camera application, or tap Choose Existing to select an existing image or movie.

    ▪ **Take Photo (or Video):** Tap the first button if you want to capture a still picture or (3GS only) video. On the iPhone 3GS, use the Camera/Video switch in the bottom-left corner of the screen to choose between capturing a still picture or video. You can't shoot video on any other model, so your single option will be to take a still picture.

    ▪ **Choose Existing:** If you tap the second button—Choose Existing— the iPhone's Photo Albums screen appears. Listed here are all the photos and videos on your iPhone.

3. Capture or choose something.

- **Still camera:** If you chose the Camera option in step 2, tap the Camera button. The iPhone will take a picture, which will appear in a preview screen with two options: Retake or Use. Tap Retake to do just that, or tap Use to use that picture in an MMS message. When you choose that latter option, you return to Messages, and the still image is placed in the Send field.

- **Video (3GS only):** If you selected Video in step 2, tap the Record button, capture what you want, and tap the Record button again to end the capture. Then you can use the iPhone's editing tools to edit the video. (I tell you everything you need to know about making, editing, and sending movies in Chapter 8.) When you're happy with your movie, tap the Use button. The video clip is inserted into the Send field, ready to send.

- **Existing image or video:** Tap the collection you want (the Camera Roll or an album you've copied to your iPhone), and in the screen that appears, tap the item you want to include in your message, which can be a still picture or a video stored in the Camera Roll. It appears in a preview screen; you can add it to a message from there by tapping the Choose button.

4. Add a subject.

   This step is optional, as is revealing the Subject field in the first place, but I find that it adds just the right amount of context to add a title to an image, video, or audio bit (**Figure 3.16**). You can use the Subject field for doing just that. After all, who wouldn't be tempted to watch an enclosed video clip titled "Me Kicking Zombie Hiney"?

Figure 3.16
*Text added to an
MMS message's
Subject field.*

Sending audio

As I mention earlier in this chapter, you can also send audio files that
you've recorded with the Voice Memos application via MMS. I cover voice
memos more extensively in Chapter 9, but while we're on the subject of
MMS, here's the gist:

1. Launch Voice Memos.

2. Tap the red Record button, and start speaking to record your memo.

3. Tap the button in the bottom-right corner of the screen (which
   displays a black square during recording) to stop recording.

4. Tap that same button, which now displays three lines, to open the
   Voice Memos screen.

5. Tap a voice memo that you'd like to use as an MMS message.

6. Tap the Share button at the bottom of the screen, and tap the MMS
   button that appears.

   Messages will launch, and your voice memo will be embedded in the
   Send field (**Figure 3.17** on the next page).

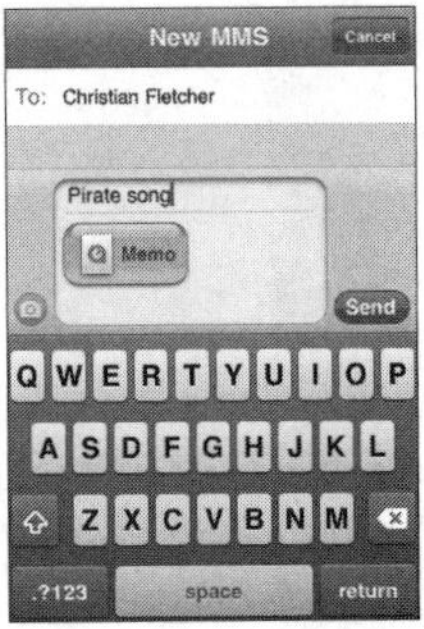

Figure 3.17
A voice memo embedded in an MMS message.

7. Address the message, enter a subject if you like, and tap Send to send the audio MMS message.

Receiving messages

When it receives an SMS or MMS message, the iPhone alerts you—either by sounding the New Text Message alert configured in the Sounds setting or (if you've switched the iPhone to silent mode by toggling the Ring/Silent switch) by vibrating. The iPhone also displays a preview of the first part of a received message. When you look at the Home screen, you'll see a red circle with a number inside denoting the number of unread text messages on your phone.

Private Previews

Having the first bit of an SMS or MMS message displayed on your phone's face isn't always ideal. Some very personal stuff can come across via SMS and MMS—personal stuff that you might prefer that your mother not see when she "accidentally" picks up your iPhone. To prevent this situation, you need to switch off previews. To do so, tap Settings and then tap Messages. Toggle the Show Preview switch to Off, and the preview won't appear.

To view your messages, just tap Messages. Any received messages appear in the Messages screen, with unread messages marked with blue dots. To read a message, just tap it. To reply to that message, enter the text in the Send field with the iPhone's keyboard, and tap Send. (The MMS Camera icon appears next to this field as well.) Similarly, you can tap any message in the list—even one in which you've already engaged in some back-and-forth (**Figure 3.18**)—and send a new message to that person simply by entering text and tapping Send. You can access that person's contact information by tapping the Contact Info button or place a voice call by tapping Call.

Figure 3.18

Tap an SMS message to view the course of your conversation.

To delete entries from the Messages list, just tap the Edit button; then tap the red minus icon, and tap Delete. The swipe-and-delete trick works here, too. Just swipe your finger to the left or right across the message entry, and tap the Delete button that appears.

You can also delete or forward portions of a message conversation. To do so, follow these steps:

1. Tap a conversation that you'd like to edit.

   It appears in a separate screen, with the name of the recipient at the top.

2. Tap the Edit button in the top-right corner.

3. Tap the circle next to the portions of the conversation that you want to delete or forward.

4. Delete the selected portion by tapping the Delete button at the bottom of the window.

5. To forward a selection, tap the Forward button.

   When you tap Forward, a New Message screen appears. Just use the To field to add the recipients and/or phone numbers for your forwarded message. When you're ready to send the forwarded message, just tap the Send button.

Messages can also contain live links. If someone places a phone number in a message, for example, you can tap it, and the iPhone will call that number. Email addresses, URLs, and physical addresses are live too. Tap an email address, and Mail opens with a message addressed to that person. Tap a URL, and Safari launches and takes you to that site. Tap a street address, and Maps opens to reveal that location on a Google map. And, of course, media such as still images, videos, and audio files will appear/play in all their glory when tapped.

Mail and Calendar

Seeking a less-immediate way to communicate than the phone or messaging? Can't figure out how to copy your notes and photos from your iPhone to a computer that's not synced with your iPhone or how to receive documents that you can view on your iPhone? Or is your life so tied to email that you can't stand to be away from your computer for more than a couple of hours? If so, you and the iPhone's Mail application are about to become best friends.

Portable email is a real boon, and so is knowing where you're supposed to be from one minute to the next. To help with the latter, the iPhone includes a Calendar application that lets you sync your schedule with your Mac or Windows PC, as well as create calendar events on the go. In this chapter, I explain the ins and outs of both applications.

Using Mail

Mail is a real email client, much like the one you use on your computer. With it, you can send and receive email messages, as well as send and receive a limited variety of email attachments. You can send photos or videos you've taken with your iPhone, for example, and receive and play such audio attachments as MP3, AAC, WAV, and AIFF. You can view received JPEG graphics files, text, and HTML; Microsoft Word, Excel, and PowerPoint documents; iWork Pages, Keynote, and Numbers files; and Adobe PDF documents. Regrettably, you can't edit any of the files you receive; they're read-only.

Mail is limited in some other ways:

- Unlike all modern computer-based email clients, the iPhone has no spam filter and no feature for managing mailing lists.

- You can't flag messages or apply rules that allow Mail to sort or copy certain messages (those from a particular sender, for example) into specific mailboxes.

- Speaking of mailboxes, you can't create new mailboxes on the iPhone, either. Instead, you must create them on your computer or on the Web, and you can do so only with IMAP accounts; they'll appear in Mail after you sync the mail accounts on your computer with the iPhone.

The iPhone is capable of sending and receiving email over a Wi-Fi connection and a carrier's 3G and EDGE networks. Other than the speed of sending and receiving messages, there's no significant difference between running Mail over these networks. Note, however, that there's a big difference if you're using your phone overseas. Wi-Fi costs nothing extra, but carriers impose punitive roaming charges for using 3G and EDGE (for email or anything else) outside their coverage areas.

tip   **Because of these roaming charges, when traveling outside your carrier's coverage area, tap Settings > General > Network and make sure that Data Roaming is off (as it is by default). Deactivating roaming will prevent your iPhone from making a connection over the cellular network and, thus, running up your bill. To access roaming again, turn Data Roaming back on.**

Now that you know what Mail can and can't do, you're ready to look at how to use it.

Creating an account

When you first synced your iPhone to your computer, you were asked whether you wanted to synchronize your email accounts to the phone. If you chose to do so, your iPhone is nearly ready to send and receive messages. All you may have to do now is enter a password for your email account in the Mail, Contacts, Calendars setting.

But I'm getting ahead of myself. Rather than start in the middle, with a nearly configured account, I'll start at the beginning so that you can follow the iPhone's account-setup procedure from start to finish. In the next few pages, I examine how to configure Exchange, Web-based (MobileMe, Gmail, Yahoo, and AOL), and IMAP and POP accounts.

Configuring an Exchange account

Let me take care of corporate readers first by outlining the steps necessary to create an Exchange account:

1. Tap the Settings icon in the iPhone's Home screen and then tap Mail, Contacts, Calendars.

2. Tap Add Account, and in the resulting screen, tap Microsoft Exchange.

3. In the Exchange screen that appears, enter your email address, user name, password, and a description along the lines of *Company Email*.

   Your IT department or manager should be able to provide this info.

4. Tap Next.

The iPhone attempts to connect to the Exchange server.

If the connection is successful, you're pretty well set. If it isn't, another Exchange screen will ask for the same information you provided before, as well as the server address. Again, the Exchange server administrator should be able to give you this information. The address in question here is the address of the front-end server—the one that greets your iPhone when it attempts to connect to the company server.

When this information is configured properly, the iPhone attempts to log on to the server via a secure (SSL) connection. If it can't do so, it tries a nonsecure connection.

If SSL isn't configured correctly, you can change those settings by tapping the name of your Exchange account in the Mail, Contacts, Calendars screen; tapping Account Info; and flipping the SSL slider to On or Off, depending on how it should be configured.

5. When you're prompted to choose the kinds of data—Mail, Contacts, and Calendars—that you want to synchronize between your iPhone and the Exchange server (**Figure 4.1**), flick the switch for those data types to On.

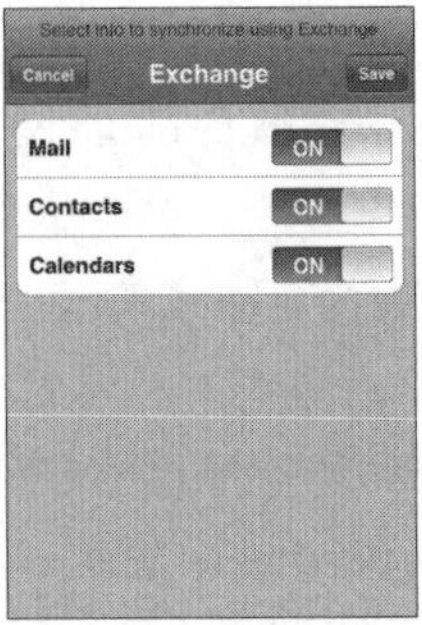

Figure 4.1
Choose the kind of data you want to sync with the Exchange server.

By default, the iPhone synchronizes just three days' worth of email. If you need to store more email on your iPhone, select your Exchange account in the Mail, Contacts, Calendars screen; tap Mail Days to Sync; and choose a new number of days' worth of email to synchronize. Your options are No Limit, 1 Day, 3 Days, 1 Week, 2 Weeks, and 1 Month.

note   When you create an Exchange account on your iPhone and choose to sync contacts and calendars, any existing contacts and calendars information on the phone will be wiped out, replaced by contacts and events from the Exchange server. Additionally, you can't synchronize this kind of data via iTunes with your computer. You can synchronize data on your phone and personal computer if you have a MobileMe account, however.

Configuring MobileMe, Gmail, Yahoo, and AOL accounts

The iPhone's designers made configuring one of these accounts really easy. Just follow these steps:

1. Tap the Settings icon in the iPhone's Home screen and then tap Mail, Contacts, Calendars.

2. Tap Add Account, and choose MobileMe, Gmail, Yahoo Mail, or AOL.

3. In the screen that appears, enter your name, the email address for this account, your account's password, and a descriptive name for the account—*My Mighty MobileMe Account*, for example.

4. Tap Save.

Unlike its practice with other kinds of accounts, the iPhone doesn't demand settings for incoming and outgoing mail servers. It's intimately familiar with these services and does all that configuration for you. But you're welcome to muck with these more-arcane settings after you create the account, if you like (and I tell you how in the "Configuring further" section later in this chapter).

Configuring POP and IMAP accounts

If you're like a lot of people and have an email account through a "regular" ISP (one that provides email via a DSL or cable broadband connection, for example), you'll configure your iPhone this way:

1. Tap the Settings icon in the iPhone's Home screen and then tap Mail, Contacts, Calendars.

2. Tap Add Account.

3. Tap Other.

   I ask you to tap Other because this option lets you set up email accounts for ISPs other than those listed above the Other entry. In the resulting screen, you have the option to add mail accounts (as well as server-based contacts and calendars, which I'll deal with later).

4. Tap Add Mail Account.

   In the resulting New Account screen, enter the information for setting up a POP or IMAP account.

5. Tap Name, and enter your real name (as opposed to your user name).

6. Tap Address, and enter your email address (such as *example@ examplemail.com*).

7. Tap Password, and enter the account's password.

8. Tap Description, and enter a description of your account.

   I often use the name of my account for this entry—*Macworld*, for example.

9. Tap Save to save your settings.

   The iPhone looks up the account settings you've entered. If you've set up an account for a common email carrier—Cox or BellSouth, for example—it checks your account and configures the server settings for you.

If the iPhone can't configure your account, or if the Internet service provider (ISP) offers IMAP and POP accounts and doesn't know which kind you have, the New Account screen displays new options.

10. Choose IMAP or POP.

   At the top of the screen, you see IMAP and POP buttons. Tap the appropriate button for the kind of account you have.

11. Enter the host name in the Incoming Mail Server area.

   This information, provided by your ISP, is in the format *mail. examplemail.com.*

12. Tap User Name, and enter the name that precedes the at (@) symbol in your email address.

   If the address is *bruno@examplemail.com*, for example, type **bruno**.

13. Tap Password, and enter the password for your email account.

> **note** Type the password very carefully. With the 2.0 and later software, password fields are a bit better about showing you what you've typed rather than displaying just black dots. When you enter a password character, the password field briefly displays the character you just typed—4 or W, for example. But the characters don't remain onscreen long, and you may miss them. Check your work before you lift your finger off the keyboard.

14. Below Outgoing Mail Server, tap Host Name; then enter the appropriate text—which, once again, will be provided by your ISP, typically in the format *smtp.examplemail.com.*

15. Enter your user name and password again, if required.

   If these fields aren't filled in for you, copy this information from the Incoming Mail Server fields and paste it in here.

16. When you've double-checked to make sure everything's correct, tap Save in the top-right corner of the screen.

The configured account (**Figure 4.2**) appears in the list of accounts in the Mail Settings screen.

Figure 4.2
Configured email POP account.

Configuring further

Most people can stop right here and get on with mucking with Mail, but your email account may require a little extra tweaking for it to work. Here's how to do just that:

1. Tap your account name in the Mail, Contacts, Calendar settings screen.

2. If you'd like that account to appear in Mail's Accounts list, be sure that the Account slider is set to On.

Why turn it off? Perhaps you've got a load of messages sitting on the server that you'd rather not download with your iPhone. Download those messages with your computer, delete them from the server, and then enable the account on your iPhone.

Putting It on the IMAP

At one time, POP accounts—accounts that require you to download email to your computer to read it—were the norm. But increasingly, IMAP email accounts—those that store messages on an ISP's central server—are becoming more popular. In the case of the iPhone, they should be, because using an IMAP account can help reduce clutter and confusion. Here's how.

Suppose that you have a POP account that's configured to download your email to both your computer and your iPhone. You read the mail once on your iPhone and delete it when you're done. A copy remains on your computer, though, so you have to delete it there too. You can avoid this double duty with an IMAP account, because IMAP email—living as it does on a central server out there in "the cloud"—can be managed by any device that can access it.

So you log on to your IMAP account with your iPhone and peruse your email. You find some messages you don't want any longer, and you delete them. When you do, they vanish from the server. When you return home to your computer, you won't see those messages, because you've deleted them. Unlike with a POP account, the contents of your email are exactly the same, regardless of which device you use to read it.

3. Verify that the information in the account's settings fields is correct; if not, tap the field you want to edit and start typing.

4. Tap the SMTP button to configure the outgoing server for your email account (see the sidebar "Out and About" for more details).

5. Tap the Advanced button at the bottom of the screen, and in the resulting Advanced screen for POP accounts (**Figure 4.3** on the next page), choose the options you want.

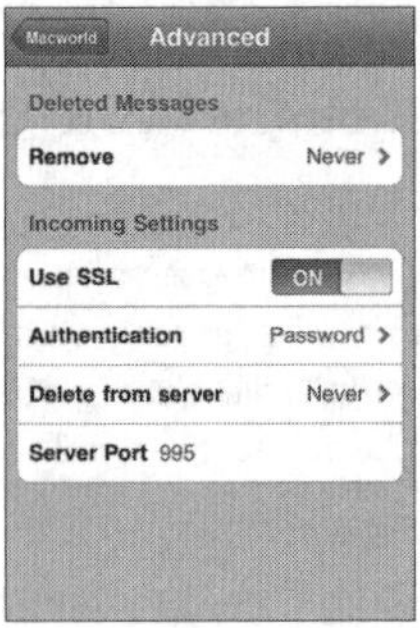

Figure 4.3
A POP account's Advanced settings.

Use these settings to specify

- The interval the iPhone will wait before it removes deleted messages from its Trash. Options are Never, After One Day, After One Week, and After One Month

- Whether your account will use Secure Sockets Layer (SSL) protection to transmit and receive email

- The kind of authentication your account requires (MD5 Challenge-Response, NTLM, HTTP MD5 Digest, or Password)

- When you want email to be deleted from the server (options include Never, Seven Days, and When Removed from Inbox)

- The incoming server port for your account

This information is individual enough that I'll leave it to your IT or ISP representative to tell you how to configure these options. Worth noting, however, is that you may be able to suss out these settings by looking at how the email client on your computer is configured.

For IMAP accounts, you have some different options in the Advanced window. You can choose which mailboxes will hold drafts, sent email, and deleted messages. You can choose when to remove deleted messages (Never, After One Day, After One Week, or After One Month). You can also turn on or off SSL (note that Yahoo Mail doesn't offer an

SSL option). You can choose the same authentication schemes as your POP-using sisters and brothers. You can enter an IMAP path prefix—a path name required by some IMAP servers so that they can show folders properly. And you can change the incoming server port.

Out and About

The iPhone 2.0 and later software is very smart about sending email. It works like this:

In the old days, you'd configure your email account with a particular SMTP server. If you took your iPhone on the road, and that SMTP server didn't work, you were stuck with an email message in the outbox that wouldn't send. This problem usually happened because of an antispam measure: The network you were connected to (in a coffee shop or hotel, for example) didn't allow messages to be relayed from one ISP's SMTP server through another's SMTP server.

This "no relaying" policy hasn't changed at all. What *has* changed is the iPhone's flexibility. Now, just select an account in the Mail, Contacts, Calendars screen and tap the SMTP button, and you'll see a list of all the SMTP servers your iPhone has settings for. At the top of the list is the primary server—the server address you entered (or that was entered for you) when you created the account. Next to this server's name is the word *On*.

Below the primary server is the Other SMTP Servers entry, listing all other SMTP servers your phone believes that it can access. By default, these entries have the word *Off* after their names. Tap one (a Gmail server, for example), and in the resulting screen, you have the option to turn that server on. When you do, if the iPhone is prevented from sending messages from the primary server, it tries to send from one of the other servers that you've enabled.

(continued on next page)

Out and About (continued)

This feature alone justifies getting a free Gmail or Yahoo account, as public Wi-Fi hotspots rarely block mail sent through Gmail's or Yahoo's SMTP servers.

One other SMTP option, while we're here: If you need to change the SMTP server port from the default setting of 25, you do it by tapping an SMTP server in the SMTP screen, tapping the Server Port entry at the bottom of the screen, and then typing a new value with the onscreen numeric keyboard that appears. Why do it? Many ISPs provide an SMTP server port (usually, 587) that can be relayed through other SMTP servers. If you find that your iPhone can't send a message, try changing your email account's SMTP port to 587 or to the public port number provided by your ISP.

Understanding Mail, Contacts, Calendars behavior

Before I leave the Mail, Contacts, Calendar screen, I should examine the options that tell the Mail, Contacts, and Calendars applications how to behave (**Figure 4.4**).

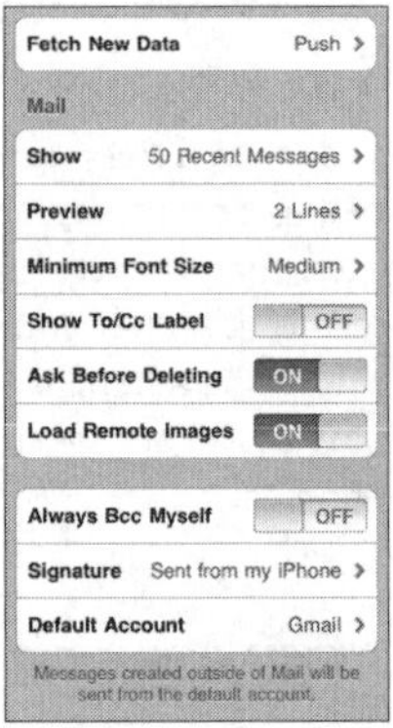

Figure 4.4
Additional Mail settings.

Fetch New Data	Push >
Mail	
Show	50 Recent Messages >
Preview	2 Lines >
Minimum Font Size	Medium >
Show To/Cc Label	OFF
Ask Before Deleting	ON
Load Remote Images	ON
Always Bcc Myself	OFF
Signature	Sent from my iPhone >
Default Account	Gmail >

Messages created outside of Mail will be sent from the default account.

View the bottom part of the screen, and you find these options below the Mail heading:

Fetch New Data. Thanks to the iPhone 2.0 and later software's Microsoft Exchange and MobileMe support, new data such as events, contacts, and email can be transferred (or *pushed*) to your phone automatically. You don't have to tell the iPhone to retrieve this data; retrieval just happens. When you tap Fetch New Data, you're taken to the screen of the same name, where you can switch off Push (**Figure 4.5**).

Figure 4.5
The Fetch New Data screen.

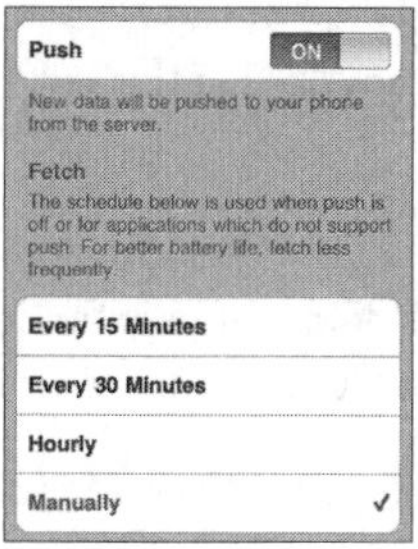

Push	ON
New data will be pushed to your phone from the server.	
Fetch	
The schedule below is used when push is off or for applications which do not support push. For better battery life, fetch less frequently.	
Every 15 Minutes	
Every 30 Minutes	
Hourly	
Manually	✓

Additionally, you find Fetch settings here. Fetch is essentially a scheduler for your iPhone; it tells the phone how often to go out and get information such as email messages from an account that can't push email, such as a POP account. (Fetch can also retrieve data from services such as MobileMe and Yahoo that push data but for which you've turned push off.) You can configure the iPhone to fetch data every 15 or 30 minutes, hourly, or manually.

If you tap the Advanced button at the bottom of the window, you're taken to an Advanced screen, where you can determine how your various email accounts behave with regard to pushing and fetching. You can configure a MobileMe or Yahoo account with a Push, Fetch, or Manual option, for example. Accounts that don't support push can be configured only for Fetch or Manual.

tip Pushing and fetching burn through a battery charge faster than using a manual setting, because your iPhone has to perform battery-draining tasks such as logging onto servers to retrieve data. Fetch demands more from a battery than push. For this reason, if you need to be miserly with your battery, fetch less often and turn push off.

Show. How many messages would you like Mail to display? Options include 25, 50, 75, 100, or 200 recent messages.

Preview. When you view message subjects within a mailbox in one of your Mail accounts, you see the first bit of text in each message. The Preview entry determines how many lines of this text you'll see: none, 1, 2, 3, 4, or 5 lines.

Minimum Font Size. This setting determines how large the text will be in your email messages: Small, Medium, Large, Extra Large, or Giant. Medium is good for most eyes, and it saves a lot of scrolling.

Show To/Cc Label. When this option is set to on, Mail plasters a *To* next to messages that were sent directly to you and a *Cc* next to messages on which you were copied.

Ask Before Deleting. When you set this option to on, if you tap the Trash icon to delete the message you're reading, you'll be asked to confirm your decision. If you swipe a message and then tap the red Delete icon that appears or use the iPhone's bulk-delete option, however, you won't be asked for confirmation.

Load Remote Images. Like the email client on your computer, the iPhone is capable of automatically showing you images embedded in messages. By default this option is on. If you routinely retrieve mail over a slow EDGE connection, you might consider turning it off, as your phone won't have to work to download this extra data.

Always Bcc Myself. If you're the kind of person who wants a copy of every message you send (but don't want the recipients of those messages to know), switch on this option. You'll get your copies.

Signature. Ever wonder where that proud *Sent from My iPhone* message comes from—the one that appears at the bottom of every message you send from your iPhone? Right here. As a new iPhone owner, you'll want to stick with this default message for a while, simply for the bragging rights. Feel free to tap this option later and enter some pithy signoff of your own.

Default Account. If you have more than one email account set up, this setting determines which account will send photos, videos, notes, and YouTube links. When you send one of these items, you can't choose which account sends it, so give this option some thought. You may discover that Wi-Fi hotspots are reluctant to send mail through your regular ISP's SMTP server, whereas Gmail accounts rarely have this problem. For this reason, you may want to make your Gmail account the default.

These Contacts settings appear next (**Figure 4.6**):

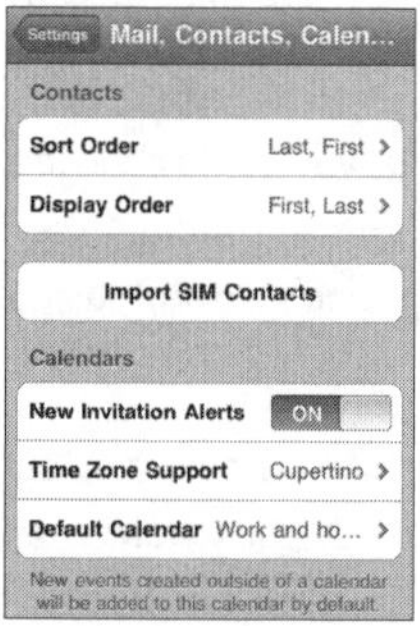

Figure 4.6
Additional Contacts and Calendar settings.

Sort Order. Tap this option to choose between sorting contacts by First, Last name or by Last, First name.

Display Order. Similar to Sort Order, this option lets you display your contacts as either First, Last or Last, First.

Import SIM Contacts. If you have another GSM phone that contains stored contacts on its SIM card, feel free to turn off both phones, extract the SIM card from the other phone, plunk it into your iPhone, and choose this command. Any contacts on that SIM card will be imported to your iPhone. If you have MobileMe and Exchange contacts on the phone, you'll be prompted to choose which of the two accounts to add them to.

Finally, you see these Calendar settings at the bottom of the screen:

New Invitation Alerts. This On/Off switch lets you view—or not—meeting invitations you've received (those pushed to you from an Exchange server, for example).

Time Zone Support. Tap this command, and you're taken to the Time Zone Support screen, where you can turn Time Zone Support on or off. Below that setting is an option to choose the time zone of a major city.

When Time Zone Support is on, Calendar's events are shown in the time of the selected city. So, for example, you could choose London even if you're in San Francisco and see events in London time. Switch this option off, and events are shown in the phone's current location (which is determined by network time).

Default Calendar. Tap this command to choose a calendar where the iPhone will add events created outside the Calendar application.

Sending and Receiving Mail

Now that your accounts are *finally* set up properly, you can send and receive messages. The process works this way.

Receiving email

Receiving email is dead simple. Just follow these steps:

1. Tap the Mail icon in the iPhone's Home screen.

   Mail will check for new messages when you first launch the application. If you have new messages, the iPhone will download them.

   When it does, a number appears next to the account name, indicating the account's number of unread messages. Any messages that contain attachments bear a paper-clip icon next to the sender's name.

2. Tap the account name.

   You'll see a list of that account's mailboxes. For POP accounts, those mailboxes include Inbox, Drafts (if you've saved any composed messages without sending them), Sent (if you've sent any messages from that account), and Trash (if you've deleted any messages from that account). For IMAP accounts, you'll most likely see Inbox, Drafts, Sent, Trash, and any folders associated with the account—folders you've added to a MobileMe or Google account, for example.

   These folder names, however, depend entirely on what the host service calls them. Gmail, for example, gathers the messages you've sent into the Sent Mail folder (**Figure 4.7** on the next page).

   In the bottom-right corner of an account screen, you'll see a Compose icon. Tap it, and a New Message screen appears, along with the iPhone's keyboard. I talk about creating new messages in "Creating and sending email" later in this chapter.

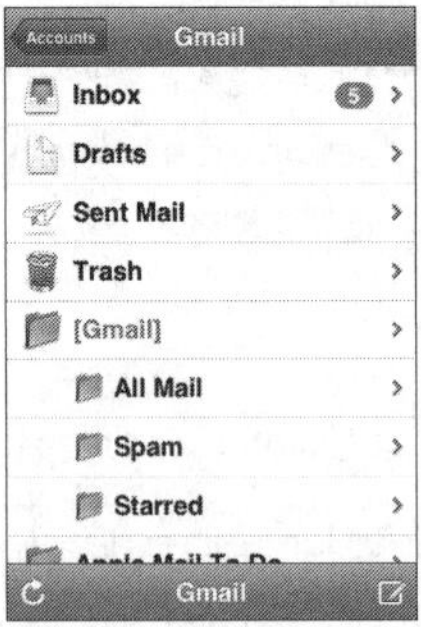

Figure 4.7
An Account screen.

3. Tap the Inbox.

Messages appear in a list, with the most recently received messages at the top. Unread messages have a blue dot next to them. The Inbox heading will have a number in parentheses next to it—*Inbox (22)*, for example. That *(22)* means that you have 22 unread messages.

This screen also bears a Compose icon and, in the bottom-left corner, a Retrieve icon, which you tap to check for new mail.

An Edit button in the top-right corner lets you delete messages. Tap it, and all the messages in the list acquire a dim gray circle next to them. This circle is for marking messages you want to delete or move. Tap one of these circles, and a red check icon appears within it. Continue tapping messages until you've selected all the messages you'd like to delete or move. Then tap the Delete button at the bottom of the screen, and all the messages will be moved to the Trash. (Alternatively, with regard to deleting messages, you can do without the Edit button. Swipe your finger across a message entry to force a Delete button to appear, and tap Delete; the message moves to the Trash.)

Tap Move, and a Mailboxes screen scrolls up from the bottom, listing all available mailboxes for that account. Choose a mailbox, and the selected messages move to it. This move feature is really useful only if you're using an IMAP account, as unlike POP accounts, IMAP accounts can have additional folders for filing email messages.

note When you delete a message, it's not really gone; it's simply moved to the Trash mailbox. To delete the message for real, you can either wait out the remove interval listed in the account's Mail setting (see "Configuring further" earlier in this chapter) or tap Trash. Then you can swipe a message and tap the Delete button that appears next to the message; tap Edit and then tap Delete All at the bottom of the screen; or cherry-pick the messages you want to delete by tapping the gray circles next to them and then tapping the Delete (#) button (where # equals the number of messages you've selected). Then—and only then—is a message truly gone.

Spam and the iPhone

As I write these words, the iPhone's Mail application lacks a spam filter—a utility that looks through your incoming email for junk mail and quarantines it in a special mailbox. This lack is a drag if you're using an account that attracts a lot of spam.

My solution? Don't use such an account on your iPhone. Google offers its free Gmail email service at www.gmail.com. Gmail provides loads of email storage (probably more than your current ISP does), and you can access it from the Web, your iPhone, and your computer's email client. Best of all, it offers excellent spam filtering. Additionally, you can set up Gmail so your other mail accounts are forwarded to it. This setup allows Gmail to filter out spam from these accounts too before the mail is delivered to your inbox. Like I said, it's free. Give it a try.

Navigating the Message screen

Simple though it may be, the Message screen packs a punch. In it, you find not only standard email elements such as From and To fields, Subject, and message body, but also icons for adding contacts and for filing, trashing, replying to, and forwarding messages. The screen breaks down this way.

Before the body

The top of the Message screen displays the number of messages in the mailbox as well as the number of the displayed message—*2 of 25,* for example. Tap the up or down arrow to the right to move quickly to the previous or next message in the mailbox (**Figure 4.8**).

Figure 4.8
Message body with document attached.

Below that, you'll see From and To fields. Each field will display at least one contact name or email address (one of which could be your own) in a blue bubble. Tap one of these bubbles, and if the name or address is in your iPhone's Contacts directory, you'll be taken to its owner's Info screen. If the name or address isn't among your contacts, a screen will appear, offering you the hidden option of emailing the person, creating a new contact or adding the address to an existing Contacts entry (**Figure 4.9**).

Hidden option? Yes. That person's email address is listed next to the Other heading. Tap that email address, and a new email message opens with that person's address in the To field. The email will be sent from the account you're currently working in.

Figure 4.9
*An unknown
contact's Info
screen.*

Tap Create New Contact, and a New Contact screen appears, with that person's name at the top and his email address filled in below. If the message has no name associated with it—if you were sent a message from a company address such as *info@example.com*, for example—no name will appear in the Name field.

Tap Add to Existing Contact, and a list of all the contacts on your iPhone appears. Tap a contact, and the address is added to that contact. If you'd like to edit the contact—indicate that the address belongs to Home or Work, for example—tap the blue bubble again to bring up the contact's Info screen, tap the Edit button, tap the email address to produce the Edit Email screen, tap Other, and choose a different label in the Label screen.

You can hide the To field by tapping the Hide entry near it. This action hides all the To fields in all the messages in all your accounts, and it changes the Hide entry to Details. To expose the To fields again, just tap Details.

tip Hiding the To field can be really helpful when someone insists on filling To fields with dozens of addresses (something that's considered to be both rude and a privacy violation). With the To field hidden, you can see the beginning of the message immediately instead of countless addresses.

Below the From and To fields, you'll see the message subject, followed by the date. If you have details showing, you'll also see a Mark As Unread entry. Tap this entry to do exactly what it suggests.

Body talk

Finally, in the area below, are the pithy words you've been waiting for. Just as in your computer's email client, you'll see the text of the message. Quoted text appears with a vertical line to its left—or more than one line, depending on how many quote "layers" the message has. If a message has several quote layers, each vertical line is a different color. (The first three layers are blue, green, and red, respectively; subsequent layers are red from there on out.)

If the message has attachments, they will appear below the message text. If Cousin Bill sends photos from his latest vacation, they'll appear here (**Figure 4.10**).

Figure 4.10
Message with attached photo.

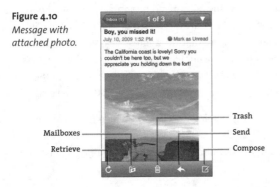

Mailboxes
Retrieve

Trash
Send
Compose

URLs, email addresses, and phone numbers contained within messages appear as blue, live links. Tap a URL, and Safari launches and takes you to that Web page. Tap an email address, and a new email message opens with that address in the To field. A tapped phone number causes a dialog box to appear. In it, you see the phone number and icons that offer to Cancel or Call.

> **tip** The iPhone is smart about URLs and phone numbers. Both http://www.example.com and www.example.com appear as live links, for example, but example.com does not. And (555) 555-1212, 555-555-1212, 555.555.1212, 5555551212, and 5551212 are all live links and produce the **Call** dialog box when tapped.

The tools below

The toolbar at the bottom of the screen contains five icons (refer to Figure 4.10):

Retrieve. Tap this circular icon, and the iPhone will check for new messages for that account.

Mailboxes. When you tap the Mailboxes icon, you're presented with a list of all the mailboxes associated with that account. Tap one of these mailboxes, and the message will be filed there. (Use this method to move a message out of the Trash.)

Trash. Tap this icon, and the cute little trash can pops its top and sucks the message into it. Like I said, to move messages out of the Trash, just tap the Trash mailbox in your account screen, tap a message, tap the Mailboxes icon, and then tap the mailbox where you'd like to put the message.

Send. The left-arrow icon is your pathway to the Reply, Reply All, Forward, and Save Image commands (**Figure 4.11** on the next page).

Figure 4.11
The Reply sheet.

When you tap the Send icon and then the Reply button that appears, a new message appears, with the Subject heading *Re: Original Message Subject,* in which *Original Message Subject* is . . . well, you know. The message is addressed to the sender of the original message, and the insertion point awaits at the top of the message body. The original text is quoted below. The message is mailed from the account you're working in.

If a message you received was sent to multiple recipients, tapping Reply All lets you reply to all the recipients of the original message.

Tap Forward, and you're responsible for filling in the To field in the resulting message. You can type it yourself with the keyboard that appears or tap the plus (+) icon to add a recipient from your iPhone's list of contacts. This message bears *Fwd:* at the beginning of the Subject heading, followed by the original heading. The original message's From and To information appear at the top of the message as quoted text followed by the original message.

Finally, if a message has images attached to it, you'll see a Save X Images button, where X is the number of images. (The button will read Save Image if there's just one image.) Tap that button, and the attached images will be added to the Camera Roll collection in the Photos application.

Compose. Last is your old friend the Compose icon. Tap it, and a New Message screen appears, ready for your input.

Creating and sending email

If it truly is better to give than receive, the following instructions for composing and delivering mail from your iPhone should enrich your life significantly. With regard to email, the iPhone can give nearly as good as it gets. Here's how to go about it.

As I mention earlier in the chapter, you can create new email messages by tapping the Compose icon that appears in every account and mailbox screen. You'll even find the Compose icon available when you've selected Trash. To create a message, follow these steps:

1. Tap the Compose icon.

   By default, Mail fills the From field with the address for this account. But you needn't use that account. Just tap From, and any other email accounts you have will appear in a scrolling list. Tap the one you want.

2. In the New Message screen that appears, type the recipient's email address, or in the To field, tap the plus icon.

   When you place the insertion point in the To or Cc/Bcc field, notice that the iPhone's keyboard adds @ and period (.) characters where the spacebar usually resides. (The spacebar is still there; it's just smaller.) This feature makes typing addresses easier, because you don't have to switch to the numbers-and-symbols keyboard.

   tip Tap and hold the period key, and—good gosh almighty!—.net, .edu, .org, and .com pop up as part of a contextual menu. How handy is that?

   When you start typing a name, the iPhone will suggest recipients based on entries in your list of contacts (**Figure 4.12** on the next page). If the recipient you want appears in the list below the To field, tap that name to add it to the field.

Figure 4.12
Begin typing to find a contact.

When you tap the plus icon, your list of contacts appears. Navigate through your contacts and tap the one you want to add to the To field. Some contacts will have multiple email addresses; tap the one you'd like to use. To add more names to the To field, type them or tap the plus icon to add them.

To delete a recipient, tap it and then tap the Delete key on the iPhone's keyboard.

3. If you'd like to Cc or Bcc someone, tap in that field, tap in the appropriate field—CC or Bcc—and then use any of the techniques in step 2 for adding a recipient.

4. Tap the Subject field, and enter a subject for your message with the iPhone's keyboard.

   That subject replaces *New Message* at the top of the screen.

5. Tap in the message body (or, if the insertion point is in the Subject field, tap Return on the iPhone's keyboard to move to the message body), and type your message.

6. Tap Send to send the message or Cancel to save or delete your message.

The Send icon, in the top-right corner, is easy enough to understand. Tap that icon, and the message is sent from the current account. You'll know that it's been sent when you hear a swoosh sound.

Cancel is a little more confusing. If you've typed anywhere in the To field, New Message screen's Subject field, or message body (even if you subsequently deleted everything you typed), a sheet will roll up when you tap Cancel, displaying Save, Don't Save, and Cancel icons. Tap Save to store the message in the account's Drafts mailbox. (If no such mailbox exists, the iPhone will create one.) When you tap Don't Save, the message is deleted. When you tap Cancel, the iPhone assumes that you made a mistake when you tapped Cancel the first time, and it removes this sheet.

If the iPhone can't send a message—when you don't have access to a Wi-Fi network or 3G or EDGE networks, for example—it creates an Outbox for the account from which you're trying to send the message. When you next use Mail and are able to send the message, the iPhone will make the connection and send any messages in the Outbox, at which point the Outbox will disappear.

Working with pushy MobileMe

Apple's $100-per-annum MobileMe Web service does a lot of things—provides 20 GB of online storage; gives you a place to post galleries of images and videos; and offers Webcentric mail, calendar, and contacts applications. For purposes of this discussion, one of the most important things it does is automatically synchronize (or *push*) mail, contact, calendar, and Internet bookmark information among your computers, your iPhone and iPod touch, and Apple's Internet-based MobileMe server. So, for example, when you enter a new event in the iPhone's Calendar application, it also soon appears within MobileMe's Calendar component on the Web, as well as on any computer that's synced with MobileMe. You set it up this way.

Configuring MobileMe on the Macintosh

You configure MobileMe through the MobileMe system preference, as follows:

1. Choose Apple > System Preferences.

2. Click the MobileMe preference in the Internet & Network section and then click the Sync tab.

3. Check the Synchronize with MobileMe box, and choose Automatically from the pop-up menu.

   When you choose Automatically, you enable MobileMe's push capabilities. This command tells MobileMe that when some new data is added to the MobileMe Web site or to your iPhone (you've uploaded a photo to a photo gallery, created a new calendar event, or added a new contact, for example), that data should be pushed almost immediately to the other devices synced with your MobileMe account.

   Note that this is not the case with data created on your computer. When you choose Automatically from this pop-up menu on your computer, any new data you create will be synchronized every 15 minutes. If you need that data synced sooner, simply click the Sync Now button.

4. In the Sync tab's scrolling pane, select the kind of data you'd like to synchronize.

   You'll see several options in this pane, but the ones you're concerned about here are Calendars and Contacts (**Figure 4.13**).

5. To synchronize this data with MobileMe immediately, click Sync Now.

   In the process, you may see a dialog box that asks how you'd like to sync your data. The options include merging your computer and MobileMe data, replacing the data on your computer with MobileMe's data, or replacing MobileMe's data with the data on your computer.

Figure 4.13
A Mac's MobileMe system preferences.

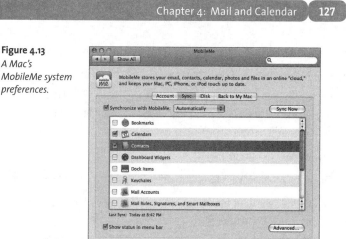

If you click the More Options button, you can choose a different option for the kinds of data you're syncing. You can choose to merge contacts but replace the calendars on your Mac with MobileMe's calendar information, for example.

Your Mac will do as you ask and synchronize your data. If the synchronization was successful, and if you chose to sync calendars and contacts, you should see the same data in iCal and Address Book that is available on the MobileMe Web site.

Configuring MobileMe in Windows

The process of syncing your data with MobileMe in Windows is similar to the Macintosh experience. The difference is that MobileMe syncs with Windows applications such as Microsoft Outlook and Windows Contacts, because Apple's iCal and Address Book don't come in Windows versions.

 For this procedure to work, you must install iTunes 8.2 or later and, of course, have a MobileMe account.

To configure MobileMe on a PC, follow these steps:

1. Download and install MobileMe Setup.

   If you don't have MobileMe installed on your PC, you'll have to get it from http://support.apple.com/downloads/MobileMe_Control_ Panel_for_Windows.

2. Choose Start > Control Panels.

3. Open the MobileMe Preferences control panel, and click the Sync tab.

4. Enable the Sync with MobileMe option, and choose Automatically from the pop-up menu.

   (See the Macintosh configuration information in the preceding section to find out why you choose Automatically.)

5. Enable the kinds of data you want to sync.

   Your choices are Contacts, Calendars, and Bookmarks. When you choose Contacts, you can sync with Outlook, Google Contacts, Yahoo Address Book, and Windows Contacts. For Calendars, you can sync only with Outlook. And Bookmarks can be synced with Internet Explorer or the Windows version of Apple's Web browser, Safari.

6. Click Sync Now.

   As with Macintosh syncing, you'll be asked how you'd like to have the sync performed. Here, too, you can choose how particular kinds of data are synced.

Configuring the iPhone

Now that your computer is configured, you're ready to add the iPhone to the mix, as follows:

1. Tap Settings and then tap Mail, Contacts, Calendars.

2. In the Accounts area, tap your MobileMe account.

3. In the account screen that appears, switch on those data types you'd like to sync with MobileMe.

   Your choices are Mail, Contacts, Calendars, and Bookmarks (**Figure 4.14**). Contacts, calendars, and bookmarks work as I describe earlier in this chapter; when contacts and calendar items are created, they're synchronized with MobileMe and any computers linked to your MobileMe account.

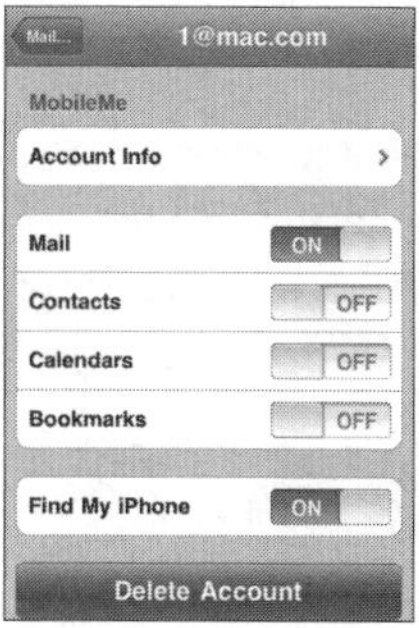

Figure 4.14
The iPhone's MobileMe syncing options.

When you switch on the Mail option, however, you're telling MobileMe to send any received messages to your iPhone immediately. When the Mail option is switched off, you'll receive that mail only when you launch the Mail application and check for it.

note When you enable MobileMe syncing for bookmarks, contacts, or calendars, the syncing option for those enabled data types will no longer be available for the iPhone in iTunes.

Below the syncing options, you see the Find My iPhone switch. This service, exclusive to MobileMe members, can help you track down a missing iPhone. I describe its workings in Chapter 10.

Using Calendar

In the old days, the only way to get events on the iPhone's calendar was to either type them on the phone or sync the iPhone with iTunes and ask it to copy your events from computer to phone. Thanks to the introduction of Exchange and MobileMe push synchronization, the iPhone's Calendar is a smarter application than it once was. In this section, I take a look at all the ways you can put life's events on your iPhone.

Managing many calendars

With the iPhone 2.0 and later software, the Calendar application can display more than one calendar—but it won't when you first launch the application. Instead, it shows your default calendar, as you configured it in the Mail, Contacts, Calendar setting. To view a list of all the calendars on your iPhone, just tap the Calendars icon in the top-left corner of the screen. To view another calendar, tap that calendar's name. Or view all your calendar events by tapping the All entry.

Viewing events

Calendar is capable of displaying events in three views: List, Day, and Month. They're laid out like so.

Month

Tap Calendar, and by default, you'll see this month's calendar, with today's date highlighted in blue. Other days maintain a gray, businesslike appearance. Tap another day, and it adopts the blue box, while the present day gains a deeper gray hue. To return to the current day, either tap it (if you're viewing the current month) or tap the Today button in the bottom-left corner of the screen. To move to the next or previous month, tap the Previous or Next arrow, respectively, next to the month heading. To scan ahead more quickly, tap and hold on one of these arrows.

Any days on the calendar that have events appended to them bear a small black dot below the date. Tap a day with a dot, and the events for that day appear in a list below the calendar (**Figure 4.15**), each preceded by its start time and colored dot, indicating the calendar to which the event is attached. (Each calendar is color-coded.) Tap an event in this list, and you're taken to the Event screen, which details the name and location of the event, its date, its start and end times, any alerts you've created, and any notes you've added to the event.

Figure 4.15
Month view with two events.

To edit or delete the event, tap the Edit icon in the top-right corner of the screen. Within the Edit screen, tap one of the fields to change its information. (I discuss these fields in "Creating events" later in this chapter.) To delete an event, tap the red Delete Event button at the bottom of the screen; then tap the Delete Event confirmation icon that appears.

Day

Tap the Day view button, and as you'd expect, you see the day laid out in a list, separated by hours. The day of the week and its date appear near the top of the screen. To move to the previous or next day, tap the Previous or Next arrow, respectively. To scan back or forward more quickly, tap and hold the appropriate arrow.

Events appear as colored bars (again, each calendar is color-coded, and that coding is reflected here) in the times they occupy and are labeled with the name of the appointment and its location (**Figure 4.16**). Just as you do with events in Month view, tap them to reveal their details; to edit them, tap the Edit button.

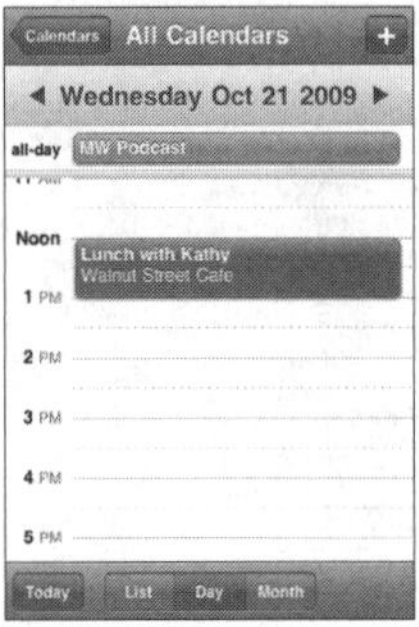

Figure 4.16
Day view with two events.

List

List view shows a list of all the events on your calendar, separated by gray date bars. Each gray bar bears the day's abbreviated name (*Fri* or *Mon*, for example) and the month, date, and year of the event. The event's title appears just below, preceded by its start time and colored dot indicating its calendar association. Once again, tap an event to view its details. Tap Edit to edit the event or delete it via the Delete Event button (**Figure 4.17**). List is the single view that provides a Search field for finding events quickly.

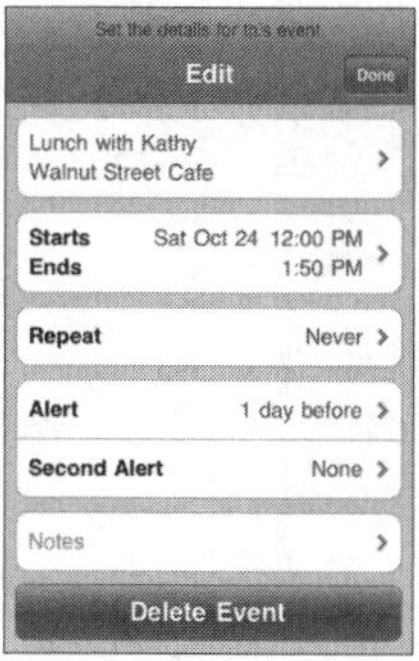

Figure 4.17
Editing an event.

Creating events

Creating events on the iPhone is simple. Just tap the plus icon in the top-right corner of the screen to produce the Add Event screen, where you'll find fields for Title & Location, Start & End, Repeat, Alert, Calendar, and Notes. In more detail:

Title & Location. The title of the event will appear when you select the event's date in Month view. Both an event's title and location appear in the Day-view list. And in List view, you see just the event's title. As with any other field on the iPhone, just type the entries and tap Save when you're done.

Start & End. The title is explanation enough. Just tap the Starts field, and enter a date and time by using the spinning wheels at the bottom of the screen (**Figure 4.18** on the next page). Ditto with the Ends field. If the event lasts all day, tap the All-Day On/Off switch.

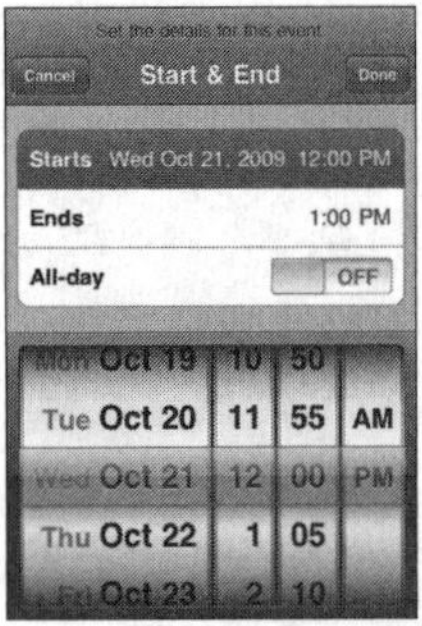

Figure 4.18
*Set the duration
of your event.*

> **tip** Unlike most calendar applications you're familiar with, this one lets
> you create events that span multiple days. Just dial in a different day
> when you tap Ends.

Repeat. You can create an event that occurs every day, week, 2 weeks,
month, or year. This method is a convenient way to remind yourself of
your kid's weekly piano lesson or your own wedding anniversary.

Alert. A fat lot of good an electronic calendar does you if you're not
paying attention to the date or time. Tap Alert and direct the iPhone to
sound an alert at a specific interval before the event's start time: 5, 15, or
30 minutes; 1 or 2 hours; 1 or 2 days before; or on the date of the event.

You can create two alerts per event—useful when you want to remind
yourself of events for the day and need another mental nudge a few
minutes before the event occurs. Regrettably, you can't change the alert
sound; you can only turn it on or off in the Sound Settings screen.

Calendar. Using this command, you can assign the new event to any
calendar you have on your iPhone.

Notes. Feel free to type a bit of text to remind yourself exactly why you're
allowing Bob Whosis to dominate your Thursday afternoon.

Syncing events

Your computer and your iPhone have a nice sharing relationship with regard to events. When you create an event on one device, it's copied to the other, complete with title, location, start and end times, alerts (likely called *alarms* in your computer's calendar program), and notes.

As I explain in Chapter 2, you can pick and choose the computer-based calendars you want to sync with the iPhone within iTunes's Info tab. If you have an Exchange or MobileMe account, calendar events associated with those accounts are pushed to your iPhone (and the iPhone pushes right back those events that you create on it).

Deleting events

Quite frankly, deleting events by using the iPhone's interface is a pain in the neck. As I mention earlier in the chapter, you tap an event, tap the Edit button in the Event screen, tap the red Delete Event button at the bottom of the screen, and then tap Delete Event again. This procedure is a very inefficient way to delete events, particularly lots of events that have expired. You're better off letting iTunes lend a hand.

To do so, plug your iPhone into the computer and then select it in iTunes' Source list. Click the Info tab, and configure the Calendars delete option to read *Do Not Sync Events Older Than X Days,* where *X* is the number of past days you're willing to keep expired events on your iPhone. When you next sync your iPhone, events that occurred more than *X* days before the current date will be removed from the phone (**Figure 4.19**).

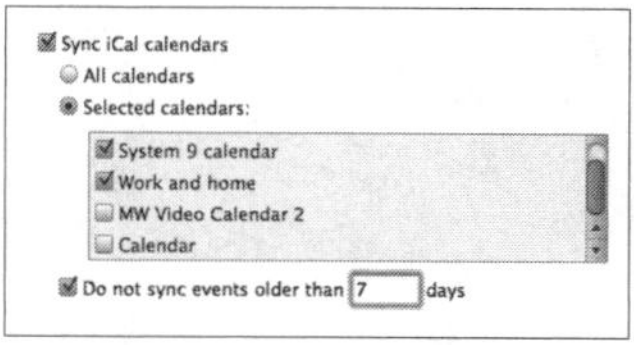

Figure 4.19
It's easier to delete lots of events through iTunes.

If you'd like to delete multiple future events, delete them from your computer's calendar. If you're using a nonpush account, when you sync your iPhone, the events will disappear from the iPhone's calendar as well. When Exchange and your MobileMe account are set up to synchronize calendars, deleting events either on the server or on the iPhone will cause the event to vanish from every synced service and device.

Subscribing to a calendar

You can also subscribe to Web-based calendars with your iPhone, which supports both CalDAV and iCal formats. To do so, follow these steps:

1. Travel to Settings > Mail, Contacts, Calendars, and tap Add Account.

2. Tap Other in the Add Account screen.

3. In the Calendars area of the Other screen, choose either Add CalDAV Account or Add Subscribed Calendar.

   Which you choose depends on the kind of calendar you want to subscribe to. iCal calendars are generally available to the public and require only that you have a server address in the form *example.com/example.ics*. iCalShare (http://icalshare.com) is a repository for such public calendars.

   CalDAV calendars are server-based and require that you know the name of the host server and have a user name and password for that server.

4. Enter the required information to subscribe to the calendar.

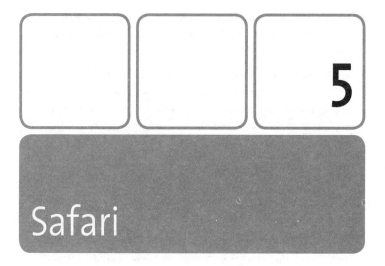

5

Safari

From Day One, the iPhone has had a real live Web browser, very much like the one on your computer. In this chapter, I show you how to use it to best advantage. Let's go surfing!

Importing Bookmarks

I know you're eager to start surfing the Web with Safari, but you'll find the experience far more pleasant if you first sync your Safari (Mac) or Safari or Internet Explorer (Windows) bookmarks to your iPhone. This is easy to do:

1. Jack your iPhone into your computer's USB 2.0 port, launch iTunes (if it doesn't launch automatically), select the iPhone in iTunes' Source list, and click the Info tab.

2. In the Web Browser area of the window, on a Mac, enable the Sync Safari Bookmarks option (**Figure 5.1**); on a Windows PC, enable the Sync Bookmarks From option and choose either Safari or Internet Explorer from the pop-up menu.

Figure 5.1
Syncing Safari within the Mac version of iTunes.

☑ Sync Safari bookmarks

3. Export your bookmarks if you're not using Safari or Internet Explorer.

   To sync your bookmarks with the phone via iTunes, your bookmarks must be in either of these two browsers. If you're using a browser such as Mozilla Firefox, check its help system for details on exporting its bookmarks.

4. Open Safari and choose File > Import Bookmarks, or fire up Internet Explorer and choose File > Import and Export.

5. Navigate to the bookmarks file you saved.

   Your bookmarks are now in a browser that's compatible with the iPhone. When you next sync your iPhone, those bookmarks will be available to the iPhone's copy of Safari.

Surfin' Safari

When you first tap the Safari icon at the bottom of the iPhone's Home screen, you may be surprised to see a full (though tiny) representation of a Web page appear before your eyes. Safari on the iPhone is nearly the real deal. (In "Safari's limits" later in this chapter, I talk about how that isn't quite the case.)

At first glance, though, it's the real *small* deal. The pages Safari displays on the iPhone are Lilliputian at first, but you have ways to make these pages legible:

- **Turn the iPhone on its side.** Yes, Safari, like nearly all the included apps, works in both portrait and landscape orientation. It displays the entire width of a Web page in either view, so when you switch to landscape orientation, you see more detail as the page enlarges to fill the iPhone's screen (**Figure 5.2**).

Figure 5.2
A Web page in landscape orientation, showing Safari's tool icons.

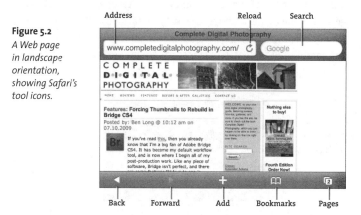

- **Stretch the page open.** You can enlarge the page by using the stretch gesture (see Chapter 1). When the page is enlarged, tap and drag to reposition it.

- **Double-tap a column.** Most Web pages include columns of text and graphics. To zoom in on a single column, double-tap it. That column expands to fill the iPhone's screen. To shrink the page to its original size, double-tap the screen again.

- **Double-tap part of the page.** If a Web page lacks columns, you can still zoom in by double-tapping the page.

Browsing the Web

Like any good browser, Safari provides numerous ways to get around the Web. Let me count the ways.

Getting addressed

Like your computer's Web browser, Safari has an Address field at the top of its main window. (If you don't see the Address field, just tap the gray menu bar at the top of the screen, and you'll be taken to the top of the page, where the Address field is revealed.) To travel to a Web site, tap in this field. When you do, the iPhone's keyboard appears. If ever there were an argument for using Safari in landscape orientation, this feature is it, because the iPhone's keyboard is far less cramped this way (**Figure 5.3**).

Figure 5.3
The landscape Safari keyboard (with the .com key held down).

Type the Web address you want to visit. The iPhone and its keyboard make this process as easy for you as possible. To begin with, you needn't type **http://www**. Safari understands that just about every Web address begins this way and doesn't require you to type the prefix. Just type **examplesite**; then tap the .com key at the bottom of the keyboard (even .com is unnecessary sometimes), and tap Go. In a short (Wi-Fi), shortish (3G), or long (EDGE) time, the page you desire will appear.

tip If a site's URL ends with something like .net or .org, you needn't key that in. Just tap and hold the keyboard's .com entry until a pop-up menu appears, offering additional .net, .edu, and .org entries. Glide your finger over to the entry you want, and let go. The address will complete with the extension you chose.

Safari offers some other convenient shortcuts for entering addresses. If you've visited the site before, for example, it's likely to be in Safari's History list. If so, just begin typing the address, and it will appear below the Address field (**Figure 5.4**). Tap the address to go to that Web site.

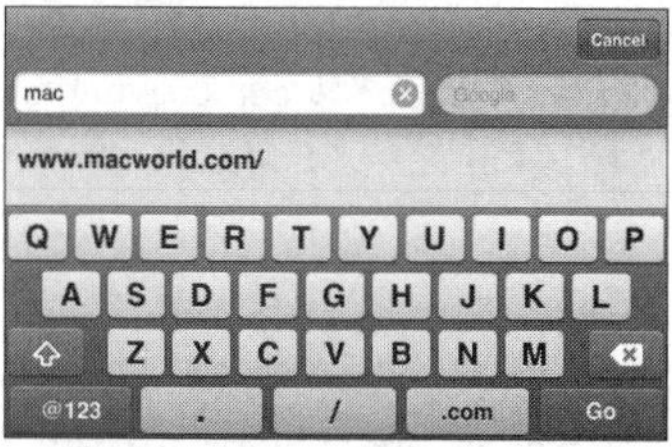

Figure 5.4
*The iPhone's
History list can
save typing.*

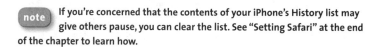

tip If the Address field is full when you tap it, you can erase its contents quickly by tapping the X icon that appears at the right edge of the field.

note If you're concerned that the contents of your iPhone's History list may give others pause, you can clear the list. See "Setting Safari" at the end of the chapter to learn how.

If you need to type a more complex address—**example.com/pictures/ vacation.html**, for example—the iPhone's default keyboard for Safari can help, because it includes both period (.) and slash (/) keys.

To leave the keyboard behind without doing anything, tap the Cancel button. If the page you're trying to visit is taking too long to load, or if you've changed your mind about visiting it, just tap the X that appears next to the Address field while the page is loading. Safari will stop

loading the page. If you'd like to reload a page that's fully loaded, tap
the Reload icon next to the Address field (the one that takes the place of
the X when a page is completely loaded).

Searching

You can also conduct Google or Yahoo searches from the keyboard. To
begin a search, just tap the magnifying-glass icon in the top-left corner of
a Safari window. This tap causes the keyboard to appear and the insertion
point to blink in the Search field. Enter your query in this field and then
tap Google or Yahoo (depending on which search engine you're using).

By default, the iPhone uses Google search. To switch to Yahoo, go to the
Settings screen, and tap Safari. Tap Search Engine and then tap Yahoo.

Navigating with links

Links work just as they do in your computer's browser. Just tap a link to
go to the associated Web page. Two things are worth noting:

- Safari is sometimes reluctant to use a link while it's still loading a Web
  page, which can be particularly infuriating when you're surfing the
  Web very slowly over EDGE. To speed things up, tap the X icon next to
  the Address field to stop the current page from loading; then tap the
  link to load its target immediately. (In some cases, you'll see a blank
  page instead of the page you were on because Safari had started to
  load the new page but hadn't completed the process. In such cases,
  tap the back-arrow icon to return to the previous page.)

- When you hover your mouse pointer over a link in your computer's
  Web browser, you can view information about where that link will take
  you. The iPhone offers a more powerful, though hidden, capability. Just
  tap and hold a link, and a sheet scrolls up from the bottom. This sheet
  displays not only the full address of the link, but also four options—
  Open, Open in New Page, Copy, and Cancel— whose names match
  their purposes (**Figure 5.5**).

Figure 5.5
*Tap and hold a
link to see these
options.*

Going back and forward

Just like your computer's Web browser, Safari has Back and Forward
arrows for moving through sites you've visited.

Saving pages

In the bottom-right corner of the Safari screen, you'll see a small Pages
icon. Tap it, and you'll see a small representation of the page you're
currently viewing. Tap the New Page button in the bottom-left corner
of the screen, and you can create a new empty Web page, saving the
page you were just viewing in the process (**Figure 5.6**). This feature is the
iPhone's equivalent of browser tabs.

Figure 5.6
*Safari lets you
save up to eight
pages.*

You can repeat this process to save as many as eight pages; the Pages
icon displays the number of pages you've stored. To visit one of your

saved pages, tap the Pages icon, and swipe your finger across the display to move back or forward through the saved pages. To view a page full-screen, tap its thumbnail or tap the Done button while its thumbnail is on view. To delete a page, tap the red X in the top-left corner of the page.

note The contents of saved pages aren't cached to the iPhone—just their locations—so you won't be able to read them if your iPhone is offline (when you can't access a Wi-Fi, 3G, or EDGE network, for example, or when your phone is in airplane mode).

Navigating with bookmarks

You heeded my advice to import your computer browser's bookmarks, right? Great. Bookmarks are another fine way to get where you want to go.

Just tap the Bookmarks icon at the bottom of Safari's screen. The Bookmarks screen will appear, replete with your bookmarks organized as they were on your computer. By this, I mean that if you've organized your computer's bookmarks in folders, that's just how they'll appear on your iPhone. Bookmarks that you've placed in Safari's Bookmarks Bar are contained in their own folder, named (aptly enough) Bookmarks Bar.

Tap a folder to view the bookmarks it contains. To travel to a bookmark's target page, tap the bookmark.

Working with bookmarks

Bookmarks are important-enough components of Safari that they deserve more than this so-far-brief mention. How, for example, do you create bookmarks, organize and edit the ones you have, and delete those you no longer need? Like this.

Creating bookmarks

You've found a Web site you like while surfing with the iPhone. To bookmark the site, follow these steps:

1. Tap the plus (+) icon at the bottom of the screen.

   In the sheet that appears, the first option is Add Bookmark. (I look at the other two options soon.)

2. Tap Add Bookmark.

   The Add Bookmark screen opens, displaying the name of the bookmark. If the name is too long for your liking, edit it with the iPhone's standard text-editing keyboard.

3. Tap the Bookmarks entry, and choose a location for your bookmark.

   When you do this, a list that contains your bookmarks-folder hierarchy appears. Tap the folder where you'd like to file your bookmark. From now on, this folder is where you'll find that bookmark (**Figure 5.7**).

Figure 5.7
*Creating a
bookmark.*

4. Tap Save to save the bookmark in this location, or tap Cancel to cancel the bookmarking operation.

Organizing and editing bookmarks

If you're as organized as I am (meaning not very), your bookmarks may be a bit of a mess. Although you're better off organizing the bookmarks on your computer and then syncing them to your iPhone, you can organize them on the phone as well. To do so, follow along:

1. Tap the Bookmarks icon.

2. In the resulting Bookmarks screen, tap the Edit button.

3. To delete an item, tap the red minus (–) icon that appears next to it.

The red minus icon appears next to all entries in the screen save History, Bookmarks Bar, and Bookmarks Menu—in short, all the items you've created but none of the items that the iPhone requires.

You'll also notice the three-line reposition icon to the right of these marked items, indicating that you can change their positions in the list by dragging the icons up or down. You can also rename your bookmark, change its URL, or file it in a different folder by tapping its name while in editing mode and then making those changes in the resulting Edit Bookmark screen.

Additionally, you can create a new folder this way:

1. Tap the New Folder icon in the bottom-right section of the screen to open an Edit Folder screen.

2. Use the onscreen keyboard to give your folder a name; then choose a location for it by tapping the field below, which displays the name of the folder you're currently in (such as Bookmarks Bar).

3. Tap this field, and up pops the bookmarks hierarchy.

4. Tap the folder in which you'd like to place this new folder.

5. Tap the arrow icon in the top-left section of the screen.

Your folder is created.

Getting more from the plus icon

As I mention in "Creating bookmarks" earlier in this chapter, when you tap the plus (+) icon at the bottom of Safari's screen, you see two options after Add Bookmark: Add to Home Screen and Mail Link to This Page. (OK, you see a Cancel button too, so technically, there are *four* options.) These two buttons work this way:

Add to Home Screen. When you tap this button, an Add to Home screen appears, displaying the name of the Web page you're currently view-ing with some kind of icon next to the page's name (**Figure 5.8**). (Some Web sites have gone to the trouble to create a cool icon that looks great on an iPhone. Other icons are just undistinguished thumbnails of a portion of the page.) You're welcome to rename the saved page by using the keyboard.

Click Add, and an icon representing that Web page is created in the iPhone's Home screen (**Figure 5.9**). In the future, when you tap that icon, Safari will launch and take you directly to that page.

Figure 5.8
Adding a Web site to your Home screen.

Figure 5.9
The icon of a Web site on the Home screen.

tip   Should you grow tired of this icon, you can remove it just as you can remove other expendable items (meaning applications other than the ones originally included with the iPhone) from the iPhone's Home screen. Tap and hold the icon until all the icons start wiggling. Then tap the X in the top-left corner of the icon you want to delete, and it's gone.

Mail Link to This Page. If you find a Web page that cries out to be shared with your nearest as well as dearest, tap Mail Link to This Page. When you do, a new, unaddressed mail message opens. The Subject heading is the name of the Web page, and the body of the message contains a link to the page. All you need to do is address the message and tap Send.

Safari and RSS

Safari supports RSS (Really Simple Syndication), the standard for distributing Web headlines. To view collections of these headlines (called *feeds*) on your iPhone, just locate a page's RSS link and tap it. The page that appears bears a blue bar at the top, along with the name of the site connected to the feed—Mac 911, for example (**Figure 5.10**). The site's headlines appear below the blue bar. Tap a headline to read the full story.

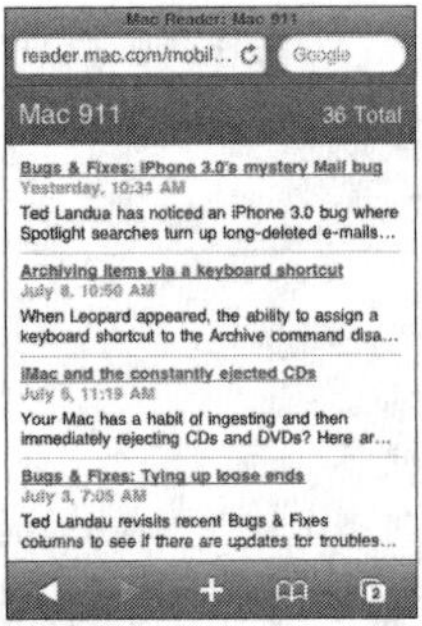

Figure 5.10
A Safari RSS feed.

> **tip** RSS URLs are clumsy to enter yourself; they're long and rarely contain real words. For this reason, bookmarking those that you intend to revisit is a good idea.

Safari's limits

Earlier in this chapter, I hint that although the iPhone's version of Safari is about as full-featured as you're likely to find on a mobile phone, it doesn't have all the capabilities of your computer's browser. The following sections discuss its limitations.

No Flash support

Many modern Web sites greet you with luxurious animations, flickering icons, and animated menus created with Adobe's Web-animation design tool, Flash. The iPhone doesn't support Flash, and because it doesn't, you may see nothing at all on such a site's home page. Ideally, the designer took into account the fact that not everyone likes (or, in the case of the iPhone, can use) Flash and inserted a Skip Animation link that takes you to a Flashless version of the site.

Similarly, many of the movies you find on the Web are Flash-based. If, while traipsing through a Web site, you see a small blue box with a question mark inside it, you're looking at the placeholder for a Flash movie. Tapping that icon will do you no good whatsoever.

The good news is that the iPhone will play a lot of QuickTime content (though not all). As the iPhone increases in popularity, Web sites likely will increase their use of QuickTime.

No downloading

You're accustomed to downloading files with computers and Web browsers. You give up that feature when using the iPhone's browser, however, because it's not supported.

No Find

Web pages can be packed with information, and the iPhone's screen is a pretty small place to view that much content. I'd love to be able to pull up a Search field and key in a word or phrase I seek. I can't.

Setting Safari

Like other iPhone applications, Safari has its own collection of settings. As you might guess, you find them by tapping Settings in the iPhone's Home screen and then tapping Safari in the Settings screen (**Figure 5.11**).

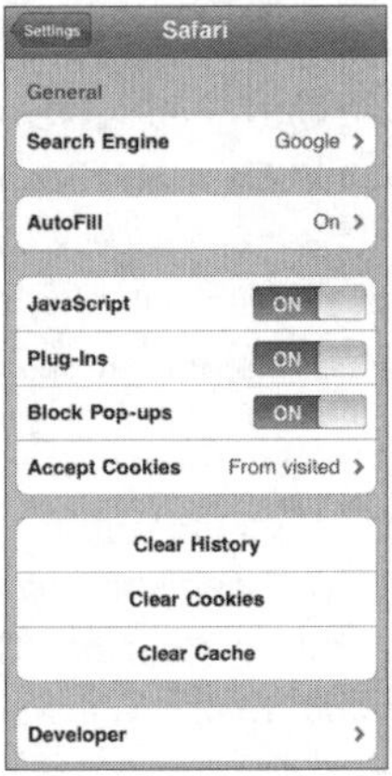

Figure 5.11
Safari settings.

These settings include the following:

Search Engine. The iPhone can use either Google or Yahoo for its Web searches. Choose the one you want here.

AutoFill. This feature is new with the 3.0 software. AutoFill, like your computer's Web browser, can fill in contact information and user names and passwords. To enable those options, tap AutoFill and toggle the Use Contact Info and Names & Passwords sliders to On.

JavaScript. JavaScript is a scripting language that helps make Web sites more interactive. By default, Safari allows JavaScript to work. If you care to disable JavaScript for some reason, you do it with this On/Off switch.

Plug-Ins. The iPhone supports some plug-ins that allow it to display or play certain Web content—QuickTime movies and audio, for example. You can turn off these plug-ins by toggling this switch to Off.

Block Pop-Ups. I make a lot of my living by writing for advertising-based Web sites, but I've yet to see a pop-up window that did more than annoy me. If you're haunted by pop-up ads, leave this option's switch set to On.

Accept Cookies. Many Web sites leave little markers called *cookies* stored in your Web browser. Cookies can store information such as when you visited the site and which pages you saw there. Sometimes, they also store information such as your user name and password for that site.

The Accept Cookies setting gives you a measure of control:

- You can choose never to accept them (which some people consider to be more secure and private, but which forces you to reenter passwords and user names each time you return).

- You can opt to accept just those cookies sent by each site you visit. (Some sites plant cookies from their advertisers, and this option prevents that behavior.)

- You can choose to always accept cookies, which means that your iPhone is now a cookie-gathering machine. The default setting is From Visited, which I think nicely balances privacy and convenience.

Clear History, Clear Cookies, and Clear Cache. This group of three buttons in the Safari Settings screen allows you to wipe your tracks:

- Earlier, I told you that when you start typing a URL in Safari's Address field, the iPhone makes suggestions based on past searches. To stop this behavior, tap Clear History.

- If you're concerned that the iPhone's stored cookies reveal more about your browsing habits than you're comfortable with, tap Clear Cookies.

- Safari's cache stores some of the contents of pages you visit so that they open faster when you revisit. If new content isn't showing up, and you believe that it should, tapping Clear Cache will help by forcing Safari to reload entire pages that were previously cached.

When you tap any of these buttons, you're asked to confirm that you really want to perform the action.

Developer. You can turn on a Debug Console within Safari if you're interested in seeing any coding errors a Web page might have. If you're an übergeek and find such errors fascinating, knock yourself out and switch it on. Everyone else, feel free to leave it off.

6

iPhone As iPod

Whether you view your iPhone as a phone that just happens to play music and videos or as a really cool iPod that you can use to make calls, the fact remains that the iPhone's media capabilities are among its greatest. You can use your iPhone to listen to the best of your music collection; play custom ringtones; check out the latest podcasts; and watch your favorite TV shows, purchased and rented movies, and music videos. This chapter shows you how to do all that and offers pointers on configuring iTunes to make the most of your iPhone's iPod functions.

Getting the Goods

"Aaack!" I hear you scream. "I've never used iTunes or owned an iPod. I have no idea how to get music into iTunes, much less put it on my iPhone. What do I do?"

Relax. I'm not going to tell you how to put your music and movies on the iPhone until you know how to assemble a music and movie library.

I'll start with music. You have three ways to get tunes into iTunes:

- Recording (or *ripping,* in today's terminology) an audio CD
- Importing music that doesn't come directly from a CD (such as an audio track you downloaded or created on your computer)
- Purchasing music from an online emporium such as Apple's iTunes Store

The following sections tell you how to use the first two methods. I devote a large hunk of Chapter 7 to the iTunes Store in both its iTunes and iPhone incarnations.

note The procedures for adding movies and videos are similar, except that iTunes offers no option for ripping commercial DVDs. You can do that, but the procedure is more complicated than ripping an audio CD.

Rip a CD

Apple intended the process of converting audio-CD music to computer data to be painless, and it is. Here's how to go about it:

1. Launch iTunes.

2. Insert an audio CD into your computer's CD or DVD drive.

   By default, iTunes tries to identify the CD you've inserted. It logs on to the Web to download the CD's track information—a very handy feature for those who find typing such minutia to be tedious.

The CD appears in iTunes' Source list under the Devices heading, and
the track info appears in the Song list to the right (**Figure 6.1**).

Figure 6.1 *A selected CD and its tracks.*

Then iTunes displays a dialog box, asking whether you'd like to import
the tracks from the CD into your iTunes Library.

3. Click Yes, and iTunes imports the songs; click No, and it doesn't.

> **note** You can change this behavior in iTunes' Preferences window. In the
> General tab, you find a When You Insert a CD pop-up menu. Make a
> choice from that menu to direct iTunes to show the CD, begin playing it, ask to
> import it (the default), import it without asking, or import it and then eject it.

4. If you decided earlier not to import the audio but want to do so now,
simply select the CD in the Source list and click the Import CD button
in the bottom-right corner of the iTunes window (**Figure 6.2**).

Figure 6.2
*Import CD
button.*

> **note** To import only certain songs, uncheck the boxes next to the titles of
> songs you don't want to import; then click the Import CD button.

iTunes begins encoding the files via the method chosen in the Import
Settings window—which you access by opening iTunes' preferences,
clicking the General tab, and clicking the Import Settings button

(**Figure 6.3**). By default, iTunes imports songs in "high quality" AAC
format at 128 Kbps. (For more on encoding methods, see the sidebar
"Import Business: File Formats and Bit Rates.")

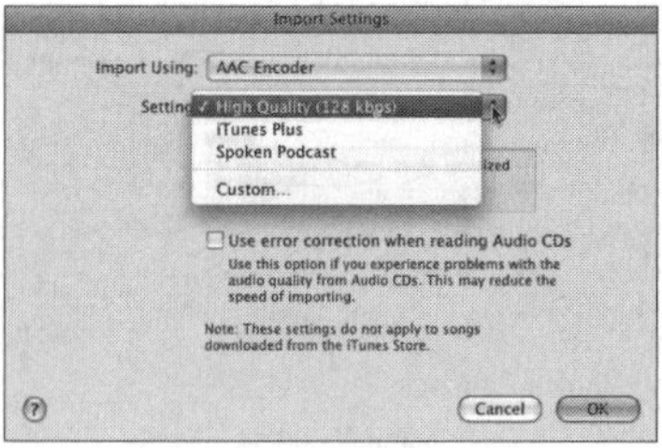

Figure 6.3
*iTunes' Import
Settings window.*

5. Click the Music entry in the Source list.

 You'll find the songs that you just imported somewhere in the list.

6. To listen to a song, click its name in the list and then click the Play
 icon or press the spacebar.

Move music into iTunes

Ripping CDs isn't the only way to put music files on your computer.
Suppose that you've downloaded some audio files from the Web and
want to put them in iTunes. You have three ways to do that:

- In iTunes, choose File > Add to Library.

 When you choose this command, the Add To Library dialog box
 appears. Navigate to the file, folder, or volume you want to add to
 iTunes, and click Open (**Figure 6.4**). iTunes determines which files it
 thinks it can play and adds them to the library.

- Drag files, folders, or entire volumes to the iTunes icon in Mac OS X's
 Dock, the iTunes icon in Windows' Start menu (if you've pinned iTunes
 to this menu), or the iTunes icon in either operating system (at which
 point iTunes launches and adds the dragged files to its library).

Figure 6.4
*Navigate to
tracks you want
to add to iTunes
via this dialog
box.*

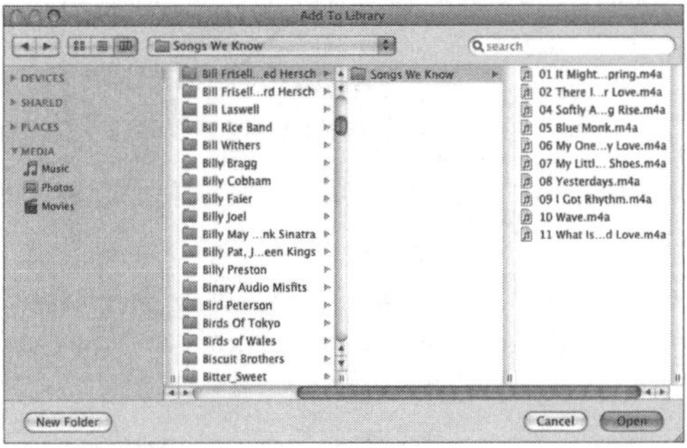

- Drag files, folders, or entire volumes into iTunes' main window or the Library entry in the Source list.

In the Mac versions of iTunes, by default you'll find songs in the iTunes Music folder within the iTunes folder inside the Music folder inside your Mac OS X user folder. The path to my iTunes music files, for example, would be chris/Music/iTunes/iTunes Music.

Windows users will find their iTunes Music folder by following this path: *yourusername*/My Music (XP) or Music (Vista)/iTunes/iTunes Music.

You can use the same methods to add compatible videos and movies to your iTunes Library. (For more on what makes those videos compatible, see "Working with supported video formats" later in the chapter.) Those videos will most likely appear in the Movies playlist in the Source list.

I say *most likely* because there are a few exceptions: Videos specifically designated as music videos appear in the Music playlist, videos designated as TV shows appear in the TV Shows playlist, and video podcasts are filed under Podcasts in iTunes' Source list. See the sidebar "Tag, You're It" later in this chapter for information on how to apply those video designations.

Import Business:
File Formats and Bit Rates

MP3, MPEG-4, AAC, AIFF, WAV . . . is the computer industry incapable of speaking plain English?

It may seem so, given the plethora of acronyms floating through modern-day Technotopia. But the lingo and the basics behind it aren't terribly difficult to understand.

MP3, AAC, AIFF, and WAV are audio file formats. The compression methods used to create MP3 and AAC files are termed *lossy* because their encoders remove information from the source sound file to create these smaller files. Fortunately, these encoders are designed to remove the information you're least likely to miss—audio frequencies that humans can't hear easily, for example.

AIFF and WAV files are *uncompressed,* which means that they contain all the data in the source audio file. When a Macintosh pulls audio from an audio CD, it does so in AIFF format, which is the native uncompressed audio format used by Apple's QuickTime technology. WAV is an AIFF variant used extensively with the Windows operating system.

iTunes supports one other compression format: Apple Lossless. This format is termed a *lossless* encoder because it shrinks files by removing redundant data without discarding any portion of the audio spectrum. This scheme yields sound files with all the audio quality of the source files at around half their size.

iTunes and the iPhone also support the H.264 and MPEG-4 video formats. These, too, are compressed formats that allow you to fit a great big movie on a tiny iPhone.

(continued on next page)

Import Business:
File Formats and Bit Rates (continued)

Now that you're familiar with these file formats, I'll touch on resolution as it applies to audio and video files.

You probably know that the more pixels per inch a digital photograph has, the crisper the image (and the larger the file). Resolution applies to audio as well. But audio defines resolution by the number of kilobits per second (Kbps) contained in an audio file. *With files encoded similarly,* the higher the kilobit rate, the better-sounding the file (and the larger the file).

I emphasize *with files encoded similarly* because the quality of the file depends a great deal on the encoder used to compress it. Many people claim that if you encode a file at 128 Kbps in both the MP3 and AAC formats, the AAC file will sound better.

The Import Using pop-up menu in the Import Settings window lets you choose to import files in AAC, AIFF, Apple Lossless, MP3, or WAV format. The Setting pop-up menu is where you choose the resolution of the AAC and MP3 files encoded by iTunes by choosing Custom from the menu. iTunes' default setting is High Quality (128 Kbps). To change this setting, choose iTunes Plus or Custom from the Setting pop-up menu. (Spoken Podcast is another option when you choose the AAC Encoder, but it produces quality that's good only for spoken-word recordings.) If you choose Custom, the AAC Encoder dialog box will appear. Choose a different setting—in a range from 16 Kbps to 320 Kbps—from the Stereo Bit Rate pop-up menu (**Figure 6.5** on the next page). Files encoded at a high bit rate sound better than those encoded at a low bit rate (such as 96 Kbps). But files encoded at higher bit rates also take up more space on your hard drive and iPhone.

(continued on next page)

Import Business:
File Formats and Bit Rates (continued)

Figure 6.5
*The Stereo Bit
Rate pop-up
menu.*

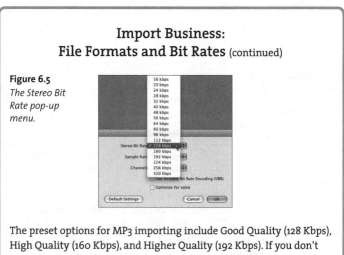

The preset options for MP3 importing include Good Quality (128 Kbps),
High Quality (160 Kbps), and Higher Quality (192 Kbps). If you don't
care to use one of these settings, choose Custom from this same
pop-up menu. In the MP3 Encoder dialog box that appears, you have
the option to choose a bit rate ranging from 16 Kbps to 320 Kbps.

Creating and Configuring a Playlist

Before you put any media files (music or video) on your iPhone, organize
them in iTunes. Doing so will make it far easier to find the media you
want, both on your computer and on your iPhone. The best way to organize that material is through the use of playlists.

A *playlist* is simply a set of tracks and/or videos that you believe should
be grouped in a list. The organizing principle is completely up to you. You
can organize songs by artist, by mood, by style, by song length . . . heck,

if you like, you can have iTunes automatically gather all your 1950s polka tunes with the letter *z* in their titles. Similarly, you can organize your videos by criteria including director, actor, and TV-series title. You can also mix videos and music tracks within playlists, combining, say, music videos and music tracks by the same artist. As far as playlists are concerned, you're the boss.

The following sections look at ways to create playlists.

Standard playlists

Standard playlists are those that you make by hand, selecting the media files you want to group. To create a standard playlist in iTunes, follow these steps:

1. Click the large plus (+) icon in the bottom-left corner of the iTunes window, or choose File > New Playlist (Command-N on the Mac, Ctrl+N in Windows).

2. In the highlighted field that appears next to that new playlist in the Source list, type a name for your new playlist (**Figure 6.6**).

Figure 6.6
Enter a name for your playlist.

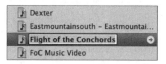

3. Click an appropriate entry in the Source list—Music, Movies, TV Shows, or Podcasts—and select the tracks or videos you want to place in the playlist you created.

4. Drag the selected tracks or videos to the new playlist's icon.

5. Arrange the order of the tracks or videos in your new playlist.

To do this, click the Number column in the main window, and drag tracks up and down in the list. When the iPhone is synchronized with iTunes, this order is how the songs will appear in the playlist on your iPhone.

If the songs in your playlist come from the same album, and you want the songs in the playlist to appear in the same order in which they do on the original album, click the Album heading.

Playlist from selection

You can also create a new playlist from selected items by following these steps:

1. Command-click (Mac) or Ctrl+click (Windows) songs or videos to select the files you'd like to appear in the new playlist.

2. Choose File > New Playlist from Selection (Command-Shift-N on a Mac; the Windows version of iTunes has no keyboard shortcut).

   A new playlist containing the selected items will appear below the Playlists heading in the iTunes Source list. If all selected tracks are from the same album, the list will bear the name of the artist and album. If the tracks are from different albums by the same artist, the playlist will be named after the artist. If you've mixed tracks from different artists or combined music with videos, the new playlist will display the name *untitled playlist*.

3. To name (or rename) the playlist, type in the highlighted field.

Tag, You're It

So how does iTunes know about tracks, artists, albums, and genres? Through something called ID3 tags. *ID3 tags* are just little bits of data included in a song file that tell programs like iTunes something about the file—not just the track's name and the album it came from, but also the composer, the album track number, the year it was recorded, and whether it is part of a compilation.

These ID3 tags are the key to creating great Smart Playlists. To view this information, select a track and choose File > Get Info. Click the Info tab in the resulting window, and you'll see fields for all kinds of things. You may find occasions when it's helpful to change the information in these fields. If you have two versions of the same song—perhaps one is a studio recording and another a live recording—you could change the title of the latter to include *(Live)*.

A really useful field to edit is the Comments field. Here, you can enter anything you like and then use that entry to sort your music. If a particular track would be great to fall asleep to, for example, enter **sleepy** in the Comments field. Do likewise with similar tracks, and when you're ready to hit the hay, create a Smart Playlist that includes *Comment is sleepy.* With this technique under your belt, you can create playlists that fit particular moods or situations, such as a playlist that gets you pumped up during a workout.

The Comments field can be useful for sorting movies as well. If you like a particular actor or director, enter his or her name in the Comments field—**Bogart** or **Huston**, for example.

Smart Playlists

Smart Playlists are slightly different beasts. They include tracks that meet certain conditions you've defined—Fountains of Wayne tracks encoded in

AAC format that are shorter than 4 minutes, for example. Here's how to work the magic of Smart Playlists:

1. In iTunes, choose File > New Smart Playlist (Command-Option-N on the Mac, Ctrl+Alt+N in Windows).

   You can also hold down the Option key on the Mac or the Shift key on a Windows PC and click the Gear icon that replaces the plus icon at the bottom of the iTunes window.

2. Choose your criteria.

   You'll spy a pop-up menu that allows you to select items by various criteria—including artist, composer, genre, podcast, bit rate, comment, date added, and last played—followed by a Contains field. To choose all songs by Elvis Presley and Elvis Costello, for example, you'd choose Artist from the pop-up menu and then enter **Elvis** in the Contains field.

   You can limit playlist selections by minutes, hours, megabytes, gigabytes, or number of songs. You may want the playlist to contain no more than 2 GB worth of songs and videos, for example.

   You'll also see a Live Updating option. When it's switched on, this option ensures that if you add any songs or videos to iTunes that meet the criteria you've set, those files will be added to the playlist. If you add a new Elvis Costello album to iTunes, for example, iTunes updates your Elvis Smart Playlist automatically.

3. Click OK.

   A new playlist that contains your smart selections appears in iTunes' Source list.

You don't have to settle for a single criterion. By clicking the plus icon next to a criterion field, you can add other conditions (**Figure 6.7**). You could create a playlist containing only songs you've never listened to by punk artists whose names contain the letter *J*, for example.

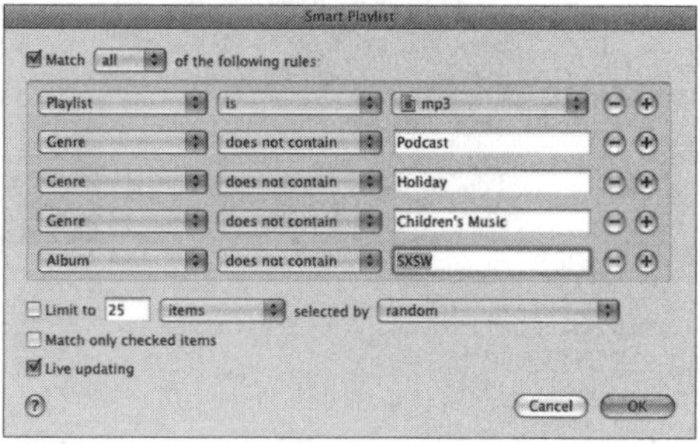

Figure 6.7
A Smart Playlist.

Using the iPod on the iPhone

Now that you've filled your iPhone with great content, you'd probably like to know how to find and play it. Follow along as I walk through the iPod area of the iPhone.

Cover Flow view

Tap the orange iPod icon near the bottom-right corner of your iPhone's Home screen, wait for the Playlists screen to appear (which it does by default when you first tap iPod), and immediately turn the iPhone on its side. You're witnessing the iPhone's Cover Flow view, which lets you browse your music collection and podcasts by their album or program artwork (**Figure 6.8** on the next page). I don't care if you never choose to browse your music this way; Cover Flow is the iPod feature you'll choose first to impress your friends. They can't help but *oooh* in awe when you flick your finger across the screen and the artwork flips by.

Figure 6.8
Cover Flow view.

Should you want to navigate your music in Cover Flow view, you can do
so easily:

1. Turn the iPhone to landscape orientation (it doesn't matter whether
   this turn places the Home button on the right or left side; the button
   works either way), and flick your finger across the display to move
   through your audio collection.

   Albums are sorted by the artist's first name, so *Al Green* appears near
   the beginning and *ZZ Top* appears close to the end.

2. When you find an album you want to listen to, tap its cover.

   The artwork flips around and reveals the track list of the album's
   contents (**Figure 6.9**).

Figure 6.9
*A track list in
Cover Flow view.*

As with other lists on the iPhone that may be longer than the screen, you're welcome to flick your finger up the display to move down through the list.

3. Tap the track you want to listen to.

Playback begins from that track and plays to the end of the list in the order presented in the track list.

To adjust volume in this view, use the Volume buttons on the side of the phone. To pause playback, tap the Play/Pause icon in the bottom-left corner of the screen or, if you're listening with the iPhone's headset, press the mic button once.

4. To move to another album, tap the album-art thumbnail in the top-right corner of the cover, swipe your finger to the right or left, or tap the *i* icon in the bottom-right corner of the screen.

Any of these actions will flip the track list back to the artwork.

note While you're listening to the contents of one album, you're free to view the contents of another. Just flick your finger across the screen to move through your collection. Go ahead and tap an album to see its contents. It won't play until you tap a track.

Music Now Playing screen

Turn your iPhone so that it's in portrait orientation, and Cover Flow disappears; it works only in landscape orientation. What you're left with when you flip the iPhone to portrait orientation is the Music Now Playing screen. This screen is what you'll use to perform several tasks, including navigating through an album, fast-forwarding, switching on shuffle or repeat play, and rating your tracks. This screen differs from the Now Playing screen that you see when playing a video, podcast, or audiobook. (I discuss how it differs later in the chapter.)

This Now Playing screen has two main views: standard play and track list.

Standard play

The view you see first is straightforward. From the bottom of the screen to the top, you see a volume slider; play controls that include Previous/ Rewind, Play/Pause, and Next/Fast Forward icons; album art; a Back icon; artist, track title, and album title information; and a Track List icon (**Figure 6.10**).

Figure 6.10
The music Now Playing screen.

Track List

Back

Previous/Rewind

Play/Pause
(displaying Pause)

Next/Fast Forward

Volume slider

The volume slider operates like its real-world equivalent. Just drag the silver ball on the slider to the right to increase volume and to the left to turn the volume down. (You can use the iPhone's mechanical volume buttons to adjust volume as well.)

The Previous/Rewind icon earns its double name because of its two jobs. Tap it once, and you're taken to the beginning of the currently playing track or chapter of the currently playing podcast or audiobook. Tap it twice, and you move to the previous track or chapter. Tap and hold, and the currently playing track rewinds.

The Play/Pause icon toggles between these two functions.

The Next/Fast Forward icon works like Previous/Rewind: Tap once to move to the next track in the track list or chapter in an audiobook or podcast; press and hold to fast-forward through the currently playing track.

I'll skip album art for a second and move to the Back icon in the top-left corner of the screen. Tap this icon, and you'll move to the currently selected track-view screen. If you've chosen to view your music by playlist, for example, you'll see your list of playlists. When you tap the Back icon and are taken to one of these screens, a Now Playing button appears in the top-right corner of the current screen. This icon appears whenever you're in the iPod area, making it easy to move to the Now Playing screen.

Track list

In the top-right corner of the Now Playing screen is the Track List icon. Tap this icon, and you get that album-cover flip effect again and a list of the current album's contents (**Figure 6.11**). (Naturally, if you have only a couple of tracks from that album on your iPhone, you'll see just those tracks.) Just as you can in Cover Flow view, tap an entry in the track list to listen to that track. Again, tracks play in order from where you tapped.

Figure 6.11
A track list in the music Now Playing screen.

The Track List screen also includes a means for rating tracks. Just above the track list, you'll see five gray dots. To assign a star rating from 1 to 5, simply tap one of the dots. Tap the fourth dot, for example, and the first four dots turn to stars. You can also wipe your finger across the dots to add or remove stars. These ratings are transferred to iTunes when you next sync your iPhone. Tap the artwork image to flip the track list and return to the Now Playing screen.

Additional controls

While you're in the Now Playing screen, tap the artwork in the middle of the screen, and additional controls drop down from above (**Figure 6.12**). Starting from the left, you'll find a Repeat icon. Tap this icon once, and the contents of the currently playing album, audiobook, or podcast will repeat from beginning to end. Tap the Repeat icon twice, and just the currently playing selection will repeat.

Figure 6.12
Additional controls in the music Now Playing screen.

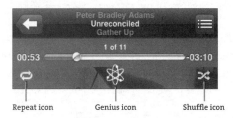

Repeat icon   Genius icon   Shuffle icon

A timeline with playhead comes next. To its left is the location of the playhead in minutes and seconds—1:40, for example. To its right is the track's remaining time. Drag the playhead with your finger to move to a different position in the currently playing track. You can do this while a track is playing and hear where you are as your drag (or *scrub*, as it's known in the iTunes business).

To the far right is the Shuffle icon. Tap this icon once so that it turns blue and the contents of the current album are shuffled; tap it again to turn shuffle off.

More-Refined Scrubbing

If you used the iPhone's scrubbing feature before the 3.0 software, you know how difficult it was to locate the exact spot you wanted in a track; scrubbing wasn't a precision operation. That's changed with the iPhone 3.0 software. Now you can scrub in smaller increments than ever before.

To do that, tap and hold the playhead. When you do (and if your thumb doesn't get in the way), you'll see the words *Hi-Speed Scrubbing*. If you drag your finger to the left or right, you move through the track in large increments. Ah, but drag your finger *down* the screen, and those words change to *Half Speed Scrubbing, Quarter Speed Scrubbing,* and *Fine Scrubbing.* Keep dragging until you find an increment you're happy with and then drag your finger to the left or right. The farther down the display your finger is, the smaller increments the playhead will jump in.

If you've added lyrics to a track (as you can in the Lyrics tab of the track's Info window in iTunes), those lyrics will appear on the iPhone's screen when you enter this view.

Below the timeline is the Genius icon. Genius is a very cool feature—so cool, in fact, that it deserves to be called out. I do that in the next section.

True Genius

iTunes 8 introduced a feature that's truly a work of genius and that's called . . . well, *Genius*. It works like this. You've got a bunch of music in your iTunes Library and on your iPod and/or iPhone. You play a track and think, "Man, I would *love* to hear more music like this!" Genius was designed for just those moments.

On your computer

When the Genius feature is turned on in iTunes (when you install it, iTunes asks whether you'd like to switch Genius on), you'll be asked to enter your Apple ID and password. iTunes then gathers information about the contents of your iTunes Library and sends it, anonymously, to Apple. The gremlins that live inside Apple's vast computer network analyze your library information and compare it with that of millions of other iTunes users who've volunteered to use Genius. Then Genius sends a file back to your computer to help iTunes recommend songs that it thinks will complement the song you select.

 If you didn't accept iTunes' offer to switch on Genius during installation, you can always turn it on another time by choosing Store > Turn on Genius.

In practice, you just select a song in your iTunes Library and click the Genius button at the bottom of the iTunes window. iTunes constructs a playlist of 24 additional songs from your iTunes Library that it thinks go really well with what you've selected. If you've got a fairly large collection of music, you'll be amazed at how accurate Genius is. Its mixes usually are very good. (If you have just a few songs, Genius obviously doesn't have much to work with, so don't expect miracles.)

 You must have an iTunes account to use Genius on your computer or your iPhone.

On the iPhone

You can also create Genius playlists on the iPhone in a couple of ways:

1. Launch the iPod app, and tap Playlists at the bottom of the screen.

2. Tap Genius.

   The Songs screen appears.

3. Tap a song that you want to use as the basis of the Genius playlist.

   The iPhone constructs a playlist of up to 25 tracks (including the one you selected) that it believes are related. The track you selected will start playing.

4. Tap the Back icon to view the playlist.

   Doing so takes you to the Genius screen, where you see the list of tracks (**Figure 6.13**). To create a new Genius playlist, tap New, and the process begins again. To have the iPhone construct a different playlist based on the same selection, tap Refresh. Finally, if you want to save your playlist, tap Save.

Figure 6.13
A Genius playlist.

When you tap Save, Genius creates a playlist that bears the name of the selected track. So, for example, if you based a Genius playlist on

"Here Comes the Sun," the playlist will be called *Here Comes the Sun.* Its name will be followed by a Genius icon in the list of playlists so that you know its origin.

Or . . .

1. While viewing the Now Playing screen, tap the Genius icon below the timeline.

   The iPhone's progress icon appears briefly, followed by a Genius screen that features, at the top, the song you selected as the basis for the playlist. The up-to-24 additional songs appear below it.

2. Create a new Genius playlist, try again, or save the playlist.

When you sync your iPhone to your Mac or PC, the Genius playlists you created on your phone appear in your computer's copy of iTunes, marked with the Genius icon.

Podcasts and audiobooks

Start a podcast or audiobook playing on your iPhone, and you'll notice that the controls at the bottom of the screen—Previous/Rewind, Play/Pause, and Next/Fast Forward—are exactly the same. The controls above are not.

Although you see the expected timeline and time readouts near the top of the screen, the icons you see just below them when playing an audio podcast, video podcast, or audiobook are different (**Figure 6.14**).

Figure 6.14
Additional elements in a podcast's Now Playing screen.

Email   30-Second Rewind   Speed

Depending on which kind of media you're playing, all these icons shake out this way.

Email

This icon appears when you're playing a video or audio podcast. Tap this icon, and in most cases an unaddressed email message opens, bearing the message *Check out this podcast on iTunes,* followed by a link to that podcast. When the recipient clicks or taps that link, iTunes launches and takes her to that podcast's page.

I say *in most cases* because sometimes the email link does nothing—presumably because the iPhone doesn't have the email address for the podcast and, therefore, can't embed it in an email message.

30-Second Rewind

Tap this icon while an audio podcast, video podcast, or audiobook plays; it jumps back 30 seconds and plays from that point.

Speed

With this icon, you can change the playback speed of an audio podcast or audiobook. By default, playback speed is set at 1x, which is normal speed. Tap the Speed icon once to change it to 2x, and the speed doubles (without changing pitch). Tap the icon again, and it changes to 1/2x, indicating that the audio plays at half speed (again, without changing pitch). One more tap takes you back to 1x.

Loop

The Loop icon appears in the far-left corner of the screen, below the timeline, when you listen to an audiobook. Tap the icon once, and the entire audiobook loops. Tap it twice, and the currently playing chapter loops.

Shuffle

The Shuffle icon appears in the far-right corner of the screen when you play a video podcast. When you activate it, when the currently playing video podcast concludes, the iPhone shuffles to another episode of that same podcast. If you have only one episode of that podcast, you return to that podcast's screen rather than shuffle to an episode of a different video podcast.

Track List

In the top-right corner of the screen is the Track List icon—which in this case isn't really a track list. Instead, when you tap it, you see an audio-book's chapters or the chapters of an "enhanced" audio podcast. (What makes these podcasts "enhanced" is their inclusion of graphics and chapter markers.) To navigate easily through an audiobook or enhanced podcast, just tap the chapter you want to move to.

iPod Voice Control

If you have an iPhone 3GS, you can control audio playback to an extent. Just press and hold the iPhone's Home button, and the iPhone's Voice Control screen appears. Wait for the double beep, and issue any the following commands to control iPod functions on the iPhone:

- **"Play" or "Play music":** The iPhone will play the last song that it believes you were listening to and then continues playing through the album or playlist that song is part of. If no last song was playing, the iPhone picks a song at random.

- **"Pause":** The iPhone pauses the currently playing track.

- **"Next song":** You get the next song in the album or playlist.

- **"Previous song":** You get the previous song in the album or playlist.

- **"Play *album*" (name of album):** If you say "Play album *Court and Spark*," and you have that album (or a portion of it) on your iPhone, that's just what the iPhone will do.

- **"Play *artist*" (name of artist):** Same idea here. Say "Play artist Jeff Lorber," and the iPhone will pick a track by the estimable jazz keyboard player and then continue playing his work in random order.

- **"Play *playlist*" (name of playlist):** Shout out "Play playlist 50 Fabulous '70s Hits by '80s Artists!" to hear that playlist played from beginning to end.

- **"Shuffle":** Use this command to shuffle the currently playing playlist.

- **"What's playing?" or "What song is this?" or "Who sings this song?" or "Who is this song by?":** All these questions provide an answer along the lines of "Now playing *name of song* by *name of artist*."

The Limits of Voice Control

Cool as Voice Control may be, it has limits. It won't respond, for example, to the following commands:

- **"Play 'Stairway to Heaven'"** (because it doesn't recognize individual track titles).

- **"Play the *Macworld Podcast*"** (because it can't be commanded to play podcasts unless those podcasts are part of a playlist).

- **"Shuffle off"** (because although you can turn shuffle on by voice, you can't turn it off the same way).

- **"Play *Gone with the Wind*"** (because Voice Control can't control videos).

- **"This song stinks!"** (which it may, but upon hearing this command, Voice Control won't assign a single-star rating to the currently playing track).

- **"Genius" or "Play more like this" or "Play more songs like this":** Any command like these directs the Genius feature to play songs in the vein of the currently playing song.

- **"Cancel":** Never mind.

iPod content views

The iPhone's iPod area provides several ways to organize your media. Look across the bottom of the screen when you're in the iPod area (anywhere but in the Now Playing screen), and you'll see five icons for doing just that: Playlists; Artists; Songs; Videos; and More, which leads you to even more options (**Figure 6.15**).

Figure 6.15
Category icons at the bottom of the iPod screens.

These icons are largely self-explanatory. When you tap Playlists, you'll see a list of all the playlists you've synced to your iPhone. Tap a playlist to move to a screen where all the tracks on the playlist appear in the order in which they were arranged in iTunes. If you tapped the Album heading when the playlist was displayed in iTunes, for example, the tracks appear in that order. Tap a track, and you're taken to the Now Playing screen, where the track begins playing.

Whenever you choose a list of tracks in one of these views, Shuffle is the obvious entry at the top of the list. (I say *obvious* because if you flick down, the Search field appears, thus becoming the first entry.) Tap Shuffle, and the contents of that collection of tracks play in random order.

Tap Artists, and you're presented with an alphabetical list of the artists represented on your iPhone. If your iPhone has tracks from more than one album by the selected artist, when you tap the artist's name, you'll be taken to that artist's screen, which displays the titles of the artist's represented albums (along with thumbnails of their cover art). To view tracks from a particular album, tap its name. To view all songs by the artist, tap All Songs in this screen.

The On-The-Go Playlist

Like the iPod, the iPhone lets you create an On-The-Go playlist, which you can create directly on the iPhone rather than syncing it from iTunes. You can add individual songs or clumps of songs to this special playlist. It works this way:

After tapping the Playlists icon, tap On-The-Go (the first entry in the Playlists screen), and a screen rises up from the bottom of the display, hinting that you've entered a special area of the iPhone. Tap one of the entries at the bottom of the screen: Playlists, Artists, Songs, Videos, or More (and then one of the selections available in the More screen). When you do this anywhere except the Videos screen, you'll see a screen that features the words *Add All Songs* followed by a list of all the songs that belong to that entry (all the songs on an album or by a particular artist, for example). If you tap Add All Songs, you do just that. To add individual songs, tap them. When you tap an item, its name turns gray to indicate that it's been added to the On-The-Go playlist. Continue tapping icons at the bottom of the screen or in the More screen until you've added all the tracks you care to; then tap Done at the top of the screen.

Again, entries in the Videos screen are the exception. When you tap Videos, you'll see your iPhone's list of movies, TV episodes, music videos, and video podcasts. And yes, you can mix audio tracks and video in an On-The-Go playlist.

(continued on next page)

The On-The-Go Playlist (continued)

When you return to the Playlists screen and tap On-The-Go, you'll see a list of all the tracks you've added through your previous endeavors. To edit the contents of this playlist, tap the Edit button at the top of the screen. In the Edit screen, you can tap the minus (–) icon next to a track to produce the Delete icon, which allows you to remove that track from the playlist (but not from your iPhone), and the List icon, which you drag to change the position of the selected track in the playlist (Figure 6.16).

Figure 6.16
An On-The-Go playlist.

While you're in the Edit screen, you can tap the plus icon to add more tracks to your On-The-Go playlist. Tap plus, and you're back to the view where you can add playlists, artists, songs, and so on.

To clear everything from the On-The-Go playlist, tap the On-The-Go playlist entry in the Playlists screen and then tap Clear in the resulting screen.

The Songs screen lists all the songs on your iPhone. Like any list that contains several dozen (or more) entries, this one displays a tiny alphabet along the right side of the screen. To navigate to a letter quickly, tap it (as best you can, as the letters are really small) or slide your finger along the alphabet listing to dash through the list.

> **note** If the first word of a list entry is *A* or *The*, the second word in the entry is used for sorting purposes. *The Beatles* is filed under *B*, for example, and *A Case of You* appears under *C*.

The Video icon is your gateway to playing movies, TV shows, music videos, and video podcasts on your iPhone. I talk about playing videos later in this chapter.

The iPhone's display has limited space, yet you have many more ways to organize your media—by albums, audiobooks, compilations, composers, and genres, for example. That's exactly what the More icon is for. Tap it, and you'll see just those items I list, as well as a Podcasts entry. Tap these entries, and most of them behave pretty much as you'd expect—with a couple of variations.

The Albums screen, for example, lists albums in alphabetical order and displays a thumbnail of the cover art next to the name of each album.

The Compilations entry lists only those albums that iTunes denotes as compilations. These items are usually greatest-hits collections, sound-tracks, or albums on which lots of artists appear—tribute albums or concert recordings, for example.

The Podcasts screen displays all the podcasts on your iPhone, along with their cover art. Tap a podcast title, and you're taken to a screen that lists all that podcast's episodes. Blue dots denote podcasts that you haven't listened to yet.

More Mucking

Unhappy that Apple chose to tuck the Albums entry in the More screen, yet left Artists easily accessible at all times? No worries. You can change what appears at the bottom of the iPod area. Simply tap More and then the Edit icon in the top-left corner of the screen. Doing so produces a Configure screen that swipes up from the bottom of the display. Here, you'll see all the iPod category entries listed. Find one you like, and drag it over a icon on the bottom of the screen that you want to replace. The new entry takes the place of the old one, and the old entry is listed in the More screen. When you're done, tap Done.

Videos

Like recent click-wheel iPods, the iPhone plays videos. Some people would say that *unlike* these iPods, the iPhone makes videos actually watchable—bright and plenty big enough for personal viewing. Here are the ins and outs of iPhone video.

Working with supported video formats

Regrettably, you can't take just any video you pull from the Web or rip from a DVD and plunk it on your iPhone. Like the iPod, the iPhone has standards the video must meet before it's allowed to touch your iPhone.

Specifically, the videos must be in either MPEG-4 or H.264 format and must fit within these limits:

MPEG-4
Resolution: 640 by 480 pixels
Data rate: Up to 2.5 Mbps
Frame rate: 30 fps
Audio: Up to 48 kHz

H.264
Resolution: 640 by 480 pixels
Data rate: Up to 1.5 Mbps
Frame rate: 30 fps
Audio: Up to 48 kHz

You can also encode H.264 movies at a resolution of 320 by 240 at 30 frames per second (fps). When you do so, the data rate is limited to 768 Kbps.

What? If you have experience encoding video, these numbers will make sense to you; if they have you confused instead, don't fret. You needn't bone up on this technology, because iTunes provides a way to make your videos compatible with the iPhone. Here's how: Drag an unprotected video (one that *isn't* a copy-protected TV show or video you haven't purchased from the iTunes Store) onto the Library entry in iTunes' Source list.

If the video is compatible with iTunes, it will be added to the library; if not, the dragged icon will zip back to its original location. If the video isn't compatible, you can convert it with a utility such as Roxio Crunch, available for Windows and Macintosh for $40 (www.roxio.com), or the free, Intel-only Video Monkey (http://videomonkey.org).

Some videos that play in iTunes may be encoded at resolutions or data rates too high for the iPhone to handle. Those files won't sync with your iPhone, but you can make them compatible with the iPhone. To do that, select a video (listed in the Movies or TV Shows entry within iTunes' Source list), and choose Advanced > Create iPod or iPhone Version (**Figure 6.17**). This command creates an iPod- and iPhone-compatible version of the video, which you can sync to your iPhone.

Figure 6.17
Convert a video for iPod and iPhone compatibility.

tip   Converting a video for iPhone compatibility doesn't replace the original, so it's not a bad idea to rename the converted version—*Casablanca (iPhone)*, for example—so that you can identify and sync the right one.

Choosing and playing videos

Playing videos within the iPod area is straightforward. Tap the Videos icon at the bottom of the screen, and you'll see your videos listed by categories: Rented Movies (if any have been copied to the iPhone), Movies, TV Shows, Music Videos, and Podcasts (**Figure 6.18**). Each video has a thumbnail image of its artwork next to it. Depending on the original source of the video, you may see title, artist, season, and episode information. The Rented Movies section, for example, tells you how many days you have left in the rental period to begin watching each movie (or how many hours you have left to finish watching a movie you've started). You'll definitely see the length of single videos—*1:56:26*, for example. If you have multiple episodes of a TV show, you'll see the name of the show as well as the number of episodes on the iPhone.

Figure 6.18
An expanded view of the Videos screen.

To play a video, tap its list entry. Videos play only in landscape orientation, regardless of which way you have the iPhone turned.

The video Now Playing screen is similar to the music Now Playing screen except that the play controls and timeline aren't visible unless you make them so. To display these controls, tap the video (**Figure 6.19**). The usual play controls—Previous/Rewind, Play/Pause, and Next/Fast Forward icons, and a volume slider—appear, as does a timeline near the top of the screen. The volume slider and timeline work just like they do in the music Now Playing screen. Drag the volume slider's volume indicator (represented by the silver dot) to increase or decrease volume, and move the timeline's playhead to a new location in the video.

Figure 6.19
The video Now Playing screen.

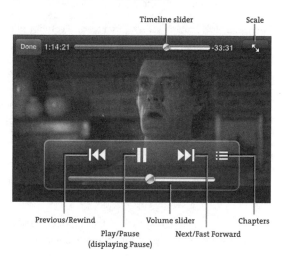

As I mention earlier in this chapter, you can advance to the next chapter in a video by tapping the Next/Fast Forward icon. (If the video has

> **tip** Cool as these controls look, you don't need to pull them up every time you want to adjust the volume. Just use the iPhone's mechanical volume buttons. Or, if you're using the headphones included with the iPhone, you can put its Volume Up and Volume Down buttons to good use.

no chapters, nothing happens when you tap this icon.) If a movie has chapters, you can also tap the Chapters icon that appears to the right of the Next/Fast Forward icon and choose the chapter you want from the Chapter Guide menu that appears. This icon won't appear when you view a movie without chapters.

If you tap and hold Next/Fast Forward, the video speeds up. To retreat a chapter, tap Previous/Rewind twice (tap once to return to the beginning of the currently playing chapter). The play controls list the chapter you're currently watching—*Chapter 13 of 32,* for example.

The video Now Playing screen has a control you haven't seen before: the Scale icon, in the top-right corner of the screen. Tapping this icon toggles the display between Fill Screen and Fit to Screen. (You can also toggle these views by double-tapping the display.)

Fill Screen is similar to DVDs you've seen that say the movie was altered to fit your TV. The iPhone's entire screen is taken up by video, but some of the content may be chopped off in the process.

Fit to Screen displays the entire video, similar to a letterbox movie you may have seen. In this view, you may see black bars at the top and bottom or on the sides.

When you finish watching a video, tap the screen and then tap the Done icon in the top-left corner of the screen. You'll return to the Videos screen.

tip By default, the iPhone remembers where you left off. When you next play this video, it will take up from the point where you stopped play-back. To change this behavior so that you always start from the beginning of a video, tap the iPod entry in the Settings screen and then tap the Start Playing entry. You can choose From Beginning or Where Left Off.

iPod settings

Like other applications and areas of the iPhone, the iPod function gets its own little entry in the iPhone's Settings screen. Tap Settings and then iPod, and **Figure 6.20** is what you see.

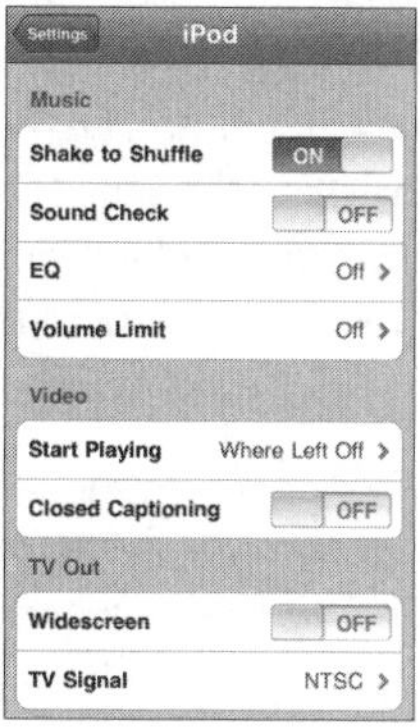

Figure 6.20
The iPod Settings screen.

Shake to Shuffle

If you'd like to engage the iPhone's shuffle feature without navigating through the iPod application, just switch on this option and give the iPhone a vigorous shake. This shake does more than shuffle; it also immediately causes the iPhone to stop playing the current song and move to another one. So even though you can't vent your frustration at a particularly awful song via Voice Control, you're free to violently shake the iPhone while shouting "*I . . . hate . . . this . . . song!*"

Sound Check

iTunes includes a Sound Check feature that you use to make the volumes of all your tracks similar. Without Sound Check, you may be listening to a Chopin prelude at a lovely, lilting volume and be scared out of your socks when the next track, AC/DC's "Highway to Hell," blasts through your brain. With Sound Check on, each track should be closer to the same relative volume.

The iPhone includes an On/Off Sound Check option, but it works only if you've first switched Sound Check on in iTunes; iTunes must evaluate your tracks and set an instruction in each track so that it works with Sound Check. To enable Sound Check in iTunes, open iTunes' Preferences window, click the Playback icon, and check the Sound Check box. Now when you sync your tracks with the iPhone and switch Sound Check on in the iPhone's iPod Settings screen, you'll experience all that is Sound Check.

EQ

EQ (or *equalization*) is the process of boosting or cutting certain frequencies in the audio spectrum—making the low frequencies louder and the high frequencies quieter, for example. If you've ever adjusted the bass and treble controls on your home or car stereo, you get the idea.

The iPhone comes with the same EQ settings as iTunes:

- Off
- Acoustic
- Bass Booster
- Bass Reducer
- Classical
- Dance
- Deep
- Electronic

- Flat
- Hip Hop
- Jazz
- Latin
- Loudness
- Lounge
- Piano
- Pop

- R & B
- Rock
- Small Speakers
- Spoken Word
- Treble Booster
- Treble Reducer
- Vocal Booster

Although you can listen to each EQ setting to get an idea of what it does, you may find it easier to open iTunes; choose Window > Equalizer; and then, in the resulting Equalizer window, choose the various EQ settings from the window's pop-up menu. The equalizer's ten band sliders will show you which frequencies have been boosted and which have been cut. Any slider that appears above the 0 dB line indicates a frequency that has been boosted. Conversely, sliders that appear below 0 dB indicate frequencies that have been cut.

Volume Limit

Though Apple takes pains to warn you in the iPhone's documentation that blasting music into your ears at full volume can lead to hearing loss, some people just can't get enough volume. If your child is one of those people, consider setting a volume limit for the iPhone's headphone port. To do so, tap Volume Limit in the iPod Settings screen, and in the resulting Volume Limit screen, use the volume slider to set an acceptable volume. (Have a track playing when you do this so that you can listen to the effect.) To keep your kid from changing your settings, tap Lock Volume Limit. You'll see a Set Code screen, where you'll enter and confirm a four-digit security code (**Figure 6.21**). When this code is set, the Lock Volume Limit icon changes to Unlock Volume Limit. Tap this button, and you'll be prompted for the security code.

Figure 6.21
Enter and confirm a four-digit code to limit the iPhone's volume.

Start Playing

I mention this setting in a little tip earlier in the chapter. Start Playing lets you choose whether videos that you return to later play from where they left off or from the beginning.

Closed Captioning

Some videos that you purchase from the iTunes Store include closed captions. You can choose to show those captions by flicking this switch to On.

Widescreen

This first option in the TV Out section of the iPod Settings screen lets you specify whether videos played on the iPhone connected to a television set with a compatible cable or Dock will play in widescreen or standard-screen view. Why wouldn't you choose widescreen if your iPhone contains a widescreen movie? If you have such a movie and are attempting to display it on a small-screen TV set, the picture could be pretty narrow and tiny. If you turn this option off, the entire TV screen will be filled with the picture (though both sides of the movie will be clipped off so that this screen-filling can take place).

TV Signal

The world has two major TV standards: NTSC (used in North and South America and much of Asia) and PAL (used in much of Europe and Australia). The iPhone can output video to a television set in either standard. You use this setting to choose NTSC or PAL.

7

The Stores

You know that constant use gives you the power to drain your iPhone's battery. In what some people might view as a turnabout-is-fair-play situation, your iPhone has the power to drain your wallet. Its means for doing so are two Apple-owned online emporiums accessible from your iPhone: the iTunes Store and the App Store. The former lets you browse, purchase, and download music, videos, podcasts, and iTunes U content over a Wi-Fi, 3G, or EDGE connection with nothing more than your iPhone and an iTunes account linked to your credit card. The App Store is where you find free and commercial add-on applications (made by Apple as well as third parties) that you can also download over EDGE, 3G, or Wi-Fi.

In this chapter, I examine the workings of each store, as well as a couple of fascinating features of the computer-based iTunes Store that you're sure to find helpful.

The iTunes Store

At one time, the iPhone's version of the iTunes Store was called the iTunes Wi-Fi Music Store, so named because you could shop only for music (to obtain videos or podcasts, you had to use iTunes on your computer), and you could do so only over a Wi-Fi connection (EDGE and 3G use were not permitted).

Today's iTunes Store is far more capable. Now you can download almost any content offered by the iTunes Store directly to the iPhone; the sole exception is HD movies (see the following note). What's more, you can download that content over any network supported by the iPhone: Wi-Fi, 3G, or EDGE. Note, however, that any content over 10 MB must be down-loaded over Wi-Fi.

note Although you can't *download* HD movies to your iPhone, you can *purchase* them on your iPhone. When you do, an iPhone-compatible standard-definition version of the movie is downloaded to your phone (if you're on a Wi-Fi network), and the HD version is made available to you within the copy of iTunes on your computer.

Although the store's face is far less crowded than that of the full-size iTunes Store, the selection is no different. You can choose among the same millions of tracks, podcasts, TV shows, music videos, movies, and iTunes U content in this pocket-size version of the store that you can in the store available via iTunes. The feature works this way.

Browsing the little store

Tap the iTunes icon on the iPhone's Home screen while you're connected to some variety of network, and the iTunes Store screen appears. Across the bottom of the screen, you see Music, Videos, Podcasts, Search, and More. Tap More, and you see Audiobooks, iTunes U, Downloads, and Redeem. Here's what to expect.

Music

Tap Music, and you're taken to the store's music section. Across the top of the screen are three buttons: New Releases, Top Tens, and Genres. These buttons work much as they do in the same-named areas of the full-grown iTunes Store's home page.

New Releases. Here, you see a list of the week's coolest additions—singles as well as albums. To preview or purchase one of these items, tap it to move to that item's screen. (I discuss the workings of this screen shortly.) In addition to the week's new releases, you're likely to see buttons for accessing free tracks and music videos and for viewing the hottest items currently available. At the very bottom of the screen is an Account button that displays your iTunes account email address—*example6@mac.com*, for example. Tap that, and you're offered the option to view your account details, sign out, or forget the whole thing by tapping Cancel.

Top Tens. This section features top songs and albums organized within particular genres. Tap Alternative, for example, and the next screen includes two large buttons: Top Songs and Top Albums (**Figure 7.1**). Tap one to see the top ten items of that kind. To see the complete list of Top Ten genres, tap the More Top Tens button near the bottom of the screen.

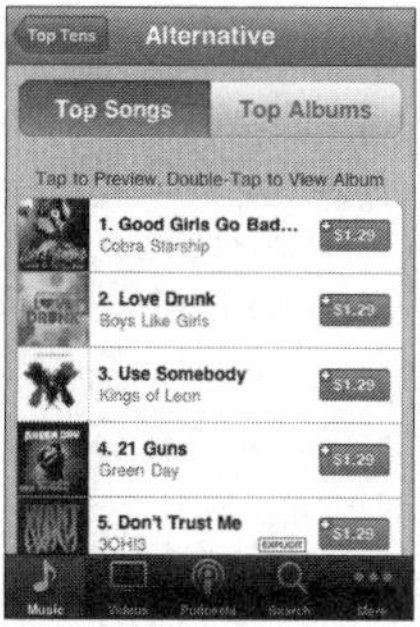

Figure 7.1
The iTunes Wi-Fi Store's Alternative Top Tens screen.

Genres. This section lists of popular genres (Pop, Alternative, Hip-Hop/ Rap, Rock, and Country, as I write this chapter). To view the complete list of genres, tap the More Genres button near the bottom of the screen. What you see when you tap a genre depends on the genre. When I tap Rock, for example, I see new releases. When I tap Soundtrack, titles are offered under an In Theaters heading. Tapping Classical, Singer/ Songwriter, or Jazz displays a list of albums. The top of each screen includes a couple of buttons that you can tap to go to albums that the Store believes worthy of your attention.

Videos

The Videos area of the Store is where you can rent or purchase movies, purchase TV shows or entire TV seasons, and purchase music videos. Tap the Videos button at the bottom of the screen, and you see a layout similar to the Music screen with three buttons across the top: Movies, TV Shows, and Music Videos.

Movies. The Movies screen displays a couple of featured movies at the top (hot new releases, as I write this chapter). Below is a New Releases area with 30 entries; below that, Top Tens and Genres entries. Each entry lists the genre (Comedy or Drama, for example), the title, its user rating (1 to 5 stars, including half-stars), and the number of ratings the movie has received—*128 Ratings*, for example.

Tap a movie and you see that movie's screen, where you can buy or rent it (if rental is an option—not all movies are for rent) as well as watch a preview of the movie. To do one of these things, tap the appropriate button. Below those buttons is a reviews link that displays a five-star scale. That scale reflects the average rating of those people who've chosen to submit a review on their iPhone, iPod touch, or within iTunes on their computer. These people may or may not have purchased or rented that movie from iTunes (and may not have seen it at all, so take some reviews with a grain of salt). Tap that button, and you'll see the average rating and the number of people who've rated the movie. Below are user reviews, complete with title, text, date, and rating.

If you'd like to write a review of your own, tap the Write a Review button at the top of the screen. You'll be prompted for your iTunes password. Enter it, and you go to the Submit Review screen, where you can enter a rating, title, and review. To submit the review, just tap Send.

TV Shows. This section works almost exactly the same way as the Movies area. The main difference is that the items in this window are entire series (*The Wire*, for example) rather than single episodes. Tap a show, and you're taken to the season screen, where you can purchase individual episodes and, sometimes, entire seasons. These screens carry no Preview button. Instead, just tap an episode title, and the movie-player window displays a preview. TV Shows screens also have a Reviews button.

Music Videos. Same idea here. You see a couple of featured items at the top of the screen, a list of music videos below, and Top Tens and Genres menus. Tap a video, and you see the Buy and Preview buttons along with the tapworthy reviews entry. In most cases, you also find a More by This Artist button. Tap it to see a screen listing other music videos by that artist.

What's the Cost?

At one time, you knew exactly what you'd pay when visiting the iTunes Store: 99 cents for a single music track and $9.99 for an album. With all the media now available in the Store and Apple's adoption of variable pricing for much of it, that situation has changed. Here's the rundown:

(continued on next page)

What's the Cost? (continued)

Music. Singles are priced at 69 cents, 99 cents, or $1.29. The most popular current tracks are $1.29. Albums cost $9.99 on average, but you can find bargains in the $7 and $8 range, as well as albums that cost $2 and $3 more. Albums that ship on two or more physical CDs cost quite a bit more, naturally.

Music Videos. Each video costs $1.99.

TV Shows. In most cases, standard-definition TV episodes are $1.99 each. (Such HBO shows as *The Sopranos* and *Rome* cost $2.99 per standard-definition episode.)

TV seasons are priced according to the number of episodes they contain and the format they're in: HD or standard definition. You sometimes get a break for buying a season, but more often than not, you pay the aggregate price of all the episodes.

Purchased movies. Apple characterizes movies as being library (meaning *older*) or new. Standard-definition library titles are $9.99; new standard-definition titles are $14.99. As I write this chapter, all HD titles are $20.

Rental movies. Standard-definition library titles are $2.99, and new library titles in standard definition are $3.99. Library HD rentals are $3.99, and new HD rentals are $4.99. After you download a rental movie, you have 30 days to watch it. After you start watching it, you have 24 hours to finish it; the movie is automatically removed from the iPhone after that period. During those 24 hours, you can watch the movie as many times as you like.

Audiobooks. The pricing of audiobooks is all over the map. You can find some for just over $10, whereas others can cost up to $50 (because, apparently, the real magic of the Harry Potter novels is that they can command these kinds of prices).

Podcasts. Free.

Podcasts

We've been through all this before, right? The Podcasts screen has its own three buttons: What's Hot, Top Tens, and Categories. If you read the section on the Music and Videos areas, you have a solid idea of how the Store works. These buttons show you exactly what they say they do: popular podcasts of the day, the top ten podcasts in specific categories (News & Politics, Sports & Recreation, Technology, Comedy, Music, and More Top Tens, at this writing), and featured podcasts in the same categories I just listed. Podcasts come in both audio and video form, and all of them are free.

Search

Search is very iPhone-like. Tap this button, and a Search field appears. Tap this field, and the iPhone's keyboard appears. Type a song title, album title, or artist name in the Search field; as you type, suggestions appear below. When the result you desire appears, tap it.

The resulting screen displays a variety of media—including some you may not expect. I searched for Led Zeppelin, and the results screen included "Stairway to Heaven" (of course), the *Mothership* album, two popular songs ("Kashmir" and "Black Dog"), two albums, three TV episodes (the TV show *NewsRadio* used "Led Zeppelin" in the title of three of its episodes), two movies, a couple of podcasts, two TV seasons (*NewsRadio* again), and two audiobooks. As you can see, a search can pull up a lot of unexpected results.

More

When you tap the More button at the bottom of the screen, you see four entries: Audiobooks, iTunes U, Downloads, and Redeem. I needn't walk you through the first two. Just understand that the Store, like

Audible.com, sells audiobooks that you can play on your iPhone, an iPod, or your computer. Like music tracks, audiobooks can be burned to CD. iTunes U is the educational area of the Store where you can download lectures, classes, and concerts offered, for the most part, by universities and colleges. iTunes U content is free.

Downloads. As you might expect, this area is where you can watch the progress of the content you're downloading. It works like this: When you tap a price, it turns into a Buy Now button. Tap that button, and the item swoops down onto the Downloads icon, at which point you're prompted for your iTunes password (the same password you use at the iTunes Store).

An icon on the Downloads button blinks, indicating the number of items that the iPhone is downloading. Tap this icon, and a screen shows you the progress of the download (**Figure 7.2**). After the item has downloaded, you can play it on the iPhone. When you next sync your iPhone, the tracks you've purchased will be transferred from the iPhone to your computer.

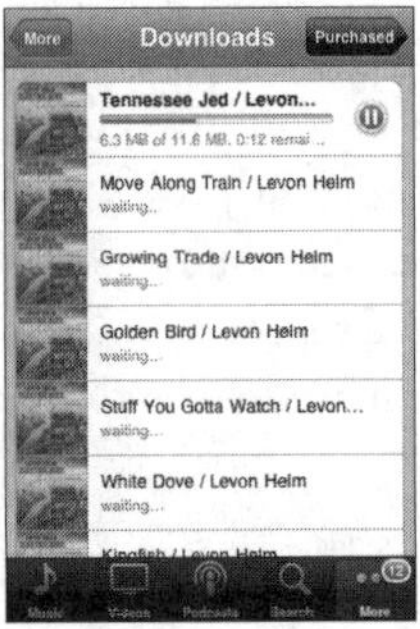

Figure 7.2
The Downloads screen details the progress of your media purchases.

When these tracks are downloaded for the first time, a new playlist appears below the Store heading in the computer-based version of iTunes' Source list. That playlist is called Purchased on *nameofiphone*, where *nameofiphone* is the name of your iPhone. After these tracks are in your iTunes Library, they behave like any others you own. You can burn music tracks to disc, and you can play any media on any of your authorized computers or any iPhones and iPods you own.

note If an album you purchase on the iPhone is bundled with extra content (such as a digital booklet and/or videos), when you sync the iPhone with your computer to download the music to it and connect to the iTunes Store, the extra content will download to iTunes automatically.

The Downloads screen also offers a shortcut to just those music tracks you've purchased on your iPhone. Tap the Purchased arrow in the top-right corner of the Downloads screen, and the iPod application opens and displays the Purchased on iPhone playlist, which contains those purchased tracks.

Redeem. Apple sells iTunes Gift Cards and Gift Certificates, which provide credit for purchases at the Store. If you have one of these things and would like to use it to pay for items at the Store, tap the Redeem entry in the More screen, tap in the Code field, type your credit code, and tap the Redeem button in the top-right corner of the screen. The amount of the gift card or certificate will be credited to your iTunes account. You can use that credit on an iPhone, an iPod touch, or a computer.

Browsing at Starbucks

Walk into a Starbucks outlet and tap the iTunes application, and your iPhone is likely to display a Starbucks button. When you tap that button, your iPhone will tell you the name of the track that's currently playing in that store, as well as recently played tracks. Using the Starbucks interface, you can purchase any of these tracks.

The App Store

The App Store is a service, hosted by Apple, that lets you download applications created by Apple and third-party developers to your iPhone, iPod touch, or (via the iTunes Store) computer.

> **note** As with large media files on the iTunes Store, when an application is larger than 10 MB, it must be downloaded over a Wi-Fi connection or from your computer. Try to do this over EDGE or 3G, and you'll be denied.

The App Store offers applications that you must pay for as well as scads of free ones, so even the most cheapskate iPhone owners among us will find lots to like at this store. In this section, I show you how it works.

Browsing the App Store

The App Store offers an interface similar to what you find at the iTunes Store. Tap the App Store icon on the iPhone's Home screen, and along the bottom of the resulting App Store screen, you'll see the five icons necessary to make your shopping experience as enjoyable as possible. The icons break down this way.

Featured

Tap the first icon in the row, and you move to the Featured screen. You'll find two buttons at the top: New and What's Hot. Tap New, and you'll see a list of notable applications—some free, some for sale—that have been added to the App Store recently (**Figure 7.3**). Each entry includes the application's name, its maker, its user review rating (one to five stars), the number of reviews it's received, and its price.

Figure 7.3
*The App Store's
Featured page.*

Tap What's Hot at the top of this screen, and you see a list of the most-
downloaded applications on the service. Each application bears the same
information: name, maker, rating, number of reviews, and price.

As I write this chapter, the top of each screen shows two applications or
categories (Our Favorite Games, for example) in a banner. In Apple's estimation, these applications are too cool or popular to miss.

Categories

If you'd like to browse the App Store for particular kinds of applications—
games, finance, or productivity, for example—tap the Categories icon
that appears in the second position at the bottom of the screen. As the
name hints, the Categories screen is where you'll find applications listed
in categories, including (at this writing) Games, Entertainment, Utilities,
Social Networking, Music, Productivity, Lifestyle, Reference, Travel, Sports,
Navigation, Healthcare & Fitness, News, Photography, Finance, Business,
Education, Weather, Books, and Medical. Tap a category, and the resulting
category screen includes three buttons that make it easier to find the
apps you want: Top Paid, Top Free, and Release Date.

Top 25

Featuring a Top Paid and a Top Free button at the top of the screen, Top 25 is what it says—a list of the 25 most-downloaded applications at the App Store (**Figure 7.4**). Scroll to the bottom of either the paid or free list, and you'll see a Show Top 50 entry. Tap it, and another 25 entries appear, slightly less "top" than the first 25.

Figure 7.4
The Top 25 area of the App Store.

Search

Search is for those times when you think, "Hmm . . . Priscilla said something about a cool new iPhone app, but the only part of its name I remember is *monkey*." Just tap Search, tap in the Search field, and type **monkey** on the iPhone's keyboard. You'll be sure to find the application you're after in the list that appears. Tap the application's name, and you'll see its listing along with the usual information—name, company, yada, as well as yada.

> **tip** Search produces results not only for product names, but company names too. If you know the company but not the name of the application, no worries—just search for the company name and tap it. Any applications offered by that company appear in the list of results.

Updates

Just like the applications you have on your computer, iPhone applications are updated by their developers to fix problems and offer new features.

When an application you've downloaded has been updated—and Apple has made that update available—the Update icon at the bottom of the App Store screen bears a red circle with a number inside it, indicating how many updates are available. The App Store icon on the Home screen also adopts this icon.

When updates are available, you can choose to update single applications or click the Update All button in the top-right corner of the screen. Your iPhone moves to the Home screen, and the updated versions of the applications begin to download. The progress of the download is shown in the form of a blue progress bar at the bottom of the application's icon.

Managing applications

Now that you've found the applications you're after, you'll want to learn more about them and then start downloading the ones you want.

Navigating the Info screen

An application's Info screen is both the gateway to downloading the thing and a source for information about it (**Figure 7.5**). Here, you'll find the name of the application, the name of

Figure 7.5
An application's Info screen.

the developer, a star rating based on user reviews, the number of reviews, a price button you tap to purchase the app, a link to those reviews, a description and screen shots of the application, developer contact information, post date, version, size, and rating.

A Tell a Friend button also appears in this screen. Tap it, and a new unaddressed email message opens, containing the name of the application in the Subject field and the words *Check out this application:* followed by a link to the application in the message body. The recipient of this message need only click the link; as long as he has a current copy of iTunes installed on his computer, iTunes will launch and take him to the iTunes Store page that's devoted to this application. (I discuss the iTunes Store's relationship with iPhone and iPod touch applications shortly.)

Reviews work similarly to the reviews for music in the iTunes app. The difference is that you're not allowed to review an app unless you've actually downloaded it. This helps prevent useless "This costs too much!" or "I hate cheese!" reviews that can drag down an app's rating.

Finally, there's the Report a Problem button. Tap it, and a Report a Problem screen appears, offering three choices: The Application Has a Bug, This Application Is Offensive, and My Concern Is Not Listed Here. These choices are followed by a Comments field where you can express yourself more thoroughly. Tap Report to send your report to Apple.

Downloading applications

To download applications, you must have an iTunes account. To obtain one, launch iTunes on your computer and choose Store > Create Account. You'll be walked through the process of creating an iTunes Store account.

 note You need both a valid email address and a credit card to create an account.

Now that you have an iTunes account, return to your iPhone, and tap the entry for the application you want to download. Tap its price (yes, even if it's marked Free) and then click Install. You'll be prompted for, at the very least, your iTunes password. (I say *at least* because if you were signed in to the iTunes Store the last time you synced your iPhone, you won't be prompted for your iTunes account when you attempt to download something from the App Store. If you're using the App Store for the first time and aren't signed in to your iTunes account within iTunes, you'll be prompted for both your account address and password.)

Enter your password with the iPhone's keyboard, and tap OK. The iPhone moves to the Home screen, shows a dimmed icon for the application you're downloading, and displays Loading and then Installing progress bars at the bottom of the screen. When the application is fully loaded, the Installing progress bar disappears, and the icon takes on its full color and brightness. To launch the application, do as you do with any applica-tion on the iPhone: Tap its icon.

The next time you sync your iPhone with iTunes, any applications you've added to it—or that have been updated on the iPhone—will be copied to iTunes' Applications area. And speaking of iTunes and applications . . .

Working with applications in iTunes

One of the slickest features of the iPhone software is the one that lets you obtain and manage applications over the phone. But the iPhone isn't the only device that bears these talents. Your computer, in league with iTunes, can do so as well, and in this way.

Downloading applications in iTunes

Why should your iPhone have all the fun? You can download applications via iTunes just by doing this:

1. Click iTunes Store in iTunes' Source list.

2. In the iTunes Store area in the top-left section of the window, click App Store.

   The resulting page looks like many other iTunes Store pages. You'll find headings for new applications, hot applications, staff favorites, top paid applications, top free applications, and a list of categories you can click to see applications organized by kind.

3. Click an application you'd like to learn more about.

   An information page appears that includes much of what you find in the iPhone's information pages: application name, developer name, price, description, ratings and reviews, and screen shots.

4. Click the Buy App button to purchase the application.

   You'll be prompted for your password. After the application has downloaded, you'll find it by clicking the Applications entry in iTunes' Source list (**Figure 7.6**).

Figure 7.6
iPhone and iPod touch applications shown in iTunes.

5. Plug your iPhone into your computer.

You can choose which applications you want to sync to your iPhone by selecting the iPhone in iTunes' Source list, clicking the Applications tab in the window that appears, and choosing either All Applications or Selected Applications.

6. Click Apply and then Sync.

Updating applications

You can also update your iPhone applications within iTunes. Select Applications in iTunes' Source list, and any applications you've down-loaded from within iTunes—or downloaded on your iPhone and then synced back to iTunes—appear as a series of icons (refer to Figure 7.6). Click one of these icons, choose File > Get Info, and click the Summary tab in the resulting window, and you'll see how large the application is, its version, who purchased it (and with which account), and the purchase date.

In the bottom-right section of the Applications window are two links: Check for Updates and Get More Applications. Click the first link, and this entry changes to *X* Updates Available (where *X* is the number of available updates). Click the Updates Available link, and you're taken to iTunes' My App Updates page, where updates for the applications you own appear. You can download individual updates by clicking the Get Update button next to the application or simply click the Download All Free Updates button in the top-right corner of the window to download all updates.

After you enter your iTunes password, the updates start downloading. You can check the progress of the downloads by clicking the Downloads entry in the Store area of iTunes' Source list. When the updates are down-loaded, just sync your iPhone to iTunes, and the updated versions of the applications will be copied to your iPhone.

Creating Custom Ringtones

iTunes on your computer is also the means for adding custom ringtones to your iPhone. Compelling as those 25 ringtones may be, some people prefer more personal sounds, which they can get by creating custom ringtones. You create a custom ringtone this way:

1. Launch iTunes, select your Music library in the Source list, and choose View > View Options.

2. In the View Options window, enable the Ringtone option, and click OK.

   Any tracks purchased from the iTunes Store that are available as ringtones display a gray bell icon in the Ringtone column.

3. Click the bell icon next to the track you'd like to create a ringtone from.

   A sound-editing pane appears at the bottom of the iTunes window (**Figure 7.7**). The entire song is represented in this pane as a sound wave, with the first 15 seconds selected by default.

Figure 7.7
The ringtone editing pane.

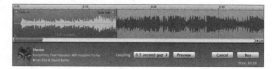

4. Click the Preview button to hear how the first 15 seconds of the song sound.

   By default, ringtones fade in and fade out. You can change this behavior by unchecking the Fade In and Fade Out boxes.

5. Edit the selection.

   To select a different part of the song, drag the blue selected area to another point in the track; then click the Preview button to hear where you are in the song.

To change the length of the selection, drag the bottom-right corner of the selected area. Drag to the right, and the selection gets longer, to a maximum 30 seconds. Drag to the left, and the selection shortens.

When a ringtone plays on the iPhone, it loops continuously until you answer the phone. To determine the period of silence between repeats, click the Looping pop-up menu and choose a gap time—0.5 seconds to 5 seconds.

6. Click Buy to purchase your edited ringtone.

   Ringtones cost 99 cents each. When you click Buy and enter your password to confirm the purchase, the ringtone will be downloaded to your computer and placed in the Ringtones area of iTunes' Source list.

7. Sync the ringtone to your iPhone.

   Select your iPhone in iTunes' Source list, click the Ringtones tab, and choose to sync all your ringtones or just selected ringtones.

8. Choose your ringtone on the iPhone.

   On the iPhone, tap Settings > Sounds > Ringtone. Your custom ringtones appear at the top of the screen in the Custom area. Tap the name of the ringtone to select it, and it will play the next time your phone rings.

Photo, Camera, and YouTube

Your iPhone is an audio wonder, handling both calls and music, but it's also a visual delight. And no, I'm not referring to its lustrous design. I'm talking pictures (both those you take and those you view), the moving pictures you can record with an iPhone 3GS, and those streamed from the free Web-based video sharing service YouTube.

The grumps among us might grouse that these features are some of the iPhone's least necessary—after all, few of us absolutely *require* a phone that can take a quick picture or movie, display gorgeous slideshows, or stream videos of piano-playing cats—but they're certainly among its most enjoyable.

In this chapter, I turn to the visual: the iPhone's photo, camera, and YouTube capabilities.

You Ought to Be in Pictures

Tapping Photos on the iPhone's Home screen is the digital equivalent of flipping open your wallet to reveal a seemingly endless stream of pictures of the kids, the dog, and that recent trip to Pago Pago. Now, thanks to the iPhone 3GS and its enhanced 3-megapixel camera, that wallet holds not just still pictures, but movies too.

The iPhone's Photos application, however, is no mere repository for pictures and movies you've shot with your phone. Flick a finger, and you're flying from photo to photo, movie to movie, or a combination of the two. If you have a more formal presentation in mind—a showing of your child's first birthday party for Grandma and Grandpa, for example— you can create something far grander in the form of a slideshow. To learn about these and other visual wonders, just follow along.

The face of Photos

When you tap Photos, you see the Photo Albums screen, which acts as the gateway to the images and iPhone-created videos stored on your camera (**Figure 8.1**). In this screen, you'll find at least one entry, and more after you sync photos to your phone.

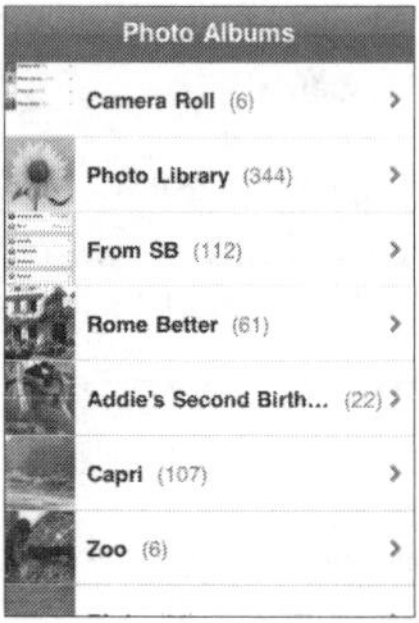

Figure 8.1
*The Photo
Albums screen.*

The first entry is Camera Roll. Tap it to see the images and movies you've captured with the iPhone's camera. To the left of this entry in the Photo Albums screen, you'll see a thumbnail image of the last picture or video taken by the camera. To the right of the entry, in parentheses, you'll see the combined number of images and movies this album contains— *Camera Roll (17)*, for example. The > character on the far-right edge of the screen indicates that when you tap this entry, you'll be taken to another screen. That other screen, called Camera Roll, contains thumbnail images of all the photos and videos in this album. Videos bear a small camera icon in the bottom-left corner of their thumbnail and the duration in the bottom-right corner—*1:07*, for example. At the bottom of the screen is an accounting of the number of photos and videos in the album—*187 Photos, 10 Videos*, for example.

The next entry, Photo Library, contains all the photos on your iPhone save for those in the Camera Roll library. It too bears a thumbnail (not one of your images, but a sunflower), and it displays the total number of images in the library—*Photo Library (584)*, for example. Tap this entry, and in the resulting Photo Library screen, you'll see thumbnail images of all the photos on your iPhone (again, excluding the Camera Roll photos). This album contains no videos.

As you learn in Chapter 2, you can sync photo albums created by such programs as iPhoto, Aperture, Photoshop Elements, and Photoshop Albums. When you do, these albums appear in the Photo Albums screen as separate entries, each featuring a thumbnail of the first image in the album as well as the number of images in the album—*Father's Day (48)* or *Family Holiday (92)*, for example. When you select your Pictures folder (Mac and Windows Vista), My Pictures (Windows XP), or a folder of your choosing within iTunes' Photos tab, any folders contained within those folders are presented as separate albums. So, for example, if your Pictures folder holds three folders that contain pictures—say, Betty's Birthday,

Dog Polisher, and Cheeses Loved and Lost—each of those items appears as a separate album in the Photo Albums screen. Again, each album lists the number of images it contains in parentheses.

If you're a Mac user and store your pictures in iPhoto '09, you're probably aware that iPhoto automatically groups pictures taken during the same general period—a single day, for example. In the Photos tab within iTunes, you can ask that iPhoto's 1, 3, 5, 10, or 20 most recent events be synced to your iPhone (**Figure 8.2**).

Figure 8.2
*Sync iPhoto's
most recent
events to your
iPhone.*

Picture and movie viewing

As I mention earlier in this chapter, when you're in an album's screen, you see all the pictures (and movies, in the case of the Camera Roll) in that album arrayed four across as thumbnail images (**Figure 8.3**). You can see 20 complete thumbnails onscreen. If your album contains more than 20 images, just flick your finger up across the display to scroll more images into view. To see a picture or movie full-screen, just tap it.

Figure 8.3
*A photo album's
thumbnail
images.*

Setting Album-screen options

When you tap the name of an album, that album appears. At the bottom of the album screen are two buttons: Options (represented by an arrow rising out of a picture frame) and Play.

The Play button. Tapping this button, regardless of the kind of album you've selected, starts a slideshow of the pictures in that library. You can view slideshows in either horizontal or vertical orientation.

The timing and transitions of your slideshow are determined by options set for the Photos entry in the iPhone's Settings screen. You have the option to play each slide for 2, 3, 5, 10, or 20 seconds, and you can choose among Cube, Dissolve, Ripple, Wipe Across, and Wipe Down transitions.

When you tap the screen during a slideshow, transparent gray bars appear briefly at the top and bottom of the screen. The top one displays a left-pointing arrow bearing the name of the currently selected photo album. As with most iPhone screens, you tap this arrow to move up one screen in the iPhone's hierarchy. You'll also see an entry such as *8 of 48*, which tells you which one of the total number of pictures you're look-ing at. The bottom bar includes an Options button along with Previous and Next buttons. (I describe these buttons in "Working with the picture screen" later in this chapter.)

note Movies don't play as part of a Camera Roll slideshow. In fact, they stop a slideshow dead in its tracks. For this reason, if you want to view these photos as a part of a slideshow, and your Camera Roll contains movies, you should sync them from the iPhone to your computer, create albums of the ones you want to keep on the phone, and then sync them back as part of an album.

The Options button. This button produces different options depending on whether you're looking at the Camera Roll album, the iPhone's Photo Album library, or another library that you've synced to the phone.

Tap the Camera Roll album and then tap the Options button, and the bottom of the screen shows three buttons: Share, Copy, and Delete. To put these buttons to good use, tap one or more pictures in the album. As you do, each button adopts a set of parentheses—*Share (5), Copy (5), Delete (5)*, for example. Share and Copy appear regardless of the album you select. Delete appears only when you select the Camera Roll library.

When you tap Share, an options screen rolls up, containing some or all of these options: Email, Send to MobileMe, Send to YouTube, and Cancel. The Send to MobileMe option appears only if you have a MobileMe account configured on the phone, and you see Send to YouTube only if you've selected a movie. If you select both a movie and image, the Share button won't work.

When you choose a movie and tap Send to YouTube, the phone compresses the movie and then prompts you for your YouTube user name and password. Enter them correctly, and you see a Publish Video screen, where you provide a title, description, tags, and category for your movie. When you're ready to rock, tap the Publish button.

You use the Copy command to copy images and movies to the iPhone's clipboard. Currently, you don't have a lot of places to paste them. Mail will take them, but if you try to paste them into something like a Notes document, for example, only their names will be pasted. The target application must support image pasting.

Selecting images and movies and then tapping Delete removes those items from your iPhone, of course. Again, this option appears only when you're looking at the Camera Roll library.

Orienteering

For those of you keeping score at home, Photos is one of those areas of the iPhone that has always worked in both portrait and landscape orientation. When viewing pictures and movies, it's best to view them in the orientation in which they were originally shot. So, for example, if you shoot a picture in the iPhone's "normal" orientation (with the top of the phone pointing up), that's also the best way to look at the picture (**Figure 8.4**). If you turn the phone sideways to view that image, you get black bars on either side of the image.

Figure 8.4
*Widescreen
picture view.*

Videos shot in portrait orientation don't produce black bars when viewed in landscape orientation. Instead, the video enlarges to fill the screen, thus cutting off the top and bottom of the frame. Movies shot in landscape orientation fare a little better when you display them in portrait view. Rather than losing part of the image, you gain black bars above and below, just as with still images.

Working with the picture screen

In addition to letting you rotate your pictures by flipping your phone around, the screen in which you view individual images offers some cool features. When viewing a picture in the Camera Roll, an album, or the Photo Albums screen, you'll briefly see a transparent gray control bar at the bottom of the screen, displaying three symbols: Options, Previous, and Next (**Figure 8.5**). This control bar conveniently disappears after a couple of seconds so you can see the complete picture without obstruction. To bring it back, just tap the display.

Figure 8.5
The picture screen.

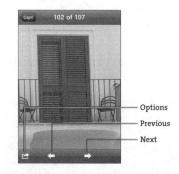

— Options
— Previous
— Next

When you view a picture in the Camera Roll album, you see one additional icon: Trash. If you've taken a picture that you now regret, just tap the Trash icon, and in the sheet that appears, tap the red Delete Photo icon.

The left- and right-arrow icons that represent the Previous and Next commands do just what they suggest. Tap the left-pointing arrow, and you move to the previous image in the album (or image or movie, if you're browsing in the Camera Roll album). Tap the right arrow, and you're on to the next image. If you tap and hold on these icons, you'll zip through your pictures at increasing speed.

Viewing pictures

Tapping those Previous and Next icons is the less impressive way to move from picture to picture. For a far more stirring demonstration of the iPhone's slickness, swipe your finger to the left to advance to the next picture or to the right to retreat one picture. You're guaranteed to get an "Oooh!" from the audience on this one.

While you've got your audience in the "Oooh"ing mood, try this: Double-tap an interesting spot in a picture. Like magic, the screen zooms and places that spot as close to the center of the screen as it can. Drag your finger on the picture to reposition it. If you'd like greater control of how large the image is, use the spread gesture (which I discuss in Chapter 1) to make it grow incrementally. Regrettably, the iPhone won't remember how you've repositioned and resized the picture. Also regrettably, you can't swipe to the next picture until you've restored the picture to its original size. You can do this by double-tapping the display again or by pinching the image down to its native size.

Swiping is good at any time, even during a slideshow. If, while viewing a slideshow, you'd like to take control, just tap the display to stop the slideshow, or swipe your finger to the left to advance or right to go back. When you manually navigate to the photo that precedes or follows the one on view, the slideshow is canceled. To restart it, you must return to the album screen and press the Play button, which starts the show from the first image.

These settings are the defaults. If you've configured Photo Settings so that the Repeat and Shuffle options are on, the slideshow will behave a bit differently. To begin with, the show will reach the end and then start over, continuing to play until you tell it to stop by tapping the display. And if Shuffle is on, the photos in the selected album will play in random order.

Using the Options button

No, I haven't forgotten about the version of this button that appears on each picture's screen. The features it provides are enough to warrant their own little section.

When you tap Options, a pane scrolls up from the bottom of the iPhone screen, displaying the entries Email Photo, Assign to Contact, Use As

Wallpaper, and Cancel (**Figure 8.6**). Mac users who subscribe to Apple's MobileMe Web service may see a fifth entry, labeled Send to MobileMe.

Figure 8.6
Options available in the picture screen.

These commands work this way:

- **Email Photo.** Tap this command, and the picture on view is placed in an empty email message. You're welcome to tap just above the picture in the message body and add text to the message. Fill in the To and Subject fields, and tap Send. Your message-with-picture-attachment is whisked away. After you send the message (or tap Cancel to forget the whole thing), you return to the picture screen rather than to the Mail application.

- **Assign to Contact.** As the name suggests, this command allows you to associate the picture on view with a contact of your choosing. Tap the command, and up scrolls your contact list. Use the Search field or the usual finger-drag or tap-a-letter method to navigate to the contact you want; then tap the contact, and a Move and Scale screen appears. Here, you can expand and drag the image into position. When you like what you've done, tap Set Photo. When you speak to that contact on your iPhone, the picture you've selected will appear.

- **Use As Wallpaper.** Tap this command, and the iPhone will offer to use the picture on display as your iPhone's wallpaper—the image that appears when your phone is locked or when you're speaking with a contact who doesn't have an associated picture. Again, you work in a Move and Scale screen. Tap the Set Wallpaper button when you're happy with your work.

- **Send to MobileMe.** If you're a Mac user who has a MobileMe account (Apple's $100-per-year subscription package of online services) and a copy of iLife '08 or iLife '09, you can use this icon to upload pictures directly from your iPhone to a MobileMe Gallery—a special MobileMe Web site that hosts pictures and movies. Note that this icon appears only if you've added a MobileMe account to Mail. If you don't have a MobileMe account or haven't added your MobileMe account to your iPhone, you won't see this button.

  For this feature to work, you must have published a MobileMe Gallery in iPhoto '08 or '09 and, when doing so, enabled the Adding of Photos Via Email option (**Figure 8.7**). When you've done all that and tapped Send to MobileMe, a MobileMe screen appears on the iPhone, listing all your published MobileMe Galleries. Select the one you want, and tap the Publish button. The image will be uploaded to the MobileMe

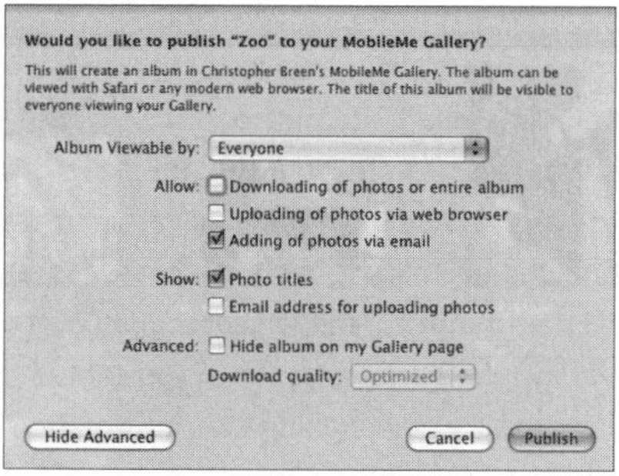

Figure 8.7
Configuring a MobileMe Gallery.

Would you like to publish "Zoo" to your MobileMe Gallery?

This will create an album in Christopher Breen's MobileMe Gallery. The album can be viewed with Safari or any modern web browser. The title of this album will be visible to everyone viewing your Gallery.

Album Viewable by: Everyone

Allow: ☐ Downloading of photos or entire album
☐ Uploading of photos via web browser
☑ Adding of photos via email

Show: ☑ Photo titles
☐ Email address for uploading photos

Advanced: ☐ Hide album on my Gallery page
Download quality: Optimized

(Hide Advanced)   (Cancel)   (Publish)

Gallery you chose. When the image has been published successfully, a window appears to tell you so and offer you the options to view it on MobileMe or tell a friend. Tapping Tell a Friend places a link to the image in an empty email message with the name of your photo in the Subject line. You know the drill: Fill in the recipient; type a cheery something in the message body, if you like; and send the message.

Snapping Pictures

The iPhone 3GS contains a 3-megapixel camera capable of capturing JPEG still images at a resolution of 1536 x 2048 pixels. The iPhone 3G has a 2-megapixel camera that shoots JPEG at 1600 x 1200. The lens is in the top-left corner of the back of the iPhone (and yes, this position does make it easy to plant your pinkie in front of it accidentally). It takes perfectly decent pictures in well-lit environments. In low-light settings— an indoor concert, outside at night, or in a poorly lit room—the results are often less than stellar, particularly with an iPhone 3G. The iPhone has no flash, and you can't zoom the camera, so it's the ultimate point-and-shoot device.

Taking a photo

To use the camera, simply tap the Camera icon on the iPhone's Home screen. In a short time, you'll see the image of a closed shutter and then a view of whatever is in front of the camera lens. If you're running iPhone 2.0 software or later, the iPhone will ask permission to use location information. It does this so that it can embed location information in the picture data—a process called *geotagging*. That way, should you later want to know where you were when you captured that breathtaking shot of the bagel, you can look up that information in a photo-editing program. You don't have to allow the camera to use location information, however. If you tell the application no, it will still work; you just won't have location information attached to the pictures you take.

note This geotagging business works only if you have Location Services switched on. I mention this option in Chapter 2, but you needn't flip back to find it; it's in the General setting on the Home screen.

To take a picture on an original or iPhone 3G, tap the camera button at the bottom of the screen (**Figure 8.8**). Its little icon rotates to show you the camera's orientation: portrait or landscape.

Figure 8.8
Tap the Camera button to take a picture.

If you have an iPhone 3GS, you have the opportunity to give the camera a helping hand. When you open the Camera application on this iPhone and point it, a box appears onscreen. This box is the iPhone's way of saying, "I believe that what I've placed in this box is the subject of this picture. My belief is so strong, in fact, that I will focus on this object and adjust my exposure to help it stand out."

If you agree with the iPhone's assessment, just tap the Camera button to take the picture. If, however, you want the iPhone to focus on some other object—say, the flower before you instead of the building behind it—just tap the object that you prefer. The box will be drawn around that object, and the iPhone will adjust its focus and exposure accordingly.

After you snap a picture, its image collapses into a box in the bottom-left corner of the iPhone screen, indicating that the image has been saved. The image in this box is a thumbnail of the last picture or movie you shot. Tap this icon, and you're taken to the Camera Roll screen, which displays the camera's captured images as thumbnails. As in the Photos application, you can tap a thumbnail for a full-screen view of the picture. To return to the camera, tap the Done button at the top of the screen.

In Camera Roll full-screen view, you have the same controls that you have in the Photos Play screen, plus the Trash icon, which you tap to discard the picture currently onscreen. And yes, the Options icon appears here too. Tap it, and you'll find the expected Email Photo, Send to MobileMe (if you have such an account), Assign to Contact, Use As Wallpaper, and Cancel buttons.

Capturing the iPhone's screen

You see the lovely shots of the iPhone's screen in this book? You can thank Apple's engineers for them. Since the release of the iPhone 2.0 software, you can capture images from the iPhone without hacking the poor thing (as I did for earlier editions of this book).

To capture whatever is on the iPhone's screen, just press the Home button and then immediately press the Sleep/Wake button on the top of the phone. The screen will briefly flash white, and the image of the screen will be placed in the Camera Roll.

All About Movies

As you've learned, among the features introduced with the iPhone 3GS are video shooting and editing. With this phone, you can record standard-definition movies at a resolution of 640 x 480 pixels and a frame rate of 30 frames per second (fps). That video is encoded as an H.264 file—a file format common on the Web and playable on all of today's computers. Not only does the 3GS capture video, but also, its microphone records the sound around you in glorious mono.

Now that you know about the iPhone's video capabilities, I'll look at the more interesting subjects of shooting, editing, and sharing video.

Shooting video

To shoot video, just tap the Camera application on the Home screen. In the resulting screen, you'll see the camera interface that you've come to expect from taking still shots. In the bottom-right corner of the screen is a Camera/Video toggle switch, which by default is switched to the Camera position for taking still shots. You want to shoot a movie, so tap this switch, and it moves to the Video position.

To focus the lens on the object you're most interested in, just tap that object. Just as it does when shooting stills, the iPhone adjusts focus and exposure so that the object you've selected is set off to its best advantage. When you're ready to record, tap the red Record button. The iPhone makes a discreet "flink" sound, a time display appears at the bottom of the screen, and the Record button blinks.

When you've had enough, tap the Record button again to stop the recording. When the video has been captured and added to the iPhone's Camera Roll album, its last frame flies down into the box in the bottom-left corner of the screen. To view the video, tap this box.

tip **The orientation in which you're holding the iPhone when you first tap the Record button determines how the video is displayed on the iPhone, on a tethered television set, and in your computer's video-editing software. If you eventually want to view the movie in the most widescreen view that the iPhone can produce, shoot in landscape orientation.**

Playing and editing video

Now that the movie is in the Camera Roll album, you can watch it as well as edit it. To watch it, just tap the large Play button in the middle of the video. Tap the screen while the video plays, and you'll see a bar at the top of the window. That bar is called the Frame Viewer, and within it, you see thumbnail images of portions of your video. Use this feature to navigate your video as well as edit it.

To move to a different position, just tap the video to expose the Frame Viewer (if it's not already exposed); then tap and drag the playhead that appears within it. When you tap the playhead. the thumbnail images expand in such a way that you see just the few seconds on either side of the playhead. This feature helps you zero in on just the frame you want to find. Now drag to the right to move forward and to the left to rewind.

To trim the video, tap either edge of the Frame Viewer until it turns yellow and a yellow Trim button appears in the top-right corner (**Figure 8.9**); then drag either edge of the viewer. When you drag the left side, you shorten the beginning of the video; drag the right side, and you shorten the end. As you drag, the Frame Viewer gets shorter, and the image that fills the iPhone's screen reflects the position of the beginning of the Frame Viewer. Let go when you've reached the spot where the good stuff starts. When you're satisfied with the selection you've made, tap the Trim button.

Figure 8.9
Editing a video.

> **note**   When you tap Trim, any video that's not within the Frame Viewer is deleted—for good. You can't undo this operation, so be careful about tapping this button.

If you've looked at your video and are unhappy with it, you can always perform the Ultimate Edit and just get rid of the thing. To do that, tap the screen and then tap the Trash button in the bottom-right corner. A screen appears, bearing a large red Delete Video button. Tap it, and the video is sucked into oblivion.

Sharing videos

Just as you can make your still pictures available to others, you can share your videos. You do so by opening that video in the Camera Roll album and tapping the Options button in the bottom-left corner of the screen.

The resulting options include Email Video, Send to MobileMe (again, this option appears only if you have a MobileMe account), Send to YouTube, and Cancel. I explain these options elsewhere in the book.

> **note**   If you came to the Camera Roll album via the Camera application, you can return to the Camera application by tapping the Done button in the top-right corner of the screen.

Syncing photos and videos to your computer

Wonderful as the iPhone may be for showing your photos, suppose that you use it to take a really great picture that you'd like to print or a video that you'd like to edit in more interesting ways than the iPhone offers. Somehow, you've got to get that stuff out of your iPhone and onto a computer.

"Ooh, ooh, ooh!", you're calling anxiously from the back of the room. "I know! I know!! *I KNOW!!!* Just tap Options and email it to yourself!"

Great idea!

But . . . no. Although you get big points for remembering what I told you about sharing pictures and video in the past few pages, the correct answer is: Plug your iPhone into your computer. When you do, in all likelihood, your computer will automatically offer to copy the pictures and movies from the iPhone's Camera Roll album to your computer.

Although you could email the pictures and videos to yourself, when you do, you send a picture that is of lower resolution than the original and movies that may be compressed in the process. Specifically, photos emailed from the iPhone are sent at a resolution of 640 x 480 pixels. When you download the pictures directly to your computer, you get full resolution of the images.

When you email videos that are, in the iPhone's estimation, too large in their native state to fit through an email gateway (meaning 10 MB and up), the iPhone tells you so by popping up a message. Then it offers you the option to trim the video to a manageable size. Take the iPhone up on its offer, and the video editing screen appears, with the Frame Viewer set to a size that the iPhone believes will fit.

The Frame Viewer starts at the beginning of the clip and cuts off the video at the end. If you don't like this placement, just drag the right end of the Frame Viewer to move it. You can also trim further, if you like. When you're ready to send the clip, tap the Email button in the top-right corner.

The video you send is not only shorter than the original, but also may be lower-resolution (480 x 360 rather than 640 x 480, for example). The iPhone wants to send as much of the video you shot as it can, and if sacrificing some resolution will make that happen, the iPhone is satisfied.

When you sync a Mac with an iPhone that contains photos and movies taken with its camera, by default, iPhoto launches and asks whether

you'd like to add those items from your iPhone to its library. On a
Windows PC, the AutoPlay option launches, listing options including importing pictures and video from your "camera." Do this, and the
pictures and movies are copied from the iPhone to your computer.

tip Some Mac users are driven to distraction by this behavior. They'd like
to import this content when *they* want to, not every time they sync
their phones. To stop this from happening, go to your Applications folder, launch
iPhoto, choose iPhoto > Preferences, click the General tab, and choose
No Application from the Connecting Camera Opens pop-up menu. From now on,
when you want to pull pictures off the camera, you must launch iPhoto. When
you do, iPhoto will see your iPhone and offer to copy its pictures.

When you copy those photos and movies, they're not removed from your
iPhone automatically. Both iPhoto and Aperture provide an option to
copy the content and then erase the card or camera on which the original
media is stored. This option applies to your iPhone. Enable it, and after
your pictures and movies are copied to your computer, the photos and
videos are deleted from the iPhone.

YouTube

YouTube remains the Big Cheese for watching politicians kill their careers
with a few ill-chosen words, frat boys set themselves on fire, and felines
impersonate Elvis. Because YouTube is so popular, it only makes sense
that the iPhone offers you a way to watch its content. It does via the
YouTube application.

Navigating YouTube

Tap the YouTube icon on the iPhone's Home screen, and you'll see a
screen that resembles the one you view when you enter the iPhone's
iPod area. Like the iPod screen, this one has five icons along the bottom.

By default, these icons are Featured, Most Viewed, Search, Favorites, and the ever-popular More (**Figure 8.10**).

Figure 8.10
Icons in the YouTube screen.

Here's what you'll find when you tap each icon.

Featured

Tap Featured, and you get a list of YouTube videos that the service believes most worthy of your attention (**Figure 8.11**). To play one, just tap it. The video will stream to your iPhone via a Wi-Fi connection (if one's available) or over 3G or EDGE. Naturally, Wi-Fi brings the video to you faster. When you scroll to the bottom of the list, you'll see a Load More entry. Tap it, and more videos are added to the list.

Figure 8.11
Featured YouTube videos.

If a video's title, such as *Simon's Cat 'Let Me In!'*, doesn't provide you enough information, feel free to tap the blue icon to the right of the video's title. When you do, you'll see the name of the movie you selected at the top of the screen and three buttons below: Add to Favorites, Add to Playlist, and Share Video.

Tap Add to Favorites, and that video is added to your list of favorites, making it easy to find it again. (I reveal more about favorites shortly.)

You can create playlists of YouTube videos via an option in the More screen. When you tap Add to Playlists, you can choose a playlist to add a video to. Alternatively, tap the plus (+) button in the Add to Playlist screen, and create a playlist right then and there.

When you tap Share, a new email message opens. The Subject line includes the title of the video, and the message body contains *Check out this video on YouTube:,* followed by a link to the video. (You can edit *Check out this video on YouTube:* to anything you like.) When you complete the To field and tap Send, the email message is sent via your default email account (as configured in Mail Settings).

The description screen also includes a Related Videos area. If YouTube has videos that it believes are similar in theme to the one you've chosen, it lists them here.

Tap yet another blue icon to the right of the movie on this screen, and you arrive at the movie's More Info screen. This screen includes a description of the video, the date when the video was added; its category (Drama or Documentary, for example); and its tags, which include anything that the poster thought appropriate, such as *poodle, waterslide,* and *ointment;* a Rate, Comment or Flag button for doing just that; and user comments below. To read more comments, tap the Load More comments button at the bottom of the screen.

If you're interested in seeing other videos uploaded by the producer of the video you're currently exploring, tap the More Videos button at the top of the More Info screen (**Figure 8.12** on the next page).

Figure 8.12
*A YouTube More
Videos screen.*

Most Viewed

The Most Viewed icon provides you the opportunity to view YouTube's
most popular videos—all videos, or the most viewed today or this week.
Like the Featured screen, this one carries a Load More entry at the bottom
of the list. To determine whether you watch all, today's most viewed,
or this week's most viewed videos, tap the appropriate icon at the top
of the screen.

Search

You can search YouTube's catalog of videos, of course, and this is the way
to go about it. Tap Search, and you get a Search field in return. Tap this
field, and up pops the iPhone's keyboard. Type a search term—*skateboard*
or *Mentos,* for example—and YouTube searches for videos that match
your query. Then it presents a list of 25 videos that it feels match what
you're after. If more than 25 videos are available that match your query,
your friend the Load More entry appears at the bottom of the list.

Favorites

As the name hints, here's where you store links to your favorite YouTube videos. To begin streaming one of these videos, just tap its name. To remove a favorite, tap the Edit icon at the top of the screen, tap the red minus sign (–) that appears next to the entry, and then tap Delete (**Figure 8.13**). When you're finished removing favorites, tap Done, and you'll return to the Favorites screen.

Figure 8.13
*YouTube
bookmarks.*

> **tip** When you sign into your YouTube account and add a favorite, that favorite appears not only on your iPhone, but also within YouTube in your computer's Web browser.

More

You've read Chapter 6, right? Then this More icon should be no mystery to you. Tap it, and you're presented with six additional choices: Most Recent, Top Rated, History, My Videos, Subscriptions, and Playlists. Most Recent offers a glimpse of the 25 videos most recently added by YouTube. Top Rated displays YouTube's 25 highest-rated videos.

History details all the videos you've chosen. Yes, *chosen*. You don't have to watch these videos in order for them to appear in your History list. Just choose them, and even if you cancel playback before they appear, they'll be part of your iPhone's YouTube History. If this list is too long, or if you're embarrassed by some of the things you've chosen, tap the red Clear icon at the top of the screen. All History entries disappear.

note The Clear icon is an all-or-nothing affair. Currently, the iPhone doesn't provide an option to delete individual videos from the History screen.

My Videos list all the videos you've uploaded to YouTube under your account. Subscriptions presents a list of the producers or channels you've subscribed to. The number of videos available from a subscription appears next to its name—*Macworld (171)*, for example.

Also, as I mention earlier, you can create playlists of YouTube videos. To create a playlist, just tap the plus (+) button in the top-left corner of the screen. An Add Playlist screen scrolls up from the bottom. Use the keyboard to name your playlist, and tap the Add button when you're done. You can remove playlists later by tapping the Edit button in the Playlists screen and using the tap-minus-and-then-Delete technique.

Playing YouTube videos

To play a YouTube video, tap it, and the video will begin loading in land-scape orientation. You'll see the now-familiar video play controls—Back, Play, and Forward—along with a volume slider, timeline, and Scale icon. Like the play controls in the iPhone's iPod area, these controls fade a few seconds after they first appear. To force them to reappear, just tap the iPhone's display.

In addition to the play controls, you'll see a Favorite icon to the left of the play controls and a Share icon to the right (**Figure 8.14**). Tap Favorite, and the currently playing video is added to your YouTube favorites. Tap Share, and you create another one of those special YouTube recommendation emails that I describe in the "Featured" section earlier in this chapter.

Figure 8.14
The YouTube play screen.

Timeline

Scale

Favorite

Back

Play/Pause

Forward

Share

Volume Slider

The video begins playing when the iPhone determines that it has down-loaded enough data for the video to play from beginning to end without pausing to download more. When the video concludes, you'll see its More Info screen.

9

The Other Applications

I've covered the iPhone's major areas—Phone, Mail, Safari, and iPod—as well as its most significant applications, including Messages, Calendar, Photos, Camera, YouTube, the iTunes Store, and the App Store. It's time to turn to the smaller applications, which by default occupy the bulk of the iPhone's Home screen: Stocks, Maps, Weather, Voice Memos, Notes, Clock, Calculator, and (on the iPhone 3GS) Compass.

If you've used Mac OS X, many of these applications are familiar to you, as most of them are offered in that operating system as *widgets*—small applications that perform limited tasks. On the iPhone, they're considered to be full-blown applications, even though they're largely single-purpose programs. They work this way.

Stocks

The Stocks application has a lot in common with the Mac OS X Stocks widget. Like that widget, the application displays your chosen stocks and market indexes (Dow Jones Industrial Average and NASDAQ, for example) in the top part of the screen and performance statistics below. Next to each index or stock ticker symbol, you'll see the almost-current share price (results are delayed by 20 minutes), such as *AAPL 152.91*, followed by the day's gain or loss, as represented by a green (gain) or red (loss) icon.

By default, the application represents gains and losses in points—*+3.89*, for example. To see the company's market cap—*136.4B*, for example—tap one of these red or green icons. You can toggle to a percentage view by tapping an icon again. Tap once more to return to point view.

note You must be connected to the Internet in some way—via a 3G network, AT&T's EDGE network, or a Wi-Fi connection—for the results to appear.

To view statistics for a particular index or stock, just tap its name. A graph at the bottom of the screen charts that index's or stock's performance over 1 day, 1 week, 1 month, 3 months, 6 months, 1 year, or 2 years (**Figure 9.1**). To choose a time period, just tap the appropriate icon (such as 1d for 1 day or 6m for 6 months).

If you flip the phone to landscape orientation, you see this graph enlarged. No, this feature isn't for the benefit of people with poor eyesight. Tap and hold on this graph, and an orange line appears that tells you the stock price on the time or day you've tapped. (The date appears at the top of the screen.) Tap with two fingers, and the iPhone tells you the change in points and percentage between one finger and another. So, for example, you might select Apple's stock in 3-month view, place your left index finger on May 13, 2009, and put your right index finger on July 20, 2009. You see that the stock rose 33.42 points, or 27.97 percent.

Figure 9.1
*Stocks
application.*

Return the iPhone to portrait orientation and swipe a graph to the left, and you'll see news headlines related to the company. (This window scrolls down if there are enough headlines to merit scrolling.) Tap a headline, and Safari launches and displays the story. Swipe once more to the left, and you'll see a table of statistics related to the company that includes such things as the day's opening and closing prices and trading volume.

For more detailed information on an index or stock, tap its name to highlight it and then tap the tiny Y! (for Yahoo) icon in the bottom-left corner of the screen. Doing so launches Safari and whisks you to a Yahoo oneSearch page with links related to that item. There, you'll find links to a Yahoo Finance page devoted to the index or stock, with related news, products, full and mobile Web pages, and Web images.

If you tap the *i* (Information) icon in the bottom-right corner of the display, the screen flips to reveal the indexes and stocks that appear on the application's front page. Click the plus (+) icon in the top-left corner and use the iPhone's keyboard to add a ticker symbol or company name. In the case of a company name, the iPhone will search for matches. If you type **Apple** and tap Search, for example, you'll get a list that includes not only Apple, Inc., but also Nicholas Applegate International and Appleseed Fund. Tap the search result you want, and it will be added to the bottom of the list. You can reorder the list by dragging an entry up or down in the list by its reorder bar to the right of the entry. To remove items, just tap the red minus (–) symbol next to the item's name and then tap the resulting Delete icon.

The Information screen also includes three icons: %, Price, and Mkt Cap. Tap one to determine the default display of gains and losses in the main Stocks screen.

This screen also offers a less-obvious icon. To have Safari take you to the Yahoo Finance page, simply tap Yahoo! Finance at the bottom of the screen.

Maps

This application is a version of Google Maps made for the iPhone, and I've found it to be one of the phone's most useful tools. You can use it to search for interesting locations (including businesses, residences, parks, and landmarks) and give those locales a call with a couple of taps. It's the showcase application for the iPhone's location technology—a technology that uses cell-tower and Wi-Fi hotspot triangulation and, if you have an iPhone 3G or 3GS, Global Positioning System (GPS) technology to pinpoint your iPhone's location. You can use it to get driving directions between here and there, and in some cases, you can check traffic conditions along your route.

The Maps application has two major components: Search and Directions. Each is available from the main Maps screen.

Searching and exploring

At the top of the Maps screen, you see a Search field (**Figure 9.2**). Tap it, and up pops the iPhone's keyboard. With that keyboard, you can enter any of a variety of search queries, including contacts in your iPhone's address book (*Joe Blow*), a business name (*Apple, Inc.*), a town name (*Springfield*), a more-specific town name (*Springfield, MO*), a street or highway name (*Route 66*), a specific street name in a particular town (*Broadway, Springfield, MO*), or a thing (*Beer*).

Figure 9.2
Maps' search feature and the results in the map below.

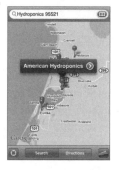

You can help Maps find its way by entering a more specific search, such as **Main St., Springfield, MO 65802** or **Beer 95521**. In short, the more specific you are in your query, the more accurate Maps will be.

Search views

You can display Maps' search results in four views:

- **Map,** which is a graphical illustration of the area

- **Satellite,** which is a photo captured by an orbiting satellite

- **Hybrid,** which is a satellite view with the names of roads overlaid

- **List,** which is a . . . well, *list* of all the locations pinpointed on the current map

These options are available when you tap the dog-eared-page icon in the bottom-right corner of the iPhone's screen. (More on other options in this screen shortly.)

In Map, Satellite, and Hybrid views, search results are denoted by red pushpins that drop onto the map. Tap one of these pins, and the name of the item appears. Again, this name can be the name of a contact's address, business, town, or highway. List items are accompanied by blue > icons; tap one of these icons to go to that location's Info screen.

Info screens

Info screens present any useful information Maps can obtain about an item, including phone number, email, address, and home-page URL (**Figure 9.3**). The phone number, email, and URL links are *live*, meaning that when you tap a phone number, your iPhone places a call to the number; when you tap an email address, Mail opens and addresses a message to that contact; and when you tap a URL, Safari opens and displays that Web site.

Figure 9.3
Maps' Info screen.

At the bottom of each Info screen, you'll see five labeled buttons: Directions To Here, Directions From Here, Add to Contacts, Share Location, and Add to Bookmarks. (You may have to scroll the screen to see all these buttons.) They work this way:

- **Directions To Here.** Tap this button to display Maps' Driving Directions interface (which I explain shortly), with the item's address in the End field.

- **Directions From Here.** This feature works similarly. The difference is that the item's address appears in the Driving Directions Start field.

- **Add to Contacts.** This produces a sheet that bears three buttons— Create New Contact, Add to Existing Contact, and Cancel. Tap the first button, and a New Contact screen appears. As its name hints, tapping this icon causes a New Contact screen to appear, with the information from the Info screen filled in. You're welcome to add any other information you like, using the standard contact-field tools.

  As for the Add to Existing Contact button, say your buddy Brabanzio has just started putting in his 8 hours at the local pickle works. You can use Maps to locate said works, tap this icon, and add its information to his contact information.

- **Share Location.** If you've found the perfect sushi joint and want to tell your friends, tap this button. An unaddressed email message pops up. The message's Subject heading includes the name of the location, and the message body contains a link that, when clicked by a recipient, launches a browser and opens Google Maps to that location.

- **Add to Bookmarks.** You can bookmark locations in Maps. Tapping this icon brings up the Add Bookmark screen, where you can rename the bookmark, if you like. When you're done, tap Save, and that location is available from Maps' Bookmarks screen (which, again, I get to shortly).

Bookmarks

The Search field includes a very helpful Bookmarks button. Tap this button to bring up a list of all the locations you've bookmarked, as well as recent search terms and your list of contacts (**Figure 9.4** on the next page).

Figure 9.4
*Maps'
Bookmarks
screen.*

To remove, rename, or reorder select bookmarks, tap the Edit button. In the resulting screen, you can tap the now-expected red minus (–) icon to produce the Delete icon, which you tap to remove the bookmark. You can also tap the bookmark to show the Edit Bookmark screen, where you can edit the bookmark's name. Finally, you can reorder bookmarks by dragging the right side of a bookmark up or down in the list.

Recents

Tap the Recents button, and you'll see a list of the previous 20 searches done on your iPhone. As you conduct a new search, the last search in this list is deleted. These queries are categorized by Search (*pizza*), Start and End (*home to Bob's house*), Location (*Grand Rapids*), and Contact (*Ebenezer Scrooge*). Tap one of these entries, and you see its location—or, in the case of driving directions, locations—on the map.

Contacts

It's swell that your Aunt Vilma sent you a change-of-address card, but where the heck is Fort Dodge, Iowa? Tap the Contacts icon, find Aunt Vilma's name in the long list of contacts, tap her name, and then tap the street address of her new cabin down by the river. Maps will pin her palace in next to no time.

Other dog-ear options

In addition to having access to the Map, Satellite, Hybrid, and List views when you tap the dog-ear icon, you have two other options (**Figure 9.5**):

Figure 9.5
*The dog-ear
screen.*

- **Drop Pin.** The first option allows you to drop your own pin on the map. Tap Drop Pin; the dog-ear flips down, and a purple pin appears on the map currently displayed onscreen. Above the pin is a box that tells you to *Drag To Move Pin*. Follow this advice by dragging the pin where you want it. The address of whatever's under the pin will appear in a gray bubble. Tap the > icon, and you're taken to the Dropped Pin's Info screen. In addition to the options offered in a regular Info screen, this screen includes a Remove Pin button for doing just that.

> **tip** Why would you want to bookmark a movable pin? I often do this
> when I'm out and about and need to enter a couple of temporary loca-
> tions. I may drop a pin, tap the blue icon, tap the Add to Bookmarks button, and
> then call the pin *Where I Parked the Car*. Then I'm at liberty to drop another pin
> during that same journey to mark a different important stop. Later, when I need
> to retrieve my car, I simply call up the appropriate bookmark.

- **Show Traffic.** If the area you're viewing in Maps supports the Traffic feature (not all areas do), tap the Show Traffic button to see colored lines that indicate how congested the roads are. Green denotes good traffic flow, yellow is somewhat congested, and red is stop-and-go traffic (or sometimes just stop). Yellow and red areas on the map throb so that they're more noticeable. If the service isn't supported in the area you're looking at, the Info screen will read "Traffic Unavailable in This Area."

tip Be sure to zoom in on the map when you see yellow and red traffic warnings. The warning may apply to only one direction of traffic—with luck, the direction you're not traveling in. A zoomed-in view will tell you what you're up against.

Getting directions

Maps' Directions component is the next-best thing to having a GPS device strapped to your wrist. Feed it the locations where you'd like to start and where you'd like to end up, and it provides a reasonable route for getting there, like so:

1. Tap Directions at the bottom of the Maps screen.

   Empty Start and End fields appear at the top of the screen.

2. Tap the Start field.

   If you've used the iPhone's Location feature to tell it where you are, the Start field automatically displays *Current Location* in blue letters. You're welcome to use that location as the start point. If you prefer to use a different start point, simply tap the field again and then tap the X icon at the right end of the field to clear it.

3. Using the iPhone's keyboard, type the location where you want to begin your journey.

   This location can be something as generic as a zip code or as specific as your home address. Alternatively, you can tap the Bookmarks icon and then tap a bookmark in the resulting screen; its location will appear in the Start field.

4. Tap the End field.

   Same idea—type a location or choose a bookmark (**Figure 9.6**).

Figure 9.6
Entering start and end points for driving directions.

5. Tap the blue Route button in the bottom-right corner.

   Maps will present an overview map of your route. At the top of the screen are three transportation icons representing driving, public transportation, and walking routes. The Driving icon (the default) displays the length of the journey and how long it should take to drive—*279.9 miles and 4 hours 57 minutes*, for example (**Figure 9.7**).

Figure 9.7
Trip overview.

The Public Transportation icon is likely to display different information from the Driving icon. It tells you when the next mode of transportation (which could be a bus, subway, train, or combination) is going to leave and when it's likely to arrive.

note The Public Transportation route is intended for local travel. If you set Arcata, California, as your departure point and Parsons, Kansas, as the destination, the iPhone will say, "Transit directions could not be found between these locations."

Tap the Walking button, and you see the most reasonable route you can make on foot (meaning no freeways), the distance, and the time it should take to get where you're going.

The Map, Satellite, and Hybrid buttons on the dog-ear page do exactly what you'd expect, but List's functionality changes when you're using the Directions feature.

Tap List, and the twists and turns of your route are laid out in numbered steps—for example, *1 Drive 0.4 miles then turn right at Old Codger Road. 2 Dive 2.6 miles then merge onto CA-94 W toward Tokyo.* Tap a step, and Maps displays that portion of your trip on a map, circling the important twist or turn outlined in the step as well as displaying the written driving directions for that step at the top of the screen.

To view the next turn in your trip, just tap the right-arrow icon at the top of the screen. To return to the map overview of your trip, tap the dog-ear icon; tap List; and then tap the Route Overview entry at the top of the Directions screen.

tip When you return to List view, a purple circle surrounds the step in the list that corresponds to the portion of the trip you just viewed. If the fourth part of the trip was to turn left on Dankhippie Road, for example, a purple circle appears around the number 4.

If you like this turn-by-turn graphic overview of your route, you can skip the List icon altogether. Just tap the Start icon in the top-right corner of the route overview screen. The first step of your journey will be shown in all its graphic glory, along with the accompanying text at the top of the screen. Tap the right-arrow icon to proceed to the next step (**Figure 9.8**). Should you want to edit your route—change the start or end point—just tap the Edit button in the top-left corner of the display. The Start and End fields appear, along with the iPhone's keyboard.

Figure 9.8
Taking a trip.

At this point, you can return to your journey by tapping the Cancel button in the top-right corner or plot a new journey by tapping Clear.

Location, Location, Location

I know—you've been staring at that small  icon in the bottom-left corner of the Maps screen, wondering what on earth it's for. Allow me to reward your patience by telling you that this is the Location icon. Tap it, and the iPhone attempts to pinpoint the iPhone's whereabouts. Tap it again on an iPhone 3GS, and the map rotates to reflect the direction in which the phone's pointing.

How Location works

The iPhone 3G and 3GS can find itself in three ways: GPS, Wi-Fi location, and cell-tower triangulation. The original iPhone, which lacks GPS, has to rely on the latter two technologies.

The iPhone 3G and 3GS can use GPS technology to obtain extremely accurate location coordinates from an orbiting satellite. For this feature to work, the iPhone must be able to "see" the satellite—meaning that you have to be outside and that the line of sight between the iPhone and the satellite can't be obscured. (In other words, GPS won't work if the phone's in your pocket or purse.)

Location's Long Reach

Maps isn't the only application that asks permission to use the iPhone's location. The Compass application and several third-party applications from the App Store use location in interesting ways— chat and Twitter clients, astronomy applications that calculate where the heavenly bodies are in relation to your position on Earth, and social-networking applications that broadcast where you are, for example. Before telling the world where your phone is, these applications should ask your permission.

At times, however, you don't want to provide your location—such as when you've told your wife that you're at the office but in reality are poised to spring out from behind a couch and shout "Surprise!" at her 37th birthday party.

More serious security and safety ramifications may apply, of course: A youngster with an iPhone may be staying late at school, for example. As with most things involving passing along personal information, grant permission wisely. If you're concerned about broadcasting your location, go to the General setting and switch Location Services off.

If you have an original iPhone, you don't have this luxury. Instead, this iPhone (and an iPhone 3G or 3GS that isn't using GPS) searches for local Wi-Fi networks. Some of these networks have registered their locations through Skyhook Wireless. When your iPhone detects one of these locations, it can glean a pretty good idea of where it is. It will be even more accurate if it detects more than one registered network.

tip   **You can register your own wireless router with Skyhook. Just go to http://skyhookwireless.com/howitworks/submit_ap.php and follow the directions to register your router's location. It takes about a month for registered routers to broadcast their location to devices like the iPhone.**

Finally, if all else fails, the original iPhone, iPhone 3G, and iPhone 3GS will attempt to use cell-tower triangulation to guess the phone's location. *Triangulation,* in this context, means that the iPhone tests the strength of any cell towers it can connect to, and after determining that it's so many miles from Tower A, so many from Tower B, and just a few yards from Tower C, it gives Maps its approximate location.

Approximate is the operative word here. If you're in an area with weak telephone reception (not a lot of cell towers around), the iPhone could plot your location miles from where you really are. (Mine occasionally tells me that I'm standing somewhere along the edge of the continental shelf when, in fact, my feet are completely dry.)

Using Location

To pinpoint (as much as possible) your location in Maps, tap the Location icon. If the Location Services option is off in the General settings screen, Maps will tell you to turn it on via a window that includes a Settings and Cancel button. Tap Settings to go the Settings screen, where you can turn Location Services on.

The iPhone will use whatever technology it can—GPS, Wi-Fi, and then cell-tower triangulation—to produce a map with a blue target that indicates where the iPhone believes you are.

If the iPhone finds you via GPS, first the blue target appears; then a throbbing blue dot haunts the middle of the target (**Figure 9.9**). Move around, and the dot moves with you.

If the iPhone uses Wi-Fi or cell-tower triangulation instead, you're likely to see a large blue target that covers a pretty broad patch of ground. The iPhone will ponder for a few seconds and then, in all likelihood, zero in on a smaller target.

Figure 9.9
GPS location symbol.

A Sense of Direction

Maps are all well and good, but it's quite possible that you don't know whether you're looking west or east down Easy Street. To find out, tap the Location button again on your iPhone 3GS. When you do, the blue circle contains a white-ish fan that indicates the direction in which the phone's pointing. Pivot, and the map pivots with you.

Weather

Weather is another iPhone application that owes more than a tip of the hat to a Mac OS X widget. Though the layout of the iPhone's Weather application is vertical rather than horizontal, it contains the same information as its namesake widget: a 6-day forecast (including the current day); current temperature in Fahrenheit or Celsius (selectable from the application's Information screen); each day's projected highs and lows; and icons that represent the current or projected weather conditions, such as sun, clouds, snow, or rain (**Figure 9.10** on the next page).

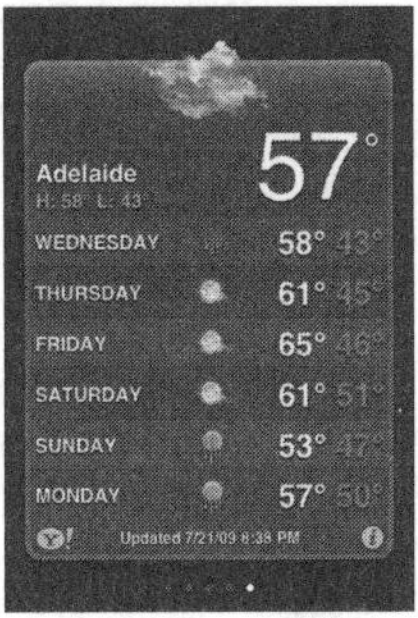

Figure 9.10
Weather application.

To move from one location screen to the next, simply swipe your finger horizontally across the screen. Alternatively, just tap to the right or left of the small white dots that appear at the bottom of the screen. (These dots indicate how many locations you have saved.)

Tap the *i* icon in the bottom-right corner of the Weather screen, and the screen flips around to display all the locations you've saved. To add a new one, tap the plus (+) icon; use the iPhone's keyboard to enter a location (again, a zip code is a handy shortcut); and tap Search. To remove a location, tap it; tap the red minus (–) icon; and then tap Delete. To switch from Fahrenheit to Celsius, tap the appropriate icon at the bottom of the screen. To reorder locations, just drag them up or down in the list.

Voice Memos

Voice Memos is an application introduced with the iPhone 3.0 software. And yes, it's for recording audio. That audio can be recorded with the iPhone's built-in microphone or the wired headset (but not a Bluetooth headset). To record and play back a memo, follow these steps:

1. Launch Voice Memos, and start talking—but don't record yet.

   Keep an eye on the VU meter at the bottom of the screen. If you see the needle move, that means the iPhone can "hear" you. This needle isn't very accurate, so don't try to push it up near the red. If it gets anywhere near the –10 mark, you're loud enough.

2. Tap the red Record icon, and start talking for real.

   A red bar appears at the top of the screen, indicating that the iPhone is recording (**Figure 9.11**).

Figure 9.11
Voice Memos application at work.

3. Pause, if you like, by tapping Record again.

   To resume, tap Record one more time.

4. Stop recording.

   Tap the silver button on the right side of the VU meter, and your recording is saved.

5. Tap the List button to play your memo.

   A Voice Memos screen appears, listing all the voice memos you've recorded. To play one, just tap it (and tap it again to pause). The timeline at the bottom of the screen displays the progress of the playback. You can tap and drag the playhead to move forward or backward in the memo.

6. Share it or delete it.

   The two buttons at the bottom of the screen—Share and Delete—are the means for doing those things. Tap Share, and a pane floats up with Email Voice Memo and Cancel buttons in it. Tap Email Voice Memo, and up pops an unaddressed email message containing the memo as an attachment.

7. Trim it.

   Tap the blue > button on the right side of a memo, and the memo's Info screen appears. Here, you can trim the memo by tapping the Trim Memo button. When you do, a pane appears that includes a yellow trim bar (similar to the Frame Viewer in the Photos application, which I cover in Chapter 8). To trim the memo, use the same method that you do to trim a video: Drag the sides of the trim bar to cut off the beginning and/or end of the memo. You can hear what's left by tapping the Play button next to the bar.

   To throw out the stuff you've trimmed, tap Trim Voice Memo. As with trimming a video, this action is permanent, so be careful.

   This Info window also contains a Share button, which saves you the trouble of backing up a screen to email the memo to someone.

8. Label it.

   Tap the name of your memo—*5:15 PM 00:17*, for example—and a
   Label screen comes into view. Tap a label that best categorizes your
   memo—Podcast, Lecture, or Idea, for example—and your memo is
   labeled. (You can also enter a custom label by tapping Custom at
   the bottom of the screen and typing a label name in the succeeding
   screen.) That label name replaces the time/date name in the Voice
   Memos screen.

When you sync your iPhone to your computer, the voice memos you've
recorded are transferred to your iTunes library. Regrettably, the label
names you've applied don't transfer as well. These memos retain their
date and time titles.

Notes

Notes is the iPhone's simple text editor—and by *simple*, I mean down-
right rudimentary. Tap Notes in the iPhone's Home screen and then tap
the Plus icon in the top-right corner of the resulting Notes screen to
create a new note. When you do, the iPhone's familiar keyboard appears.
Start typing your new novel (OK, novelette). If you make a mistake, use
the usual text-editing tricks to repair your work.

Each individual Notes screen has four icons at the bottom. The left-arrow
and right-arrow icons do exactly what you'd expect: move to the previous
or next note. Tap the Mail icon, and a new, unaddressed email message
opens in Mail, with the note's text appearing in the message body. Tap
the Trash icon, and you'll be offered the option to Delete Note or Cancel.

To view a list of all your notes (**Figure 9.12**), tap the Notes icon in the top-
left corner of the screen. Each note is titled with up to the first 30 characters of the note. (If you entered a return character after the first line, only

the text in that first line appears as the note's title.) Next to each note is the date of its creation (or time, if it was created that day). Time and date information also appears at the top of each note.

Figure 9.12
Notes application.

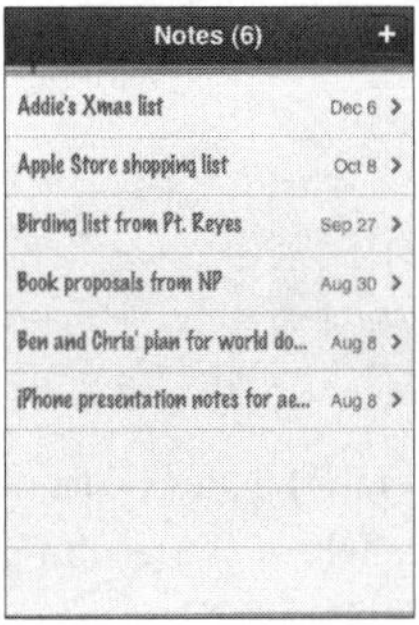

Notes (6)	+
Addie's Xmas list	Dec 6 >
Apple Store shopping list	Oct 8 >
Birding list from Pt. Reyes	Sep 27 >
Book proposals from NP	Aug 30 >
Ben and Chris' plan for world do...	Aug 8 >
iPhone presentation notes for ae...	Aug 8 >

With the iPhone 3.0 software, now you can sync notes to your computer. If you've enabled the Sync Notes option in the Info tab in iTunes, your notes will be copied to your computer, appearing in Apple's Mail application on a Mac and in Microsoft Outlook on a Windows PC.

Clock

More than just a simple timepiece, the iPhone's Clock application includes four components—World Clock, Alarm, Stopwatch, and Timer— that are available as icons arrayed across the bottom of the application's screen. Here's what they do.

World Clock

Just as its name implies, World Clock allows you to track time in multiple locations. Clocks are presented in both analog and digital form (**Figure 9.13** on the next page). On analog clocks, day is indicated by a white clock and night by a black one.

Figure 9.13
World Clock.

To add a new clock to the list, just tap the plus (+) icon in the top-right corner of the screen. In the Search field of the resulting keyboard screen, enter the name of a reasonably significant city or a country. The iPhone includes a database of such cities and offers suggestions as you type.

You can remove or reorder these clocks. Tap Edit and use the red minus (–) icon to delete a clock. To reposition a clock, tap its right side and drag it up or down in the list.

Alarm

Your iPhone can get you out of bed in the morning or remind you of important events. Just tap Alarm at the bottom of the screen and then tap the plus (+) icon to add an alarm.

In the Add Alarm screen, you'll find a Repeat entry, which lets you order an alarm to repeat each week on a particular day; a Sound entry, where you assign one of the iPhone's 25 default ringtones or a custom ringtone to your alarm; an On/Off Snooze entry, which tells the iPhone to give you 10 more minutes of shuteye when you press the Home button; and a Label entry that lets you assign a message to an alarm (*Get Up, Meeting This Morning,* or *Take That Big Purple Pill,* for example).

To create a new alarm, just flick the hour, minute, and AM/PM wheels to set a time for the alarm. Tap Save to save the alarm. When you save at least one alarm and switch that alarm on, a small clock icon appears in the iPhone's status bar.

> **tip** You can create an alarm only for the current 24-hour period. If you'd like an alarm to go off at a time later than that, use the Calendar application to create a new event, and attach an alert to that event.

Stopwatch

Similar to the iPod's Stopwatch feature, the iPhone's Stopwatch includes a timer that displays hours, seconds, and tenths of seconds. Tap Start, and the timer begins to run. Tap Stop, and the timer pauses. Tap Start again, and the timer takes up where it left off. Tap Reset, and the timer resets to 00:00.0.

While the timer runs, you can tap Lap, and a lap time will be recorded in the list below. Subsequent taps of Lap add more lap times to the list. When you tap Lap, the counter resets to 0.

Timer

The iPhone's Clock application includes a timer that will tick down from as little as 1 minute to as much as 23 hours and 59 minutes. To work the timer, just use the hour and minute wheels to select the amount of time you'd like the timer to run; then tap Start (**Figure 9.14** on the next page). (Alternatively, you can tap a number on the wheel, and the wheel advances to the "go" position.) The timer displays a countdown in hours, minutes, and seconds, and the label on the Start button changes to Cancel. Tap Cancel to stop the countdown.

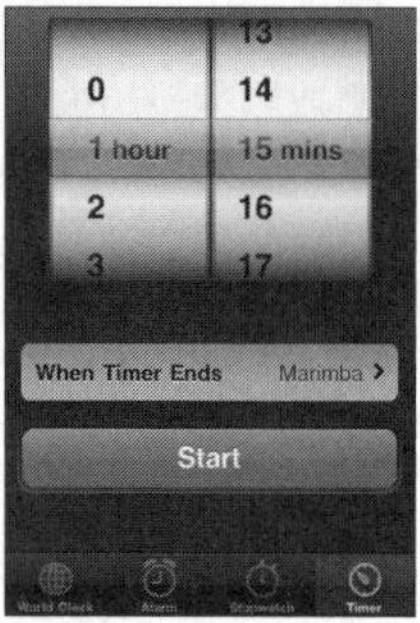

Figure 9.14
Time keeps on tickin', tickin', tickin' into the future....

The iPhone offers two actions when the timer ends: Either it plays one of its ringtones (and vibrates, and displays a Timer Done dialog box), or it activates the iPhone's Sleep iPod feature. The latter option isn't as odd as it first sounds. Many people like to listen to soothing music or ambient sounds as they drift off to sleep. The Sleep iPod option allows them to do just that without playing the iPhone all night (and needlessly running down the battery).

Calculator

Unless you've stubbornly clung to your grandfather's abacus, you've used an electronic calculator like this before. Similar to the dime-a-dozen calculators you can find on your computer or at the local Bean Counters "R" Us, the iPhone's Calculator application performs addition, subtraction, division, and multiplication operations up to nine places when you hold the phone in portrait orientation. When you choose an operation (addition or subtraction, for example), Calculator highlights the appropriate symbol by circling it.

In addition to the 0–9 digits and the divide, multiply, add, subtract, and equal keys, you find these keys:

- **mc.** For "memory clear." This key clears out any number stored in the calculator's memory.

- **m+.** Tap m+ to add the displayed number to the number in memory. If no number is in memory, tapping m+ stores the displayed number in memory.

- **m–.** Tap m– to subtract the displayed number from the memorized number.

- **mr.** Tap mr, and the displayed number replaces the currently memorized number. A white ring appears around this key if a number is in memory.

- **C.** Tap C to clear the total.

Ah, but wait—there's more. Flip the iPhone to landscape orientation, and you get a full-featured scientific calculator (**Figure 9.15**). When you rotate the iPhone, any number stored in the calculator remains, so you can move quickly from simple to complex calculations and back again without losing your work.

Figure 9.15
The Calculator application's scientific calculator.

Compass (iPhone 3GS Only)

The iPhone 3GS has a built-in magnetometer—a bit of circuitry that measures the direction of the Earth's magnetic field. Launch this application, and the iPhone will tell you which direction it's pointing by using a traditional compass face (**Figure 9.16**).

Figure 9.16
Compass application.

note I say *likely* because it may not. Instead, the iPhone may tell you that it has no idea where it is and that you need to wave it in a figure-8 pattern to bring it to its directional senses. You'll feel stupid doing it, but this trick works.

At the bottom of the screen are the geographic coordinates (in degrees, minutes, and seconds indicating where the iPhone believes that it is). To the left of these coordinates is the Location button. Tap it, and Maps opens, showing you your location as determined by the iPhone. To the bottom right of the Compass screen is the Info button. Tap it, and you can choose whether the iPhone points to True North or Magnetic North.

note Compass doesn't work unless you have Location Services turned on.

10

Tips and Troubleshooting

Compared with just about any other mobile phone you've owned, the iPhone is a dream of intuitive design and ease of use. Yet nothing in this world (save you, dear reader, and I) is completely foolproof or infallible, which is why this chapter is necessary.

Within these pages, I offer ways to get things done more expeditiously, provide hints for operating the iPhone in ways that may not seem obvious, and (of course) tell you what to do when your iPhone does the Bad Thing and stops behaving as it should.

Getting Tipsy

I've sprinkled tips and hints throughout the book, but I saved a few good ones for this chapter. In the following sections, I show you how to control text, manage the battery, and sync your iPhone efficiently.

The word on text

If one iPhone feature frustrates the greatest number of people from the get-go, it's text entry. These tips will help make you a better iPhone typist.

Keep going

I've mentioned this before, but I'll say it again here: Typing on the iPhone's keyboard isn't like typing on your computer keyboard, a process in which you type, make a mistake, backspace to correct the mistake, and continue typing. Use that technique on the iPhone, and you'll go nuts making the constant corrections.

Typing the first letter correctly is important, as mistyping that first letter is likely to send the iPhone's predictive powers in the wrong direction. But after that, get as close as you can to the correct letters and continue typing even if you make a mistake. More often than not, the iPhone's predictive typing will correct the mistake for you (**Figure 10.1**). To take the suggestion, tap the spacebar; the iPhone will fill in the (ideally) correct word.

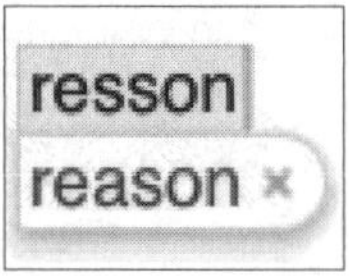

Figure 10.1
More often than not, the iPhone knows what you meant to type.

Sure, you may need to go back and correct a word or two in a couple of sentences by pressing and holding the display to bring up the magnifying-glass icon, but doing this for two mistakes is far more efficient than retyping half a dozen words.

Move to the correct letter

You need to type as carefully as possible in one specific instance: when you're entering a password. As I mention elsewhere, for security reasons the iPhone very briefly displays the last letter you typed in a password field before turning that letter into a black dot. This brevity makes it nigh-on impossible to correct your work, because you can't see where you've made a mistake.

For this reason, when you're entering passwords (or just typing carefully), tap a character and wait for the letter to pop up on the display. If you've hit the wrong character, keep your finger on the display and move it to the correct character. Only when you release your finger will the iPhone accept the character.

Adjust the dictionary

Irked because the iPhone invariably suggests *candle* when you intended to type *dandle* (**Figure 10.2**)? You have the power to modify the iPhone's built-in dictionary. If you type *d-a-n-d-l-e*, but the iPhone displays *candle*, simply tap the *candle* suggestion, and it disappears. Then finish typing.

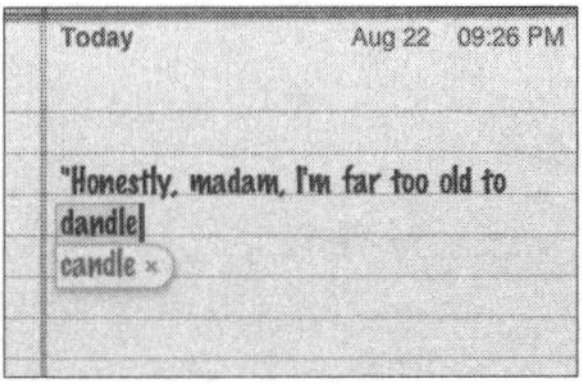

Figure 10.2
Correct the dictionary by tapping incorrect suggestions.

When you next get a good way into typing *dandle*, the iPhone will propose it as the word to use. When it does, just tap the spacebar to autocomplete the word. The iPhone's not stupid, so it won't suggest *dandle* when you next type *candle*, but it may not autocomplete *candle* that first time. In subsequent entries, however, it probably will.

Avoid unnecessary capitalizations and contractions

The iPhone tries to make as much sense as possible from your typing. When it's willing to, let it carry the load. You probably won't type the letter *i* all by itself unless you mean *I*, for example. The iPhone knows this and will make a lone *i* a capital *I*. Similarly, type *ill*, and even if you're trying to say that you're not feeling well, the iPhone will suggest *I'll*. Conversely, if you're feeling fine, the iPhone allows you to type *well* without suggesting *we'll*. Knowing that both *its* and *it's* are common, the iPhone will never suggest the contraction.

Rule of thumb: When a word that can also be spelled as a contraction is tossed at the iPhone, it will suggest the more commonly used word (**Figure 10.3**).

Figure 10.3
You can often skip the apostrophes when typing on the iPhone.

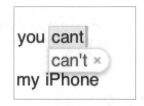

Space out your periods

No, I don't mean place spaces between them. I mean when you reach the end of a sentence, don't bother going to the .?123 keyboard to enter a period. Just tap the Space key twice in succession. The iPhone will end the last word you typed with a period, insert a space, and configure the Shift key so that the next letter you type will be capitalized. Now you're ready to type the next sentence.

 You can turn off this double-tap Space-key behavior by switching the setting off in the Keyboard portion of the General setting.

Use Pogue's punctuation tip

The New York Times' technology columnist, David Pogue, revealed this tip scant days after the first version of the iPhone was released, and in doing so, he proclaimed that other technology writers would use it in a heartbeat because it's so good.

Darn tootin', say I. It goes like this:

You may find it distracting to have to tap in and tap out of the iPhone's number/punctuation screen whenever you want to add a stray comma or type *9* rather than *nine*. This dance isn't necessary. Just tap and hold on the .?123 key in the bottom-left corner of the keyboard. While holding down your finger, drag to the punctuation symbol or number you want to type. When that item is selected, let go. The keyboard will return to the alphabetical keyboard.

Power management

Wonderful as it is to have a mobile phone that can play full-length movies, you do *not* want to board a cross-country flight, enjoy the latest Harry Potter flick on your phone, jump off the plane with the expectation of alerting a key client to your arrival, and be greeted with a dead battery. Power can be paramount in such situations. To help ensure that your battery will still have something to offer, try these tips.

Treat it right

Your iPhone's battery performs its best in these conditions:

- **It's warm.** Lithium batteries perform best when they're run at around room temperature. If they get cold—below 24°F—they don't hold a charge as long.

- **But not too warm.** Running a cool iPhone won't damage the battery, but storing it somewhere that's really hot—say, your car's glove compartment when it's 95°F outside—can. Also, the iPhone gets warm when you charge it and extra-warm when you charge it in a case. Therefore, don't leave your iPhone in a hot place, and remove it from a case before charging.

Lock it

The iPhone isn't supposed to do anything unless you touch its display or push its Home button, but you might accidentally do one thing or the other if the iPhone is rattling around loose in your pocket or pocketbook. Rather than project all 216 minutes of *Lawrence of Arabia* to the inside of your pants pocket, quickly press the Sleep/Wake button to lock your iPhone.

Turn off Sound Check and EQ

The iPod features Sound Check and EQ (equalizer) require more processing power from your iPhone, in turn pulling more power from your battery. If you've applied EQ settings in iTunes to the tracks that will play on your iPhone, you must set the iPhone's EQ setting to Flat, which essentially tells the iPhone to ignore any EQ settings imposed by iTunes. To make EQ Flat, choose Settings > iPod > EQ, and tap Flat in the EQ screen.

Turn on airplane mode

If you don't need to make or receive calls or to use the iPhone's Internet or Bluetooth capabilities, switch the iPhone to airplane mode (go to the Settings screen, and toggle the Airplane Mode switch to Off).

Turn off Wi-Fi

Although it doesn't save you as much juice as switching the iPhone to airplane mode, turning off Wi-Fi can help you get more life from your iPhone charge. To turn off Wi-Fi, go to the Settings screen, tap Wi-Fi, and flip the toggle switch to Off.

Turn off 3G

As it says in the Network area of the General setting, "Using 3G loads data faster, but may decrease battery life." If you don't need 3G—if you're not within range of a 3G network, for example—switching off this feature will give you a longer battery charge.

Turn off Bluetooth

Yes, Bluetooth can stress a battery too. Turn it off by going to the General setting, tapping Bluetooth, and flicking the switch in the resulting Bluetooth screen to Off.

Turn off Location Services

This option is another one that can drain a battery as the iPhone looks around every so often to see where it is. You can turn Location Services off in the General setting.

Fetch mail less often

Push mail and accounts configured to fetch messages automatically every 15 minutes will tax your battery's charge. If you don't need your mail Right Now, turn push mail off and configure mail fetching so that it's done manually (when you launch the Mail application). You do this in the Fetch New Data screen within the Mail, Contacts, Calendars setting.

Plug it in

If you're accustomed to the way an iPod works, you may be under the impression that when you jack your iPhone into your computer's USB port, you can't use it. Wrong. When it's plugged into its power supply, your computer, or an accessory device that supplies power, the iPhone is completely usable. Make calls, watch movies, surf the Net, get email—everything works.

note If you plug the iPhone into an audio device such as an FM transmitter or speaker system, you'll be prompted to switch on airplane mode, as using the iPhone in this fashion with the telephone features switched on can cause ugly audio artifacts to come out of your speakers.

Use the charger

Those who are accustomed to the iPod often charge the iPhone by plugging it into a computer's USB 2.0 port. This method isn't the best charging solution, though, because if your computer goes to sleep, the iPhone won't charge; it charges over USB only when the computer it's attached to is up, running, and awake.

Apple provides a small power supply with the iPhone. If you get into the habit of using the power supply, you'll never be caught unawares by an iPhone that's failed to charge.

Use your iPod

We're nearly to the point now where babies are issued iPods at birth; everyone has at least one of the things nowadays. If you have both an iPhone and an iPod, and you hope to spend some quality time listening to music or watching videos, use the iPod instead. Save your iPhone's battery for chores that only the iPhone can perform.

iPhone Battery: How Long and How Much?

When the iPhone was unveiled, many people worried because it doesn't have a removable battery. How long will the battery last before it gives up the ghost? And will you have to buy a new phone when the battery dies?

To answer the first question, Apple claims that after 400 full charge cycles—that's a charge from dead to fully charged—the iPhone's battery will function at approximately 80 percent of its original capacity.

As for the second question, just as you can with an iPod (another device that's not designed for easy battery replacement), you can have your iPhone's battery replaced. If the iPhone is out of warranty—meaning that it's more than 1 year old and you haven't added an AppleCare Protection Plan, which extends the hardware repair coverage to 2 years—Apple will do the job for $79 plus $6.95 shipping. The job takes 3 days. During that time, Apple will give you a loaner phone for $29 if you take your iPhone to an Apple Store. (The loaner phone is not available with mail-in service.)

By the time you read this book, you should see several third-party vendors jumping into the iPhone battery-replacement business, just as they did for the iPod. It's worth noting, however, that although some vendors may offer a "user-replaceable" battery, successfully replacing an iPhone's battery on your own is more than a little challenging. The battery is soldered in place. Unless you're *very* good with a soldering iron or couldn't care less about destroying your iPhone, have a professional do the job.

Sync different

Ask Apple about syncing your iPhone, and the answer you get is simple: One iPhone, one computer. But that answer's not entirely correct. To avoid that sinking feeling, keep these syncing tips in mind.

Sync to multiple computers

When you plug your iPhone into your computer, select it in iTunes' Source list, and click the Summary tab, you'll see (under Options) that you can Manually Manage Music and Videos. On any iPod other than an iPod touch, enabling this option means that on any computer to which the iPod is connected, you can add music to the iPod by dragging it from the iTunes Library to the iPhone's icon in the Source list.

This isn't the case with the iPhone. You can use this technique on only one computer: the computer that the iPhone is synced with. Try it on a different computer, and you'll be told that the iPhone can be synced with only one iTunes Library. To add music from the currently connected computer, you must erase all the media from the iPhone.

Although the iPhone lacks the iPod's manual-syncing option, you *can* sync your iPhone with different computers—to a point. The trick is that in nearly all cases, each computer will sync a different kind of media. You can sync music and videos from Computer A, photos from Computer B, podcasts from Computer C, and contacts and calendars from all three.

For this technique to work, you must enable the sync option in iTunes for just the media you intend to sync from a particular computer. So on Computer A, enable just the Sync Music, Sync TV Shows, and Sync Movies options. On Computer B, uncheck these options but check Sync Photos. Disable all these sync options on Computer C but enable the sync option for podcasts.

You can add contact, calendar, mail-account, and bookmark data from all these computers to a single iPhone. To do so, follow these steps:

1. Click the Info tab in iTunes' iPhone Preferences window, and enable the sync options you want (Sync Address Book Contacts and Sync iCal Calendars, for example).

2. In the Advanced area at the bottom of this window, where you see *Replace Information on This iPhone*, do *not* enable the options for contacts and calendars.

3. Click Apply.

    A dialog box will appear, asking whether you'd like to replace the information on your iPhone with the information on the currently connected computer or to merge the data on this computer with the data that's currently on the iPhone.

4. Click Merge.

    The chosen information on the computer will be merged with the existing information on the iPhone.

iPhone gone missing

The iPhone is small enough and out of your pocket enough that it's easy to misplace. Whether it slipped behind a couch cushion, or you left it in the back of a cab, you'd like to know where it is. The Find My iPhone feature lets you do just that.

To use Find My iPhone, you must have a MobileMe account, which costs $99 a year. Also, before you can use this feature, you must switch it on (meaning that you have to do this *before* you lose your iPhone). Just follow these steps:

1. Choose Settings > Mail, Contacts, Calendars, and tap your MobileMe account.

I tell you how to set up a MobileMe account in Chapter 2, in case you haven't done this yet.

2. Enable Find My iPhone by flicking the On/Off switch to On.

3. Open your computer's Web browser and travel to http://me.com, which is MobileMe's log-in page.

4. Log into MobileMe by entering your user name and password.

5. Click the Settings button (the button near the top of the page that bears a gear icon), and verify your password.

6. On the next page, enter your MobileMe password again.

7. Enable Find My iPhone by clicking the Find My iPhone link in the list on the left side of the window.

8. Locate your phone.

   In the page that appears, you'll see a world map with the words *Trying to Locate . . .* on top of it. If your iPhone is switched on, and the Find My iPhone is option enabled, you should soon see a map with a blue circle imposed on it. This circle indicates the iPhone's location (**Figure 10.4**).

Figure 10.4
Find My iPhone has found my iPhone.

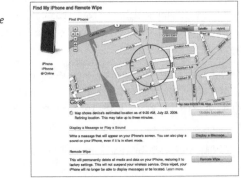

tip Again, if the iPhone's not switched on, Find My iPhone won't work; your iPhone won't be located.

9. Communicate with the phone.

   Click the Display a Message button, and a window appears where you can type as many as 160 characters. If you know that you've left your phone in a place where someone may find it—a restaurant or doctor's office, for example—type something polite in this field, such as "Please return my phone by calling 555-555-1212. Thank you."

   To help get the finder's attention, enable the Play a Sound for 2 Minutes with This Message option in this window. The message appears on the iPhone's display with an OK button below that dismisses the window (**Figure 10.5**).

Figure 10.5
Let the iPhone's finder know that you're on his trail.

tip The Play a Sound for 2 Minutes with This Message option is perfect for those times when you know the phone is in your house somewhere, but you can't find it. Even if you have the iPhone muted, it will play this bell-like alert sound.

10. If all else fails, wipe the phone.

If you're certain that the iPhone is lost or in the wrong hands, you should wipe its data. To do that, click the Remote Wipe button in the Find My iPhone screen (refer to Figure 10.4). This feature permanently deletes all the media and data on the iPhone.

> **tip** If you wipe the phone remotely and later recover it, you can always restore its data and media by plugging it into your computer. Remember, iTunes keeps a backup when you sync.

Troubleshooting

The iPhone may be an engineering marvel, but even engineering marvels get moody from time to time, and when your iPhone misbehaves, you're bound to be in a hurry to put things right. Allow me to lend a hand by suggesting the following troubleshooting techniques.

The basics

If your iPhone acts up in a general way—won't turn on, won't appear in iTunes, or quits and locks up—try these techniques.

No iPhone startup

Is your phone just sitting there, with its cold black screen mocking you? Try charging it with the included charger rather than a USB 2.0 port. If you get no response after about 10 minutes, try another electrical outlet. Still nothing? Try a different iPhone cable.

Still no go, even though you've had that iPhone for a long time and use it constantly? The battery may be dead (but this shouldn't happen in your first year of ownership, regardless of how much you use the phone).

The Four Rs

In the following pages, I repeatedly refer to four troubleshooting techniques: resign, restart, reset, and restore. In order of seriousness (and desirability), they are

- **Resign.** Force-quit the current application by holding down the Home button for about 6 seconds. This step should get you out of a frozen application and return you to the iPhone's Home screen.

- **Restart.** Turn the phone off and then on. Hold down the Sleep/Wake button until a red slider appears that reads *Slide to Power Off*. Slide the slider, and the iPhone shuts off. Now press the Sleep/Wake button to turn on the iPhone.

- **Reset.** Press and hold the Home and Sleep/Wake buttons for about 10 seconds—until the Apple logo appears—and then let go. This step is akin to resetting your computer by holding down its power switch until it's forced to reboot.

- **Restore.** Plug your iPhone into your computer, launch iTunes, select the iPhone in iTunes' Source list, click the Summary tab, and click the Restore button. This step wipes out all the data on your iPhone and installs a clean version of its operating system.

If iTunes can't see the iPhone, you need to throw the phone into DFU (Device Firmware Upgrade) mode. To do that, plug the iPhone into your computer with the USB cable, and press and hold Sleep/Wake and Home until you see the Apple logo. Then let go of the Sleep/Wake button and continue holding the Home button for 10 seconds. iTunes should tell you that the iPhone is in recovery mode, and you should be able to restore it.

(continued on next page)

The Four Rs (continued)

Fortunately, iTunes makes a backup of your information data (contacts, calendar events, notes, applications, and so on) when it syncs the iPhone. After restoring the iPhone, you'll be asked whether you want to restore it from this previously saved data. In most cases, you do. If, after restoring from your backup, the iPhone continues to misbehave, restore again—but this time, when you're offered the chance to restore from a backup, choose to set the iPhone up as a new iPhone.

No iPhone in iTunes

If your iPhone doesn't appear in iTunes when you connect it to your computer, try these steps:

1. Make sure that your iPhone is charged.

   If the battery is completely dead, it may need about 10 minutes of charging before it can be roused enough to make an iTunes appearance.

2. Be sure that the iPhone is plugged into a USB 2.0 port.

   Your computer won't recognize the phone when it's attached to a USB 1.0 port or a FireWire port.

3. Plug your iPhone into a different USB 2.0 port.

4. Unplug the iPhone, turn it off and then on, and plug it back in.

5. Throw the phone into DFU mode (described in the sidebar "The Four Rs").

6. Use a different iPhone cable, if you have one.

7. Restart your computer, and try again.

8. Reinstall iTunes.

Unresponsive (and uncooperative) applications

Just like the programs running on your computer, your iPhone's applications—both those from Apple and third-party applications that you obtain from the App Store—can act up, freezing or quitting unexpectedly. You can try a few things to nudge your iPhone into action. If the first step doesn't work, march to the next.

1. Resign from the application.

   If an application refuses to do anything, it's likely frozen. The only way to thaw it is to force it to quit. Press and hold the Home button until you return to the Home screen.

2. Restart your iPhone.

   Some applications misbehave until you shut down the iPhone and then restart it.

3. Clear Safari's cache.

   If you find that Safari quits suddenly, something in its cache may be corrupted, and clearing the cache may solve the problem. To do so, tap Settings in the Home screen; then tap Safari; and in the Safari Settings screen, tap Clear Cache.

4. Reset the iPhone by holding down the Home and Sleep/Wake buttons until you see the Apple logo.

5. Delete and reinstall troublesome third-party applications.

   If a third-party application quits time and again, tap and hold on it until it and the other icons start wiggling. Tap the X in the application icon's top-left corner to remove it from the iPhone. Go to the App Store, locate the application, and download it again. Apple keeps a record of your application purchases, so don't worry; you won't have to pay for it again.

6. On the iPhone, go to the General setting; tap Reset; and then tap Reset All Settings.

    This step resets the iPhone's preferences but doesn't delete any of your data or media.

7. In that same Reset screen, tap Erase All Content and Settings (**Figure 10.6**).

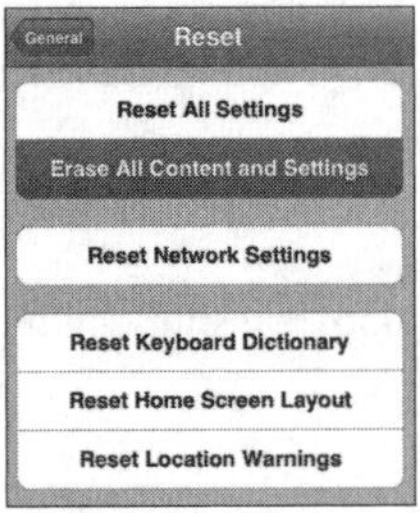

Figure 10.6
Erasing all the content and settings from your phone is the next-to-last resort.

General	Reset
Reset All Settings	
Erase All Content and Settings	
Reset Network Settings	
Reset Keyboard Dictionary	
Reset Home Screen Layout	
Reset Location Warnings	

 note This step vaporizes not only the iPhone's preferences, but its media content as well. Before doing this, try to sync your iPhone so that you can save any events, contacts, bookmarks, and photos you've created, as well as the third-party applications.

tip You want to try to back up third-party applications in particular because all the data for those applications is stored within the applications themselves. If you're unable to back up these applications and then lose them because you erased them, any data files you created with them are lost as well.

8. Restore the iPhone.

   As I suggest in the sidebar "The Four Rs," try restoring from your most recent backup first. If the problem persists, something in the backup may be corrupted.

9. Restore yet again, but choose *not* to restore from a backup; instead, start as though you're configuring a new iPhone.

   iTunes will install everything afresh, which means that you'll have to resync your data.

Mail issues

Are your attachments not opening? Is the iPhone refusing to send your mail? Are you getting far too many offers for questionable nostrums and shady real estate deals? Read on for solutions.

Can't read attachments

You can read certain kinds of documents that arrive as attachments in email messages—specifically, Microsoft Word, Microsoft Excel, PDF, JPEG, and text files. But Word, Excel, PowerPoint, iWork, and PDF files won't open unless they carry the proper extensions: .doc or .docx, .xls or .xlxs, .ppt or .pptx, .key, .numbers, .pages, and .pdf, respectively. Also, if the message body is formatted in rich text format (RTF) and includes an attachment, you won't be able to read the attachment. Try forwarding the message to yourself. This method should convert the rich text to plain text and allow you to view the attachment.

Can't send mail

Try configuring the email account on your iPhone rather than syncing it from iTunes. To do so, first copy the settings you'll need from your email client (account name; password; and POP, SMTP, or IMAP information).

Then delete the account that was synced from iTunes, go to the Settings screen, turn off Wi-Fi, and tap the Mail setting. In Mail, tap Add Account; configure the account; and tap Save. The iPhone will attempt to confirm your account over 3G or EDGE. If it does so, you're good to go. Turn Wi-Fi back on.

If you can't send mail because your ISP prohibits you from *relaying* (sending mail through another ISP), as it may when you're connected to a Wi-Fi network other than your own, you can use AT&T's cwmx.com outgoing server to send mail over 3G or EDGE. (cwmx.com doesn't work with Wi-Fi.) Or consider adding a free Gmail (http://mail.google.com), Yahoo (http://mail.yahoo.com), or AOL (http://mail.aol.com) account and sending mail via its server.

Can't cope with spam overload

The iPhone's Mail program offers no spam filtering. If your computer's email client removes the bulk of the spam you receive, you'll be shocked when you download your first batch of mail on the iPhone, because it's likely to be choked with spam.

If your ISP can't impose some kind of filtering on your email so that the spam doesn't reach you in the first place, sign up for a free Gmail account, and switch to it for email you intend to receive on your iPhone. Gmail has great spam filtering, so you'll get just the mail you want without the excess junk. (You can also configure Gmail to forward mail from other accounts through your Gmail account and remove the spam in the process.)

Index

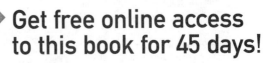